In *Landscape, natural beauty and the arts*, a distinguished group of scholars probes the complex structure of aesthetic responses to nature. Each of the chapters refines and expands the terms of discussion, and together they enrich the debate with insights from art history, literary criticism, geography and philosophy.

To explore the interrelation between our conceptions of nature, beauty, and art, the contributors consider the social construction of nature, the determination of our appreciation by artistic media, and the duality of nature's determining in gardening. Showing that natural beauty is impregnated with concepts derived from the arts and from particular accounts of nature, the volume occasions questions of the distinction and relation between art and nature generally, and culminates in a set of philosophical studies of the role of scientific understanding, engagement, and emotion in the aesthetic appreciation of nature.

CAMBRIDGE STUDIES IN PHILOSOPHY AND THE ARTS

Series editors:
SALIM KEMAL *and* IVAN GASKELL

Landscape, natural beauty and the arts

CAMBRIDGE STUDIES IN PHILOSOPHY AND THE ARTS

Series editors:

SÁLIM KEMAL *and* IVAN GASKELL

Advisory board:

Stanley Cavell, R. K. Elliott, Stanley E. Fish, David Freedberg, Hans-Georg Gadamer, John Gage, Carl Hausman, Ronald Hepburn, Mary Hesse, Hans-Robert Jauss, Martin Kemp, Jean Michel Massing, Michael Podro, Edward S. Said, Michael Tanner.

"Cambridge Studies in Philosophy and the Arts" is a forum for examining issues common to philosophy and critical disciplines that deal with the history of art, literature, film, music and drama. In order to inform and advance both critical practice and philosophical approaches, the series analyses the aims, procedures, language and results of inquiry in the critical fields, and examines philosophical theories by reference to the needs of arts disciplines. This interaction of ideas and findings, and the ensuing discussion, brings into focus new perspectives and expands the terms in which the debate is conducted.

Forthcoming volumes in the series include:

Explanation and value in the arts
Authenticity and the performing arts
Politics, aesthetics and the arts

Landscape, natural beauty and the arts

Edited by

SALIM KEMAL
Pennsylvania State University

and

IVAN GASKELL
Harvard University Art Museums

CAMBRIDGE
UNIVERSITY PRESS

Published by the Press Syndicate of the University of Cambridge
The Pitt Building, Trumpington Street, Cambridge CB2 1RP
40 West 20th Street, New York, NY 10011–4211, USA
10 Stamford Road, Oakleigh, Victoria 3166, Australia

First published 1993

Printed in Great Britain at the University Press, Cambridge

A catalogue record for this book is available from the British Library

Library of Congress cataloguing in publication data

Landscape, natural beauty, and the arts / edited by Salim Kemal and Ivan Gaskell.
p.   cm. – (Cambridge studies in philosophy and the arts)
Includes index.
ISBN 0 521 43279 0
1. Landscape.   2. Nature (Aesthetics)
I. Kemal, Salim.   II. Gaskell, Ivan.   III. Series.
BH 301.L3L36   1993
111′.85–dc20   92–13792   CIP

ISBN 0 521 43279 0 hardback

Contents

Contributors

JOHN BARRELL
University of Sussex

ARNOLD BERLEANT
Long Island University, C. W. Post

ALLEN CARLSON
University of Alberta

NOËL CARROLL
University of Wisconsin

DONALD W. CRAWFORD
University of California, Santa Barbara

T. J. DIFFEY
University of Sussex

DON GIFFORD
Williams College

RONALD W. HEPBURN
University of Edinburgh

STEPHANIE ROSS
University of Missouri, St. Louis

P. ADAMS SITNEY
Princeton University

YI-FU TUAN
University of Wisconsin

Editors' acknowledgments

Several members of the series' Advisory Board have given us a great deal of help and advice. We should particularly like to thank R. W. Hepburn.

John Barrell's essay first appeared in *Projecting the Landscape*, HRC Monograph no. 4 published by the Humanities Research Centre, Australian National University. We are grateful to them and to Professor Barrell for permission to publish it in this collection.

At Cambridge University Press Terence Moore (New York), Judith Ayling and Catherine Max (Cambridge) have been very patient and helpful, and we should like to thank them for their support.

Again we owe a great deal to Jane Whitehead and Jane Baston. This volume is for them.

Nature, fine arts, and aesthetics

SALIM KEMAL *and* IVAN GASKELL

Our starting point is Lindisfarne, or Holy Island.

The island is off the coast of Northumbria and connects to the mainland by a causeway that floods at high tide. Much of its early history is known only through Bede's *Historia Ecclesiastica Gentis Anglorum*. In 635 King Oswald granted the island to Bishop Aidan to found a monastery. A cult grew around the king following his death in battle against the heathen Mercians in 642. Bede writes that people began to collect dust from where the king had fallen with which to cure sicknesses in themselves and their stock.

About this time, another man, who was of the British nation, is said to have been crossing the place where this battle had been fought; and seeing that one spot was more green and more beautiful than the rest of the field, he came to the wise conclusion that there could be no other explanation for this exceptional greenness than that some person of greater sanctity than anyone else in the army had been killed there. So he took away some of that earth wrapped up in a linen cloth...[1]

The Briton found that piece of earth valuable because the color and beauty he saw signified something more. The depth of color and quality of that patch of grass had moral magnitude because the earth, nature, and its workings were affects of divinity. Bede goes on to relate that the house where the Briton spent the next night caught fire. Only the beam from which he had hung the earth in its linen wrap remained undamaged – miraculously. Subsequent inquiry established that that particular part of the field was where the martyred King Oswald had fallen. For Bede this confirmed the Briton's wisdom in thinking that the site was holy because it was green and beautiful.

Bede's history of the land and its people came to have its own importance. King Alfred ordered scholars to translate the *History* into

English, intending its study to sustain a cultural identity against the encroaching Danish forces. Thereby he invested the *Historia* with a cultic resonance. The Christian myths, the land, its aesthetic qualities, and its people became united in the construction of an identity.

Such associations of nature, beauty, and a sense of order, together with the secular role they play, still structure the understanding of landscape in nature and painting. Our conceptions of nature may vary and each version may find independent reasons for thinking its object beautiful and purposeful. Perhaps the more verdant is not straightforwardly more beautiful when it results from a spillage of nitrogen fertiliser. Nor need aesthetic values signify sanctity at all, since science,[2] politics,[3] and commerce[4] provide alternative readings of nature. Nevertheless, the understanding of nature and its beauty depends on our construction of order and purpose.

At present, natural beauty is so riddled with conceptions derived from painting and poetry that landscape refers ambiguously to parts of nature *and* representations of nature in paintings, photographs, and film.[5] Perhaps this is a result of the history of landscape. In his seminal paper on "The Renaissance Theory of Art and the Rise of Landscape,"[6] Professor Sir Ernst Gombrich argues that the theory of landscape painting, denoting the artists' creative genius, among other things, preceded the practice of representing actual instances of natural beauty. Passages in Leonardo's notes explore "the motive powers of the creative process itself," issuing in the claim in the *Paragone* that if an artist "desires valleys or wishes to discover vast tracts of land from mountain peaks and look to the sea on the distant horizon beyond them, it is in his power;...In fact, whatever exists in the universe either potentially or actually or in the imagination, he has it first in his mind and then in his hands, and these [images] are of such excellence, that they present the same proportional harmony to a single glance as belongs to the things themselves."[7] The apocryphal story of the "invention" of landscape is that an artist in his studio set down on canvas his friend's recollections of his travels: his landscape owed little to the painter's eye and much to his imagination.[8]

What deserves to be accounted for in this understanding of landscape is "this movement in a 'deductive' direction from artistic theory to artistic practice, from artistic practice to artistic feeling" – until by the eighteenth century artistic categories were read into nature. Gombrich cites a guide book through the Lake District that promises to lead the tourist "from the delicate touches of Claude,

2

verified at Coniston Lake, to the noble senses of Poussin, exhibited at Windermere Water, and from that to the stupendous romantic ideas of Salvator Rosa, realized in the Lake of Derwent."[9]

The result of these developments is that human creation and nature so interpenetrate in our understanding that they apparently preclude the likelihood of producing clear conceptual distinctions. Human beings are a fragment of nature, and nature is a figment of humanity. Similarly, the painterly and representational perspective that landscape ordinarily connotes, that determines the natural "prospect," loses its authority when ascribed to the work of the artist's imagination. It suggests, instead, a concern with constructing landscapes, both on canvas (or film) and in the land itself. Prospects in representations depend on the artist's imaginative construction and, in reality, look out onto land whose cultivation requires laborers, artisans, animals, tools, and a whole aesthetic, economic, and social order.

These characteristics of the conception of landscape, natural beauty, and nature, and the difficulties they suggest in the way of making clear conceptual distinctions, undermine any attempt to produce an hierarchy of concepts that will constitute a definitive foundationalist grasp of their complex interaction. Nature is not *the* most fundamental concept of natural beauty or landscape, and the attempt to resolve issues about the experience of natural beauty by deriving its vocabulary from such concepts is likely to fail. Better then to deal with natural beauty by showing the cluster of concepts that make up the parameters of our present understanding, without worrying about the metaphysical certainties that a determinate foundationalist schema promises.

To set out these parameters, this volume begins with essays by T. J. Diffey and Ronald Hepburn. One way to develop the problematic of natural beauty and landscape is to ask how people must talk of nature in the context of aesthetic values. For Bede nature was charged with a meaning derived from God and an appropriate eschatology. Such metaphysical commitments no longer determine conceptions of nature as clearly as they might once have done; nor is there obvious need for a commonsensical damper on thinking of earth as anything but "dirt."[10] In this context, some clarification of how "Nature" operates without metaphysics is surely welcome, especially if it promotes sense on the relation of natural to artistic beauty.

In his exploratory essay on "Natural Beauty without Metaphysics,"

T. J. Diffey considers that problematic from a particular perspective. He begins by attending to a present-day popular account of beauty. This avoids many of the "metaphysical lucubrations" that have engaged past thinkers while it also clarifies our conception of natural beauty by comparison at times with fine art. He finds that most people accede to a relativism and subjectivism about beauty that ascribes complete autonomy to individuals. They are very reluctant to give any external or public criteria authority over their own certainty about their own relation to objects, especially as a general agreement about which objects or landscapes are beautiful seems to validate their own independent choices.

Philosophers usually think this subjectivism and relativism untenable. Indeed, they seem unable to make a space for natural beauty at all. Its territory is carved up "between three leading ideas: beauty as the object of biological or sexual interest; beauty as disinterested appreciation of a rational mind; and an idealist rating of art above beauty in importance."[11] Yet none of these offers very substantial appreciations of natural beauty: neither sexual interest in nature nor the privileging of art seem germane or helpful, and a disinterested delight, in its desacralized contemporary version, seems too thin to generate much significance.

Diffey does not intend his inquiry to secure firm and final answers. But to counter the lack just outlined, to make some headway into grasping natural beauty, yet without any traditional metaphysical commitments, he begins with a claim with which everyone must agree, regardless of how they choose to explain its validity: a prospect of the Sussex downs "is *undoubtedly* beautiful...I have never heard it doubted nor would I understand anyone who did deny it..."[12] He then asks how "natural" this object can be. Very few prospects dominate areas that lack all signs of human agency (and this determines any human perceiver's interest), and unspoilt terrain is not beautiful simply by virtue of being unspoilt. Nor is there a neutral account of nature as a component of natural beauty. Diffey refers to Arthur Lovejoy's " 'Nature' as an Aesthetic Norm," which argues that there is no unequivocally identifiable subject of attribution. Nature in natural beauty operates in association with concepts such as landscape, view, and prospect, all of which are already aesthetically evaluative.

These ambiguities may suggest that perhaps people should look more closely at works of art. Nature's beauty became accessible in part because poets and painters made it clear through their work and made it plausible through its implicit contrast with and relation to artistic beauty. However, the same difficulties infect any attempt to determine the latter independently of the former: it is not some uniform thing; people consider the aesthetic issues of art just because beauty in nature seems too nebulous; the decline in talk of beauty coincides with the emphasis on art. All these suggest that the aesthetic issues about art have their source in aesthetic issues about nature, implying a need to understand artistic beauty through natural beauty rather than the other way around.

This still leaves open the issue of the basis for finding nature beautiful. Subjectivity and relativism ill serve attempts to protect beautiful places; but, in any case, these concepts may not grasp the popular conception wholly, since people also find sustenance in natural beauty.[13] If contemporary materialist philosophers are reluctant to identify that sustenance as religious or spiritual, Diffey suggests, it is because they too easily identify Christianity with all religion and reject the latter because of their problems with the former. Once spirituality is unhooked from its particular Western Christian version, by contrast, nature may appear as the repository of transcendent values.

Art may not seem to be the obvious model for exploring that transcendence: talk of beauty became unseemly because of the post-Hegelian stress on art. Yet art too has become a refuge for "religious and noumenal truth,"[14] even for atheists. Both art and nature make available a notion that "through the senses paradoxically one is in the presence of something supersensible." This sense of the ineffable, of the broad issue of whether the order of nature has room for humanity and its highest aspirations, underlies popular reverence for the countryside, and appears in philosophical and literary reflections. Poems like Wordsworth's "Lines Composed a Few Miles above Tintern Abbey" or Auden's "In Praise of Limestone," while they resonate with intensely private (and sometimes subterranean) sensibilities, make the latter transcendent by referring them to nature – and this to such an extent that references to nature not only seem completely appropriate to thought of beauty, Diffey suggests, but that at times its beauty seems enough to inform nature with a transcendent meaning.

Yet the last claim does not fully answer the issue. While beauty and nature gain stature and depth through their reference to each other, art seems to develop best when unfettered by beauty. The ineffable quality of natural beauty is incapable of clear expression in the sense that "beauty, and therefore natural beauty, is *dumb*," whereas by contrast "art *speaks*, is or is like *language*."[15] Art can be true in a way that a prospect or a segment of countryside cannot. The inarticulateness of natural beauty, its simply *being*, seems to prevent it from being "about anything," whereas art embodies a process of reflection and construction that gives it fluency, even about the nature of its beauty. That fluency is the basis of an interest in art; but if a combination of beauty and transcendence in nature allows beauty to substitute for transcendence, when "there is only [nature's] beauty to contemplate and enjoy," then there is need for some further justification of our interest in natural beauty.

Traditional answers rely on a spiritual transcendence that is less useful in this more faithless age. Any more satisfactory answer, a critic may hold, must conserve advances in scientific knowledge, its technological control of nature, and a moral sensitivity for their proper relation to the environment. Ronald Hepburn leads to some of these issues by considering what it is to talk about "The Serious and Trivial in Aesthetic Appreciation of Nature." He too takes up the theme of the interaction between talk of nature and of art. The fluency of art and the corpus of writing and thinking about its production, reception, and character suggest criteria for discerning serious appreciation. Conceptions of art are fluid too, of course, but that seems to follow from the reflectiveness that art has always claimed. Natural beauty has much less to go on: its vocabulary until recently depended too much on metaphysical and other assumptions because nature was supposed to be the permanent crucible for human endeavor and being. If that conception now seems redundant, there is still a lack of clearly non-metaphysical vocabulary or tradition for talking about nature and exploring the seriousness of its beauty.

Yet without the last, its preservation has little foundation or value. Certainly, nature must include more than English pastorals and their American variants. It must take cognizance of the freedom of the percipients, who are themselves a part of nature. Similarly, Hepburn proposes, beauty must cover much more than delight and wonderment in the look, feel, or formal quality of things. Sensuous and thought components are both necessary, as is some sense of the "life enhancing" quality of beauty.

Do these, though, unequivocally ground ascriptions of seriousness to natural beauty? Hepburn argues that the sensuous element can reveal detailed or indiscriminate access to natural objects; reflection can be feeble, immature, or haphazard; yet rejection of either component trivializes by impoverishing the full possible range of subjects' relations to nature. Perhaps a trivial approach falsifies the conception available in a fuller account of nature or in a deeper grasp of the subjects' participation in constructing that conception.[16] Yet this does not imply that a fuller thought content will necessarily make an experience more serious: a work that succinctly refers the viewer "to quite fundamental features of the lived human state" can be more serious than one that fritters all its energy at some arbitrary node. Superficiality can enter also from the side of perception, when it fails to give due weight to the objects of nature themselves, and ends by anthropomorphizing them. Sentimental approaches posit in nature a *"failed human life and human attitudes instead of successfully attained nonhuman life."*[17] Further, a deep appreciation must include the nourishment that images of the natural world have given to human inner life.

These two elements – the autonomy of nature and the human annexation of natural forms – raise distinctive issues of seriousness and triviality. To understand nature "in its own terms" can invite a scientific understanding, given that many other systematic accounts of nature seem obviously metaphysical. But that cannot be necessary, so far as "thinking-in" these explanations may also disrupt rather than promote aesthetic appreciation. Nor can an "undifferentiated consciousness of nature's dysteleology. . .always predominate in any aesthetic experience."[18] Even though a truthfulness to nature requires cognizance of the ephemerality of an individual, too rigid a hold on this thought seems to preclude an appreciation of the beauty of a butterfly before a bird snaps out its life or of the lithe balance of a leopard's movements before it springs to kill a gazelle.[19] Perhaps, then, nature becomes an aesthetic object only by falsifying its scientific or dysteleological character – which surely militates against the seriousness of an aesthetic appreciation of nature.

One way to escape this impasse, Hepburn proposes, is to construct a less simplistic account of nature. Aesthetic appreciation too can stand more scrutiny. Some aestheticians prefer to stress the perceptual qualities of objects over the thought component and its problems. But that yields a very thin account of natural beauty just because its conceptions of nature and beauty lack depth. Perhaps the answer lies in the practice of aesthetic discrimination: between the extremes of too little thought or too little sensuousness. "We might find an acceptable ideal for serious aesthetic perception in encouraging ourselves to enhance the thought-load *almost* to the point, but not *beyond* the point, at which it begins to overwhelm the vivacity of the particular perception."[20]

7

The attempt to interiorize or annex nature raises its own issues of seriousness and triviality. Hepburn identifies metaphor as "the essence of such appropriations," in which natural forms articulate inner events – for example we suffer dark nights of the soul – and argues that their seriousness depends on their power. Metaphors mold and make that interiority powerfully or merely perfunctorily, with those borrowed from nature's power being perhaps less restrictive or anxious than ones derived from a human-made environment. This appropriation yields an experience that is both distant and intimate. Arguably, so far as it fragments the experience of nature to incorporate it into the alternative wholeness of aesthetic valuation, the meaningfulness of natural beauty has some of the intensity of dreams. While he does not explain this dreamlike quality in the way just suggested, Hepburn cites that quality to explain how in natural beauty "the interiorization seems half completed in nature itself," its figures "apprehended with a mysterious sense that the components ... deeply matter to us, though one cannot say how."[21] Similarly, imaginative comparisons unify diverse features of nature in our experience – clouds with sand, hills with waves in the sea.

These associations can be trivial or serious when they are more or less arbitrary and more or less appropriate. Perhaps seriousness here resides in recognizing the continuing otherness of nature, its incongruity with our capacity for aesthetic response. If every one of its features signaled some precise and determinate relation with some deeper meaning, natural beauty would not merit any special attention. Its instances would merely repeat the same determination. Rather, its seriousness consists in part at least in trading on the real possibility that nature has no regard for human sensibility or aspiration.

Both these approaches, of annexation and autonomy, while they may indicate distinctive senses of seriousness, can together fall victim to a scepticism about natural beauty generally: that it is so closely tied to a human scale, is so Κατ᾽ ἄνθρωπον, that it is quite superficial when considered from any larger measure. A cliff face that appears awesome when viewed from its foot may seem inconsequential when seen from an airplane at thirty thousand feet.[22]

Hepburn suggests that this kind of criticism relies on some sense of what things are *really* like, that undermines the validity of a human viewpoint. And rather than entertain this skepticism, he warns that "our aesthetic experience of nature is thoroughly dependent on scale and on individual viewpoint. To fail to realize *how* deeply would surely trivialize." Moreover, the central assumption that there is some single perspective that yields what things are really like – and that establishes authoritatively *the* meaning of nature – is highly contentious. Just as the subject matter of art is not restricted, so too the aesthetic appreciation of nature can attend to any qualities, and that precludes privileging some single perspective on a part or whole of nature.

The recognition of parity between perspectives, when seen in relation to the respect for truth set out earlier, generates apparently irresolvable pressures in the conception of natural beauty. One militates towards an exploratory interrogation of nature and a consequent subjectivization of its various orders, undetermined by any single explanatory principle. The other pushes towards an exteriorization of sensibility, interrogating human interiority as a by-product of acknowledging nature's separateness. The notion of truth or some determinate explanatory principle seems to apply less easily to this second sense. Each approach promotes a distinctive method for grasping natural beauty, which is not obviously commensurable with the other. But perhaps that is as much as a philosophical reflection on method can deliver. A choice between the approaches depends on what the actual instance needs in order to merit serious consideration, and it may be that the seriousness or triviality of aesthetic appreciation follows not simply from the texture of experience – its sensuousness or rationality, the ordering that results from a privileged explanatory principle or the engagement that allows an annexation of nature – but from the uses it makes available.

Be that as it may, the essays by Diffey and Hepburn raise a number of issues. Both suggest that too simple a conception of nature, especially one that tries to establish *the* meaning of nature and thence of natural beauty, trivializes its experience. In addition, both essays usually explain natural beauty by reference to art. Arguably, this is more than accidental, since the more thoroughly developed vocabulary of art should cast light on the other, recently released from connotations of sanctity and piety, and since both engage with the matter of beauty. Hepburn's distinction between a sensuous and thought component of aesthetic responses to nature, for example, echoes Schiller's division between feeling and rational form in understanding fine art.

That extrapolation from art to nature invites consideration of the concept of nature as it emerges in art. Natural beauty draws on the conventions that constitute artistic beauty – which, like its counterpart, exists in the way people talk about it and the means they can use to represent it. In the two essays immediately following, "The Public Prospect and the Private View: The Politics of Taste in Eighteenth Century Britain," by John Barrell and "Landscape in the Cinema: The Rhythms of the World and the Camera" by Philip Sitney, the authors explore nature's appearance in the visual arts of painting and film. These modes of representation allow a particular access to nature that determines the object and the texture of its appreciation. The needs and conventions of society and media, the critics' concerns and the technology available for representing objects, determine the conception of nature and so of natural beauty.

In "The Public Prospect and the Private View" Barrell explores the social construction of nature and the viewing subject. He argues that a correct taste for landscapes in nature and art came to legitimate political authority. The latter needed people "capable of thinking in general terms, of producing abstract ideas out of the raw data of experience," writers maintained, and a proper taste for natural beauty evinced possession of the necessary disposition. Only men have this ability by nature, and only some of them have the opportunity to nurture and realize that ability.[23] The opportunity fails to occur if a man has to work to support himself and his dependents: his occupation will cause a narrowing of his interest; his sensibility, determined by his experiences at work, will not allow for ideas of wide enough scope; and, as mechanical work deals with objects, it does not sustain abstract reasoning. Only those of independent means have the disinterested public sensibility – a capacity for gaining a prospect of the whole social order – needed for participation in a government that serves the public interest. Only they have the capacity for engaging in the liberal arts – which, Barrell says were then still the arts of those who were free or liberal. The others, including mechanicals, women, and children, are thwarted by a sensuality that leads them to an interest in "consumption and possession."[24]

Barrell argues that this political distinction between the governors and those they govern correlates with an equally complex distinction between two kinds of landscape. Citing the work of Coleridge, Reynolds, and Hazlitt, he focuses on Sir Joshua Reynolds' riddle of whether or not a painter should represent accidents of nature such as rainbows, storms, and movements. Accidents signify the occurrence of changes: by representing trees bent over by the wind, the artist reminds his audience that the state depicted in the painting will be followed in nature by a different state. Nature cannot then appear as the basis for well founded truths, constituted of "substantial representative forms," all "arranged in a wide extent of land," but attracts attention for its particularities. In eighteenth-century Britain critics understood these two different types of landscape as produced by and for "two different spheres of life, and even of two different kinds of people."[25]

The prospect suited those who could recognize abstract ideas, when they were presented in a painting, by analyzing their essential features. These people were not waylaid by attending only to the details, from whose attractions their attention could not escape. Reynolds, Coleridge, and Thomas Tickell, for example, supposed that the ability to think the whole, the general and abstract relation between things, is more valuable than the inability to eliminate details that results in a failure to "comprehend a whole, not even what it means."[26]

This distinction between the landscape as either "ideal, panoramic prospect, the analogue of the social and the universal, which is surveyed, organized, and understood by disinterested public man," or as "occluded…representing the 'confined views' of the private man, whose experience is too narrow to permit him to abstract" is complicated by its interrelation with another distinction, between two different spheres of a citizen's life: "the public sphere, where he is enjoined to consult only the public interest, and the private sphere, where he is temporarily released from his obligation as a citizen."[27] This suggests that landscape art of either kind remains private when compared with the public art of history painting. Public here means a grand style, depicting what concerns everyone "as universal men, as men considered in the light of what is common to all of them, their substantial nature, and not what is of concern to their private and accidental identities." In effect, landscape, of whatever kind, denotes the sensibility, private feelings, and private virtues.

These distinctions explain how Hazlitt solves Reynolds' riddle. Unfortunately, Barrell suggests, he does so by denying the relation between art and the public or communal sphere. That denial may have set the tone for aesthetics in the next century. In any case, Barrell's essay clarifies how the concepts of nature and subject are shot through with tensions born of the political and aesthetic concerns of critics of painting.

These social concerns are not the only factors determining the meaning of nature and landscape. Critics identified political issues in

11

terms of visual characteristics because of the power visual representations possessed to articulate theses about nature. This led to talk of
nature and its politics by using the aesthetic terms of prospect,
landscape, perspective, universality, detail, figure, public, private,
history, and so on. Other crucial elements of the present aesthetic
vocabulary came from photography and, especially, cinema. Landscape, landscape painting, and the search for a harmony change with
the sense of, and access to, nature. Paintings explored that relation in
a particular way. Gainsborough and Constable gave way to Turner's
impressions and glimpses, which Courbet in turn counterpointed
with his representations of the construction of landscape. A newer
mode makes a newer meaning possible: cinema raises issues of how
to conceive of landscape without the painterly constraints of static
viewpoint and unmoving representations. The concept of nature that
emerges from representation in this medium will require an appropriate sense of beauty. Prospects take on an added dimension when
the camera can enter into their space; the camera can educate its
audience to move from detail to prospect through cuts and zooms.
Perhaps the argument that detail and abstraction attract different
groups and sensibilities can find purchase despite these differences
and even if those works of art as a whole cannot any longer claim the
aura of the original.[28] In any case, the contribution of cinema to the
conception of nature in art is well worth following.

In his essay "Landscape in the Cinema," Philip Sitney explores the
newer vocabulary that cinema eventually gave to landscapes and
nature in its representations. The topic of cinematic landscapes, he
maintains, "is virtually an unconscious issue of film theory." The
vast literature on film considers "montage, language, the human face,
the city, sound and silence, faith and truth," but includes "almost
nothing on natural beauty." In his reappraisal, Sitney follows the
historical evolution of evocations of landscape beauty that results
from changes in cinematic technology. This leads him to study the
integration of landscape issues into narratives and culminates in an
account of *avant-garde* film where, in the 1970s and 1980s, the
aesthetic issues of landscape films emerged more clearly. Thus the
essay's narration of landscape in cinema explores how landscape
changes its meaning when it surfaces in a new medium among novel
interconnections. This deepens the conception of nature and compli-
cates the interaction between art and nature that determines aesthetic
evaluation. Now images, time, and movement interact; change
becomes a visible feature, to be choreographed into the represen-

tation; movement is more than the eye following and being led or arrested by strokes and blocks of color, but includes advancing into space. All this requires a distinctive or, at least, larger vocabulary that, in turn, effects the possibility of relating a controlled representation of nature to its beauty in the search for authenticity.

"Landscape entered the cinema as one of the arenas of human action."[29] That register continues to appear in mainstream cinema: in the last shot of *The Searchers* Ethan remains outside the house, stepping back into the harsh and arid landscape. There are also variations: in *Mirror* Tarkovsky uses shots of ripened corn fields being whipped into waves by the wind and of a broken fence to announce Lenin's appearance in Russian history; Renoir uses rain to signify passages of time fraught with emotional currents. These depend on a syntax of representations of nature and its beauty in cinema that was formed quite early. The moving camera, the panoramic sweep, the long shot combined with closer shots from different perspectives, all appeared in the early twentieth century. Their use determined different cinematic genres: the Western, travelogues, and adventures set on the seas, among others. Film technology allowed further refinements, so that orthochromatic film, with strong contrasts between black and white, sustained a story of conflict with nature more acutely than the panchromatic stock with its tonal variations of gray. The invention of sound and color, and advances in technology such as the zoom lens, added to the richness of texture and vocabulary. All this gave the films of, say, Anthony Mann, Mizoguchi, and Dreyer the means to integrate landscape into narratives as an element of meaning, loading them with a moral power or ambiguity as the films dictated.

Sitney shows how this complexity of movement, meaning, space, and imagery allowed theorists to talk of the "rhythmical pressure of natural beauty" in cinema – of the "music of landscape"(Eisenstein) or "the cinema of poetry" (Pasolini) – and also opened up another approach to landscape in the *avant-garde* cinema of Europe and North America. The work of Stan Brakhage eschews actors, documentary subjects, narration or voice, and forces the images alone to develop emotional resonances. Brakhage argues that cinema is the only art that can embody the relation between vision and time – through "the shifts in focus, reaction to peripheral vision, superimposed memory scenes and eye movements, while maintaining a sense of the body's movement in space."[30] And his use of visual images alone strips them of the usual epistemic frame that, through sound, narration or music, etc., gives a film its systematic organization into a story. Brakhage's presence behind the camera brings the audience what he sees, but leaves this in an ambiguous relation to his expectations of those sights. "The compensation of this sacrifice is the inheritance of a rich tradition of landscape painting and photography susceptible to reconception in terms of cinematic rhythm."

Central to this movement, Sitney proposes, is the use of montage. But while people like Brakhage, Menken, Hutton, Kobland, Kubelka, and Sombert, in their different ways, used montage, sometimes to register the presence of a subject viewer, others pursued the automation of the camera in order to emphasize the independence of the world of objects. These alternatives also borrowed from an already encoded approach to landscape,[31] but they did not simply repeat or try to reproduce those codes. The possibilities of cinema simply make that impossible; instead, by reappropriating those codes, *avant-garde* film made "landscape" into "a term in the epistemology of the cinema, essentially because *avant-garde* film making. . .conjoined the representation of natural beauty with exploration of how the film-making tools 'see' and 'know' their subjects."[32] Thereby they develop the concept of landscape.

The analyses by Barrell and Sitney suggest by implication that an understanding of natural beauty and landscape that ignores their construction will end in nostalgia. Landscape's beginnings in Dutch painting arise from a particular organization of perceptions that yields a distinctively textured experience. Its mode of seeing is based in the techniques of linear perspective, surveying and mapping, though this is still bound up with an irreducible sense of wonder and awe towards nature that escapes mathematical perspectives. Instead of being simply absorbed into that quantifying organization of land and sight, landscape still represents an escape to the world of nature, where life, body, and soul are in harmony. The landscape provides the most telling arena for action against which to judge the history that human beings construct.

Dutch landscape is not alone in resting on this interaction between human history and primeval nature. In some English landscape art that relation of human beings to nature was suffused with a nostalgia for some older and more "authentic" history. Patterns of agriculture and ownership determined the order of the land. Roads followed the outlines of fields; tillage took the form of straight furrows on flat land or raised sections cultivated with hoes; spinneys and fallow fields dotted the land. People lived in villages that gave them easy access to their work, maintaining an ordered rhythm in continuous communities. These locations, even if now co-opted into advertisements promoting a bogus authenticity and togetherness, yet bear some imprint of a history that, emerging from nature, redounds with human engagements.

In the late eighteenth and early nineteenth centuries, in England, this nostalgia took the form of including in landscapes figures of rustics, their implements, and their work on the land. Barrell argues that the point of including these figures was to suggest that no "disjunction" existed between "an ideal image of the rural life and its actuality," and to "offer a reassurance about the state of the poor in England."[33] Here the "raggedness of the poor became of aesthetic interest, and they became the objects of our pity," to be replaced eventually by more efficient representations of laborers "merged-...with their surroundings, too far away from us for the questions about how contented or ragged they were to arise."[34]

Talk of the idyllic grace of nature is caught up with this politics of nostalgia. These are elegies for impossible lives. Like the connections Bede makes between nature, beauty, and divinity, and which King Alfred promulgated for Bede's *Historia*, they no longer seem quite plausible. Cult, theodicy, and nostalgia now seem unduly sentimental because they are usually sustained only at the cost of refusing to recognize material and cultural changes.[35] The relations of good earth, nature, and God-givenness do not easily retain their timbre when people conceive of earth as dirt or as geological and botanical formations, when they use this vocabulary to establish their "down to earth" common sense or scientific credentials. Natural beauty seems to have been without momentum for some time, perhaps as much because art now shorn of beauty is a powerful tool for examining a human life almost entirely mediated by social formations as because nature has become the object of a scientific probing that is little enchanted with its mysterious processes. Those now impossible lives only become possible by selecting a particular kind of observer's point of view: the latter gave substance to the language of prospects and, later, of "tourism" as the cultivation of nature extended beyond producing food. The observer's viewpoint, once reserved for those who owned the land but did not work on it, was more and more occupied by people who rented the space for a short while, on holiday, and cultivated a taste for escaping back to nature from the city.

Underlying this truck with nature was the fact that it had been cultivated, its harshness and jaggedness removed by the work of centuries and thousands of laborers. It was a conception of nature that would not do for America. To this tradition, this land was largely unpeopled and uncultivated. It was a wilderness in which the European immigrants could not simply take up a viewpoint with its attendant prepackaging of a cosy nature. Rather they had to penetrate its unknown contours to construct – or reconstruct – their communities. The shape of nature was seemingly primeval here, in turn both promising and threatening, and was unmediated by any sense of other peoples' work on its order. Nostalgia became more difficult; landscape bore again the imprint of God's grace and gift, but wrapped in some deadly threat that people felt they had to overcome by taming and ordering nature.

In "The Touch of Landscape" Don Gifford maps out some of the changes the New World brought into the mother country's tamed conception of a countryside. Jefferson laid out Monticello under the influence of English gardens but needed to add cognizance of the wilderness that framed his prospects in order to avoid showing "too much of art." Thoreau sought "the preservation of the world" in wildness but was exhausted by "the vast, Titanic, inhuman Nature" of Mount Katahdin: it robbed him of "his divine faculty." Faulkner laments the passing of wilderness, but signals its presence in the imagination as a fear that "the wildness within" matches "the wildness without," still lying beneath the flatness imposed by a "juggernaut civilization."

So total was the threat of this encroachment that the need to rescue nature became an element of politics. Fredrick Law Olmsted won a prize "to humanize the physical environment of cities and to secure precious scenic regions" by designing New York's Central Park; and later, when Lincoln decreed the preservation of Yosemite Valley as a public nature reserve "for all time," Olmstead was one of the Park's first commissioners. This democratization of nature, though, has increasingly taken the form of individuals consuming the product "natural landscape." Crowds oppress these natural spots: their deeper involvement would destroy the spectacle, and the alternative seems to be to present only a spectacle at a nearby site. Gifford points out that commercial companies propose to construct super cinemas at sites like Tusayan, Arizona, by the Grand Canyon, and Zion National Park at Springdale, Utah. These will have screens seventy feet wide and fifty feet high, that almost surround the viewers and give them a sense of being in the middle of the scene. Unburdening nature of the impact of history, of human engagement, or of grace, landscape is simply another collection of sensations to have had, without the encumbrance of reality, as the cinema becomes another monumental sight.[36]

Although this sounds like an unseemly nostalgia for a predemocratic age in which only the sensitive few merited access to nature, it is more correctly seen as a reminder of a genuine need for authenticity. Perhaps the mainstream sense of beauty and nature has failed that need. Most of the examples used to generate issues in the papers so far discussed are from fairly usual landscapes. If nature is to be beautiful, if it is to grant transcendence, if issues of seriousness and triviality in aesthetic appreciation of nature arise from given conceptions of nature, if sensuousness and thought must encompass nature, then, having considered the contribution of art to natural beauty, this volume should consider how nature structures that aesthetic estimation, how its genuine otherness, say in its climatic extremes or in its action on art, enlarges the concept of beauty. In "Desert and Ice: Ambivalent Aesthetics," Yi-Fu Tuan develops the conception of natural beauty by turning to the experience of nature in its extremities.

These water-scarce and frigid regions seem eccentric to the tradition from which landscape and natural beauty arise. Yet their very extremity also has a power to attract those who, dissatisfied with the pace and texture of a tamed landscape, are in search of authenticity in the far edges of nature. The Eurocentricity of "landscape," the attachment to it of those whose home it is, is a reminder that deserts and ice-scapes are home to others. They have attracted people from the mainstream with a longing to be taken out of themselves into "something vast, overpowering, and indifferent."[37] But this is not so much a rejection of home as transporting a kind of home-space to an unfamiliar location in which some deeper sense of human reality emerges. Tuan cites the examples of Wilfrid Thesiger, T. E. Lawrence, and Charles Doughty, among desert explorers, and Fridtjof Nansen and Robert Byrd among polar explorers. Both groups sought "the peace that comes from solitude." They looked for "the effortless, empty, eddyless wind of the desert," or "to taste peace and quiet and solitude to find out how good they are."[38] This isolation may bring them closer to themselves, free of the abiding pull of society and its demands.

Byrd describes observing the sky while listening to music:

17

as the notes swelled, the dull aurora on the horizon pulsed and quickened and draped itself into arches and fanning beams which reached across the sky until at my zenith the display attained its crescendo. The music and the night became one; and I told myself that all beauty was akin and sprang from the same substance. I recalled a gallant, unselfish act that was of the same essence as the music and the aurora.[39]

This last classical reference to goodness, beauty, and truth placed him in an harmony that appeared clearly because it was uninterrupted by others. And if the desert explorers seemed more uniformly misanthropic, their hope was still to discover their authentic being by engaging with a nature apparently indifferent to human beings.

But they did not reject home for this pursuit: "camp is a home-away-from home, which can seem all the more homelike in the way that it caters to and satisfies the body's demand for comfort by contrast with the indifference or active hostility of...nature outside."[40] This was the arctic explorers' response; and although people like T. E. Lawrence felt fettered by their bodies and shunned those home comforts, nevertheless, their aim was still to find themselves a deeper home, a real place, even in nature at its most extreme.

That extremity was metonymic with death. They seemed to test their humanity at its most mortal. Roosevelt writes feelingly of the plains in winter that the "terrible cold that broods over the earth like the shadow of silent death seems even more dreadful in its gloomy rigor than is the lawless madness of storms."[41] Lawrence wants that of "death and life, or less finally, leisure and subsistence, we should shun subsistence (which is the stuff of life) in all save its faintest degree."[42] And Nansen describes the polar region as the "kingdom" or "realm" of death.

Few of these explorers were religious, even though their behavior followed a pattern already established in Christianity. As religious institutions became more like secular ones, individuals sometimes sought more extreme tests of their felt religiosity. The move was meaningful within the taxonomy of Christian virtues: the deserts result from Adam's fall from grace; Moses wandered the desert for forty years, in a time when his people were closest to their God; Christ's temptation by Satan was in the wilderness, his transformation occurred on a mountain. It was not a big step from there to Jerome's claim that "a town is a prison, and the desert loveliness a paradise."[43] The desert provided greater simplicity before God and a more intense experience of His presence.

The sense of death that accompanied twentieth-century explorers was, in its religious context, ameliorated by the gift of eternal life under God's laws. Nevertheless, some of the secular explorers shared a distaste for the inauthenticity of well-ordered social life. Patterns and given designs, with their connotations of repetition and therefore of success, smooth over the raw energy of human lives; the framed prospect or picture, implying a set location for the viewer, rob them of the possibility of creating their own spaces and orders. The risks attached to gaining authenticity are extreme, but no value is easily wrought, and they are willing to face ultimate failure.

A notion of landscape or natural beauty that confines nature to the realm of mainstream existence also lacks the richness of creative experience. The constant openness of the social order that nature can signify is closed off if nature is always encoded, even in its representations, in conventional ways. Nature then becomes less than home, not so much a harmony with man as a signal of the constraints that social life imposes. An expanded notion of nature, we may suggest, will bring an extended notion of natural beauty that will more fruitfully explore the deep and changing relation of human beings to their environment.

This otherness of nature, its presenting subjects with qualities that lead them to question accepted conceptions of beauty, gives primacy to natural beauty. The conception of beauty that emerged from landscape art, on the other hand, encoded nature through artistic conventions and their social bases, using standards that are not clearly native to nature. Perhaps the strongest contrast to the otherness of nature lies in the determination of nature in gardening, which can justifiably be considered an art among others like painting and sculpture. Here art intrudes most directly, not simply singling out significant features on the model of landscape painting, but actually intervening in the natural order to control and reorder it. It seems to be the opposite of that escape to extreme climates that Tuan's essay described. In some cases, such as Versailles or the Taj Mahal, the formal gardens overpower the rudeness of nature with an extended and careful civilization that reproduces the king's authority over his land and subjects. The suburban garden, by extension, even as it may intend to rescue some pieces of earth from the continuous carpeting of asphalt, shares this determining thrust, but constrained to a domestic scale. The thoroughness of that asphalt carpeting robs the suburban garden of its natural context and meaning.

Nature may seem to continue to have a part in these determinations, in some sense, because gardens cultivate natural shrubs and

19

plants, whose characteristics determine what can be done. But that seems no different from painting having to rely on the characteristics of oils or acrylic, sculpture on stone or steel, and poetry on the sounds and meanings available in any language. The art of gardening consists in part of making the most of the possibilities available in materials, just as in painting or sculpture. In *this* context, perhaps the opposite of gardening lies in environmental art, where nature enters significantly into art, resulting in works that owe a great deal to their sites. The meaning of the final work includes its interaction with those natural surroundings that it does not simply supplant. Yet explaining the opposition in this way serves at best to remind viewers that neither pole of art or nature can be overpowered completely. The nature and development of an art depends on what materials artists explore and the conditions in which they work. Gardens in a temperate climate offer possibilities for the nature of the art that a tropical climate can neither sustain nor accept; the topology of a particular place will suit some features of landscape better than others; the light in different places may suit watercolors better than oils: nature will constrain art, even as art determines how people construe nature. Given this interaction, environmental art may be much closer to gardening than the last paragraph proposed. In her essay on "Gardens, Earthworks, and Environmental Art," Stephanie Ross argues that environmental art works may be the *avant-garde* of gardening, that emerged after the decline of the main art.

To make her argument, Ross begins by examining the nature of gardens. A definition seems impossible, since there is a large variety of gardens, including those with or without flowers, lawns, streams, trees, shrubs, herbs, layers, extensions, borders, walls, privacy, fountains, bulbs, or purposes. These variations permit a range of emblematic and semantic possibilities, that will disrupt any expectation that gardens simply reproduce some Edenic bliss. Ross points out that English reactions to the manifest order of the French garden consisted in giving their gardens a more natural look. They were not necessarily introducing entirely new elements into the parameters of man and animal or nature and civilization by that means, but they represented different conceptions of how much the land could be cultivated or socialized without loss of authenticity – without suppressing nature as a repository of creative energies.

English garden owners used the emblematic properties of trees and shrubs to make particular statements. Rather than signify only the domination of civilization over nature, gardens in the early eighteenth century used shrubs, trees, and architecture to construct messages. Ross cites the example of Stowe, Cobham's estate in Buckinghamshire, that uses temples in Classical, Gothic and Modern styles, with the last constructed downhill and downstream, combined with other commissions of statuary, quotation and herbiage, to set out an "anti-Stuart, anti-Catholic, pro-British" stance.[44]

This use of gardens changed rapidly during the course of that century, as the influence of Romanticism overtook that of Classicism. These changes included varying accounts of nature and beauty because they relied on distinctive conceptions of human and external nature. Under the influence of Kant, Coleridge thought an interest in natural beauty evinced the health of the observer's soul. This concern with nature and its beauty is surely crucial to the fluency of English landscape.

At first gardens seem to be only an indirect part of that concern for landscape. Owners cultivated their land – landscaped it – to produce preferred relations between its natural features and their sense of aesthetic order. The garden formed the background of their conversations, walks, rides, and society; it could be "representational in the broad sense of saying something, having a subject matter, and requiring interpretation."[45] Yet gardens seemed to remain outside the compass of the kind of representation that landscape paintings could embody. Ross contends that gardens like Stowe were not "of (about) some other natural scene," in the way that paintings were of their subjects, even though their designs incorporated such "painterly concerns as color, texture, balance, form, perspective, and light and shade in laying out grounds."[46] However, later developments – the cult of the picturesque – occluded that distinction too, as Uvedale Price and Richard Payne Knight, for example, came to think of natural scenes in terms of pictures and valued natural features when they were suitable for painting. The weight of gardening as an art supported an exploration of the art of landscape painting by exploring aesthetic aspects of the domestication of nature.

With the decline in the art of gardening, one tool for thinking through the human relation to nature may seem to have vanished. But Ross argues against such pessimism. Conceptions of landscape and natural beauty may still interact with and feel the influence of practices that succeeded the high art of gardening. These include earth works and environmental art. Ross divides the latter into broad and overlapping categories such as architectural installations, didactic art, proto-gardens, sculpture gardens, and art parks, among others. The last two perhaps resemble gardens more obviously than the others. Alan Sonfist's *Time Landscapes* reproduces the vanished flora of a particular area, for example, while Robert Irwin's Wellesley College installation, a long steel wall that reflects the play of light shining through trees on a nearby lake, alters perceptions by returning attention to the grounds where it is placed. Both artists construct proto-gardens by engaging with the land and its order. Similarly, sculpture gardens and art parks seem very straightforwardly like gardens for including works of art in a natural landscape.

For all these cases, Ross argues, what makes them like gardens is that the relation between objects and their site is a vital feature in understanding and interpreting the works. These are not the only similarities: gardens and some environmental art engage with and disrupt the land; blossoms are as ephemeral as some environmental works; paths and trees control perceptions as much as the rules some environmental artists use to construct the narrative of their works; gardens privilege some foliage over others for their texture and color and for their contribution to the texture, solidity, and depth of the whole just as do some works of environmental art. But similarities also remain arbitrary until some principle of relevance makes them significant to both gardens and environmental art. One such criterion of relevance lies in the influence of the first upon the construction of the second; another closely related criterion, which Ross prefers, lies in this: "if, in understanding and interpreting later works, we see them as fulfilling some of the important functions of their predecessors, then it is proper to see the later works as descendants of those which came before."[47] By this second criterion, because twentieth-century environmental works "perform some of the [same] aesthetic tasks," they link with eighteenth-century gardens. And their central aesthetic task is to "build landscapes in the environment:" to think through the relation between the works and their sites.

Using these parameters of site and work, Ross draws on the work of Robert Irwin – who contends that works can be site dominant, site adjusted, site specific, or site determined – to argue that gardens which fail to address their sites are of merely botanical interest because they ignore the features which trade on prospects, viewpoints, contours, and textures to determine their order. Their success lies in measures other than the aesthetic. Nor need engagement with the setting always be a mutually respectful one: Le Nôtre fought the local swampland to produce Versailles. Nevertheless, even as the gardens signify the king's self-understanding, they are still sensitive to the site that emerged from swampland. All these works – gardens and environmental art – "are in the landscape, they all manipulate that landscape, and they all make us take into account our relation to the landscape."[48]

The more complex that relation between work and site, the richer the work is, and the greater its stature. The distinctions and lineages Ross provides in developing this argument suggest a vocabulary for talking about gardens and environmental art. Her essay does not explicitly intend to rejuvenate gardening's membership of the fine arts; nevertheless, by comparing gardens and environmental art, she expands the current conceptions of nature, beauty, and the landscape. It therefore shares the enterprise of Tuan's essay, which in effect also questioned the constraints guiding received notions of beauty based on accepted conceptions of nature.

Her essay also raises again an issue that appears in the preceding essay. The duality of gardens, their close reference to nature, and their construction out of nature under the aegis of fine art, occasions questions about distinctions between art and nature generally: are there important differences in understanding and appreciating each? Perhaps natural beauty is only an extension of the principles of ordering and response that govern fine art. Nature is as much a construct, and natural beauty is as dependent on human perspective, as any landscape painting. Diffey raised this issue when he suggested that to understand art it was necessary to look to natural beauty but also accepted that natural beauty became clearer in some respects through comparison with fine art. Hepburn explains crucial distinctive features of natural beauty by using a distinction that, for example in Schiller, explained fine art – again suggesting a close interaction between the two. The essays by Barrell, Sitney, Gifford, and Tuan, in examining the characteristics of nature in representations in different arts and enterprises, show that Nature is itself a construction, and so seems aptly construed in terms borrowed from art.

The possibility of this and other construals of nature raises yet another matter. Given the overwhelming power of the scientific and technological understandings of nature, and the success they can claim, their vocabulary seems inescapable in any grasp of nature, including an aesthetic one. Perhaps its use will allow for a more mature explanation of natural beauty and its place in the system of human life. Conversely, that scientific vocabulary may ultimately prove inadequate. In some versions it may suppose that the human

23

relation to nature must be contemplative – a mode that unnecessarily restricts the greater sophistication that is in fact available to us. A combination of a scientific vocabulary and an engaged sense of beauty could yield powerful results without any metaphysical commitments. Yet perhaps that too attractive move remains unsatisfactory because it rejects too much – the emotional, annexing impulse, that interiorized nature, still seems vital, and a complete rejection of it for the sake of scientificity, rather than being a rejection of sentimentality, too easily becomes a dismissal of the important matter of feeling human.

In "Comparing Natural and Artistic Beauty" Donald Crawford takes up the first issue directly. He does not intend to defend a particular way of comparing art and nature aesthetically but explores their relation to suggest that ultimately we do not seem to have clear reasons for finding such comparisons idle. He begins with a classical sense of beauty, that conceives of natural beauty as "the sensuous embodiment of seemingly intelligent design," with all the associated notions of perfection, due proportion, form, and regularity. Here nature is an ideal for art, which succeeds so far as it represents beautiful natural forms. Both are of the same genus and so easily comparable. The most influential classical authority, Aristotle, explains works of art as organisms because of their manner of imitating the reality of nature.[49]

A number of theses from this theory continued to gain adherents for some time, and Aristotle's authority remained largely intact for some centuries in Europe. Nevertheless, Crawford argues that this conception of beauty is untenable on its own grounds. In any case, shifting attention to the eighteenth century, his essay introduces the challenge that "the picturesque" issued to the classical formalists' requirement of regularity and proportion. This did not reject Aristotelian organicism outright but certainly complicated it by acknowledging a need for figures – carts, people, animals, and other varieties of objects – in fairly determinate positions in paintings, represented as being in calculated but not overly manipulative control of land. Leaving aside the issues of the social and political commitments that explain the aesthetic choices artists made in paintings by including figures of rustics, their implements, and their work on the land – an issue raised earlier – the interaction between art and nature in the picturesque seems to preclude any clear comparison between the two kinds of beauty. Designed landscapes also relied on principles of perspective to produce a picturesque "natural" scene, and while some landscapes may acquire those qualities independently of human action, nevertheless, if the perception of it as a picturesque landscape borrows its modes from appreciating constructed landscapes, then regardless of how the landscape came into being, it neither clearly yields a beauty that is entirely "natural" nor permits a comparison between two completely distinctive elements. Comparisons are still meaningful here, as Crawford says, but they "are not straightforward comparisons between art and nature as one might assume."[50]

This criticism of the feasibility of comparisons in the picturesque clearly implies a much wider doubt about any attempt to distinguish and compare art and nature. It trades on the need to recognize the mind's participation in conceptions of nature according to artistic rules, but also opens the possibility of denying the naturalness of any experience that imports an explanatory overview of the order of nature. A religious view of the natural order arguably also interferes with grasping nature for itself, and can vitiate comparisons between art and nature. Pressed further, this position may raise doubts about whether any account of a "pure" nature is available or any comparison meaningful at all.

Be that as it may, Crawford goes on to consider other criticisms of the meaningfulness of comparisons between artistic and natural beauty. One difficulty is that whereas works of art are intentional objects constituted of meanings and requiring interpretation and criticism, the "aesthetic appreciation of nature...is restricted to an appreciation of their sensuous surface."[51] No intention literally constructs these objects; therefore they are qualitatively distinct from their artistic counterparts, and no meaningful comparison between surface elements and expressive or semantic meaningfulness is available. At least two responses to this claim are possible: to argue that natural beauty possesses the expressive and semantic properties that art does, or to understand art and nature on a continuum based on some more general principle that makes comparisons between them meaningful.

Those who want to defend the expressiveness of nature can contend that nature is God's creation, and needs interpretation just as any work of art does; that analogies between artifacts and natural objects allow the one to determine conceptions of the other; or that events and objects in nature are part of a whole complex, whose relation to the particular stands in as much need of interpretation as any work of art and its cultural context. Crawford identifies the

25

following problems with these claims. As every part of nature is as significant of the whole complex, any part will be as expressive, and that eliminates all comparative aesthetic evaluations. Moreover, finding a natural complex for natural objects leaves open the additional cultural context of works, whose distinctiveness thwarts direct comparisons. Finally, discovering analogies between natural and artistic beauty is of little help until some criteria of relevance allow focus. But that, the suggestion is, is just what is missing.

Perhaps the general principle promised by thinking of art and nature as a continuum will provide the needed standard. This claim derives from Hegel, for whom perceptual forms embody greater or lesser rational self-consciousness. "Natural beauty is always less developed than art by this conception, though there are varying degrees of perfection within nature as well as within art."[52] Crawford focuses on three problems with this system: its basic principle is the classical one, that beauty is the sensuous embodiment of perfection, but with perfection now explained in terms of stages of developing spirit and rational self-consciousness; its comparative judgments rely on broad categories that do not facilitate any subtle discriminations; indeed, arguably the reason for, say, the inferiority of rocks against statues depends on characteristics of art forms which more or less guarantee that even the more unsuccessful work of art will claim a greater perfection than the most beautiful rocks, regardless of how the two objects look. The result of these problems is that the comparisons between nature and art promised by the general principle do not obtain.

An alternative mode of comparison may emphasize the interdependence of fine art and natural beauty. Some works such as landscape-art relate to nature in that they depict it. Others "directly make use of the natural environment in their artistic realization" and "are best interpreted as being at least in part about that very environment, or about our relationship to it. Here the more general concept of reference replaces resemblance or imitation as the important category in appreciating these works, and the classical model of beauty is left far behind."[53] But do these works allow for informative comparisons between natural beauty and art? Crawford distinguishes three "aesthetically dynamic relations between art and nature:" a symbiotic one in which each adds sense to the other and they merge together; a dialectical relation in which a work and its site gain resonance from each other without merging together: Crawford proposes that Smithson's *Spiral Jetty* or Christo's *Valley Curtain* exemplify this relation;

26

a parasitic interaction, in which art dominates nature or vice versa, as when "endless rows of tract homes eradicat[e] the natural land-scape." Each of these works becomes meaningful because of its interaction with nature, leaving little room for any clear comparison between natural and artistic beauty.

These reflections, then, situate the relation between natural beauty and the arts. The ancient assumption, with its modernist, even Christian variant in Hegel, found the comparisons meaningful, holding that people understood the arts better through their relation to natural beauty. Crawford's arguments suggest that this kind of claim involves a cluster of concepts, including particular concep-tions of aesthetic appreciation, value, and their interaction. As a result of this complication the applicability of these concepts to present day concerns remains unclear. An alternative is to accept the expressiveness of nature and then compare that with the additional and distinctive cultural context of works of art. There is no guarantee, however, that such a comparison will be significant: it will depend on the reasons given for valuing beauty. More importantly, the context that nature provides for beautiful natural objects can itself be a cultural product. Whether nature embodies God's intentions or a scientific understanding, the coherence of each depends on finding such practices plausible. Not every account of either concept will permit the same associations; but, conversely, a particular culture may suppose the comparison between fine art and natural beauty to be itself meaningful. There, the culture provides some principle that makes the comparison relevant.

The dominant culture at present seems to be a scientific-technological one. It subscribes to a particular conception of nature. In his essay on "Appreciating Art and Appreciating Nature," Allen Carlson proposes that an appreciation of nature must construe its objects in terms of suitable scientific categories. By developing this possibility, Carlson not only considers the issue of the relation between art and nature that the last essays have addressed, but he also develops at least two of the suggestions made by Diffey and Hepburn. The latter sought a sense of natural beauty that allowed people to "enhance the thought-load" in the appreciation of nature "*almost* to the point, but not *beyond* the point at which it begins to overwhelm the vivacity of the particular perception."[54] Carlson's essay explores the appropriateness and necessity of a scientific understanding of nature – the thought-load – in natural beauty. Further, a scientific understanding of nature is free of metaphysics in Diffey's sense of the term. And the need for a scientific construal of nature complements the political, historical, and other construals of nature that motivated the essays by Barrell, Sitney, Gifford, Tuan, and Ross.

As the title of his essay indicates, Carlson's arguments occur in the context of a more general comparison of the appreciation of art and nature. The notion of appreciation is little discussed. By clarifying it Carlson hopes to illuminate aspects of our grasp of natural beauty and to show the relation between art and nature appreciation. He begins by examining a tradition of aesthetics that, relying on the "aesthetic attitude," defined as the "disinterested and sympathetic attention to and contemplation of any object whatever, for its own sake alone,"[55] yields insights into the nature of appreciation. A central implication is that the scope of appreciation seems limitless – the attitude needed for appreciation, on the face of it, seems to assimilate almost any of the many different kinds of objects within the compass of the aesthetic because it attends to the state of the subject rather more than that of the object.

Another quality of appreciation contrasts with some features of that aesthetic tradition: whereas disinterestedness often means con- templation and a corresponding passivity, appreciation connotes an active discerning and engagement with an object. The active nature of appreciation raises an issue of the criteria of relevance that guide its engagement with the object. In the main, Carlson argues, the tradition of disinterestedness offers little help with this issue. Perhaps as a result of its critics defining the issues, the tradition rarely attended to the implications of this concept for defining the aesthetic. The consequence is that rejecting the feasibility of defining the aesthetic by reference to its disinterestedness leads to a loss of some insights about aesthetic appreciation, including the recognition that relevant knowledge of the object informs appreciation.

Later writers defined how "the way of attending to an object...in part constitutes its appreciation."[56] Variations in kind, style, school, period, or materials, among other things, determine appreciation. Since all these make complex and interrelated demands on appreci- ation, there are no general criteria for aesthetic relevance by which to distinguish absolutely what is aesthetic from what is not. Rather, the object indicates what might be relevant to its understanding and, therefore, what would constitute its aesthetic appreciation. The object and its properties thus gain primacy: to appreciate something aesthet- ically is to appreciate it as and for "what it is, and not another thing."[57]

This leaves open the class of things capable of being appreciated aesthetically, including both works of art and natural objects. Indeed, taking seriously the nature of the object promises to enrich the sense of the aesthetic. "As Ronald Hepburn points out in a classical discussion of appreciating nature: If our 'aesthetic education' instills in us 'the attitudes, the tactics of approach, the expectations proper to appreciation of art works only,' then 'we either pay very little aesthetic heed to natural objects or else heed them in the wrong way.' We 'look – and of course look in vain – for what can be found and enjoyed only in art.'"[58]

One question, then, is: what is paradigmatic of art appreciation? Carlson proposes that the appreciation of design and order are crucial. Although appreciation of art varies with its objects, which will make distinctive demands of the viewer's mental and physical capacities, nevertheless, all such works share the fact that they are designed. This seems to follow from the concept of art in that it presupposes an agent. But the relation between a particular work and a particular artist is a causal one, with all the contingencies that involves. Accordingly, while the concept of art may imply an artist, it does not follow that the only way to understand a particular work is by understanding the artist who caused it. This leaves open the possibility of anti-intentionalism. Carlson diagnoses anti-intentionalism as a figment of the disinterestedness tradition, contending that even a work that satisfies the demand for an "isolated, pure aesthetic object" must still be "*designed by its creator* to be that way." Since appreciation follows the lead of the object, it must reckon with the object being designed to be the way it is.

Design is crucial to most art historical and critical analysis, Carlson explains, citing such authorities as E. H. Gombrich and H. W. Janson. Design appreciation involves "three key entities: the initial design, the object embodying this design, and the individual who embodies the design in the object."[59] The interplay between them constitutes the object by embodying its design. It makes room for judging the success or failure of the object, the problems it was trying to solve, whether the designer helped or hindered the fulfillment of a design, and so on.

The suggestion is also that too insistent an affirmation of these aspects of design should not *a priori* exclude less paradigmatic cases of art appreciation. A term that addresses those less usual art forms, carrying implications for an appreciation of nature, is order appreciation. Action painting, instanced by the work of Jackson Pollock, relies neither on a given design that becomes embodied in the work,[60] nor on the artist as an agent in complete and decisive control of the material. Instead, the artist becomes the selector of ordered and appreciable objects. Similarly, Dadaist randomness and spontaneity, although they distance the work from the artists' fully conscious and controlled production, still allow a measure of selection. The same reference to order appears in the work of Duchamp and surrealists like Dali who, for all their rejection of the constraints of paradigmatic art, selected objects for display. The "fact of selection...is significant" here, where "selection itself becomes the heart of the process."[61] The objects become significant choices because they embody patterns and purposes, even if the latter do not already have to do with aesthetic qualities or fine arts in a traditional sense.

They call for something other than design appreciation of the kind identified as native to art: they need order appreciation. Instead of an initial design, order appreciation uses the ideas and beliefs determining selection to indicate what the object is doing. Similarly, instead of a direct relation between a designer and an object embodying design, order appreciation acknowledges determinations of an object by a wider range of forces and agencies, and sees the artist as a selector who "by means of a general account, a story, or a theory...helps make the object appreciable."[62] This last role, of course, seems as appropriate to the spectator as to the artist. Even if the meaning of a work is distinct from the "artist's" intention, so that the artist does not have a privileged knowledge of the work's meaning, the activity of grasping the work and its meaning will trade on the design and order which that object signals to the spectator.

This switch of focus to an order selected by an appreciator moves art appreciation closer to the appreciation of nature. But Carlson warns that any assimilation between the two is "a theoretical mistake and an appreciative pity."[63] Again he diagnoses the preference of disinterestedness for an isolated object, divorced from its relation to other "extraneous" factors, as the source of that assimilation – usually of art into nature appreciation. To avoid collapsing the two into one, he suggests emphasizing the object-orientedness of appreciation. Disinterestedness cannot abide that emphasis. Nor can another assimilationist doctrine, which treats nature as if it were created by a designer, bear that object-orientation. Certainly, the latter doctrine has its own drawbacks: it must construe God anthropomorphically for the appreciations to collapse into one; but that also destroys any really distinctive conception of God.

Rejecting these assimilationist claims leaves the problem of articulating a positive conception of nature appreciation. One claim is that nature cannot be appreciated aesthetically since it cannot satisfy the central requirement of designed or intended order, and questions of the success or failure of nature seem inappropriate. Yet that seems to preclude the possibility that *any* kind of object may be appreciated aesthetically. Moreover, Carlson argues, the rejection of nature appreciation ignores the possibility of responding to aspects of objects other than their design. The theist points the way by construing nature in a particular way, thereby highlighting how construals of objects determine their appreciation. Design-orientated responses are but one type; others become possible depending on the alternative stories told. With nature "the story told about it, the ideas and beliefs we have about it, are pivotal factors in its appreciation."[64] And these may make order appreciation a more appropriate response.

By this account, nature appreciation in part involves selecting objects by focusing on the forces that determine their order and make the latter intelligible and appreciable. Acknowledgment of the interplay between the order, the determining forces, and the story that illuminates that order, guides the appreciative response. In addition, a focus on the object, such as order appreciation needs, brings out other features of nature appreciation. The stories told about nature are various: where these rely on gods, demons, spirits, or heroes to signify its active forces, their anthropomorphizing of nature also robs the latter of its distinctiveness. What plays "a crucial role in our aesthetic appreciation of nature," and "has increasingly done so in the West since the seventeenth century," is the account of nature "given by science."[65] And so far as order appreciation depends on giving an account of the object, science is the paradigm for the aesthetic appreciation of nature. It provides the forces that determine the geological, biological, and meteorological characteristics of the natural order, and thereby makes the latter "visible and intelligible." In this context, "awareness and understanding of evolutionary theory, for example, is relevant to appreciating the natural order as revealed in flora and fauna; without such knowledge the biosphere may strike us as chaotic."[66]

Similarly, selection becomes less interesting in nature appreciation, since any part of nature can relate to the same story. This implies also that the designer's part is correspondingly less significant in nature appreciation, while it remains vital to assessing the success and failure of art works. By contrast with that interrelation of design and designer, nature appreciation invites the responder to assess objects as ordered according to stories that give them meaning, significance, and beauty. And also by contrast with the supposition of *other* designers like ourselves that underlies art appreciation, Carlson contends, in nature appreciation "all that lies behind an ordered object is a story, the account which illuminates the order."[67] An implication here may be that the most fruitful story, the one that affirms a universal community of appreciators because it seeks some objective truth, is that of science. While folkloric or other stories generate responses from the cultures that follow them, scientific conceptions of nature may be more and other than culture bound. In turn, that depends on the conception of science at work and the viability of the folkloric explanations of nature.

These paragraphs summarize Carlson's argument for the distinction of art from nature appreciation and his call for a scientific grasp of nature in its beauty. His essay examines issues that address the matters raised by Diffey, Hepburn, and a number of the preceding essays about the nature of our appreciation of art and nature and the interaction between these two facets of aesthetic experience. Two issues from Carlson's essay provoke responses from the authors of the following essays.[68] The first issue concerns in part his distinction of appreciation from disinterestedness; the second questions his advocacy of a scientific understanding of the natural order. In his essay on "The Aesthetics of Art and Nature," Arnold Berleant considers whether aesthetics harbors two distinctive kinds of experience, requiring two different theories, or whether the experience of art and nature is of a single kind amenable to a comprehensive theory of response. He sees this as part of a larger issue, provoking some of the central concerns of aesthetics: "the nature of art, the identifying features of aesthetic appreciation, and the larger connections of such experience with matters once regarded as philosophically central but now largely consigned to the margins, matters Diffey calls noumenal and transcendent and Tuan identifies in the aesthetic response to extreme environments."[69] Berleant's purpose is to argue for a single theory that will allow for individual and cultural variations and accommodate itself to changes in the objects and events that occasion aesthetic interest.

To characterize this more elastic sense of the aesthetic, Berleant begins by examining the notion of disinterestedness. Carlson has already identified it as the villain preventing a proper understanding of appreciation and imposing a restrictive aesthetic. The concept originated with Shaftesbury, and has since been associated principally with one particular reading of Kant. Shaftesbury argued that "art must be enclosed within borders. . .so that it may be grasped in a single view,"[70] thereby isolating the object in order to signify its distinctive aesthetic qualities and focusing on its internal qualities and relations. The analyses this conception made possible constituted "the new discipline of aesthetics" but also raised problems about its foundations: of how to account for practices like architecture, with distinctive concerns for the active use of space to facilitate particular activities, that were not simply amenable to single views or capable of being isolated from other interests. Utility and form, perception and use, performance and response, are difficult to separate, yet interfere with the contemplative ideal.

The engagement these works call for also occurs in responses to natural beauty. Contemplation by itself seems to preclude appreciation of numerous factors. Gardens draw strollers into views and changing positions, where their appreciation depends on their stages in a journey through the landscape. By contrast, the purity of nature has a price. George Falconer, gardener to Lord Covehill, explains how that purity of contemplative aesthetic experience was maintained. "We must never be seen from the house, it was forbidden. And if people were sitting on the terrace or on the lawn, and you had a great barrow-load of weeds, you might have to push it as much as a mile to keep out of view. If you were seen you were always told about it and warned, and as you walked away Ladyship would call after you, 'Swing your arms.' It was terrible. You felt like somebody with a disease."[71] A concern for the object for itself occludes the care and work, the process by which it comes about, until the object is no longer construed as a product, but gains some etiolated purity in separation from the gardeners, their work, and the weeds which are in fact continuous with the garden.

Similarly Jane Austen describes Abbey-Mill farm in *Emma*, saying "It was a sweet view – sweet to the eye and the mind. English verdure, English culture, English comfort, seen under a sun bright, without being oppressive."[72] But this sensibility appears more sanguinary from the perspective of the English Jacobeans subjected to the laws promulgated by Pitt the Younger – laws that sought to preserve a particular conception of England's verdure, culture and comfort from the effects of the French Revolution.[73]

These politics make possible and also interfere with that purity. Indeed, perhaps a real purity is not available in nature. Berleant jokes that the ideal contemplation of nature may occur at a remove from the object itself: in a painting or photograph that frames the scene, excluding extraneous factors. Among the latter we may include the physical distractions of being outdoors, of gardeners hiding in the shrubbery, and of the innocence that makes this sense of a pure nature available to appreciation.

Another problem with the traditional aesthetic appreciation of nature results from the attempt to discover its distinctive features. Art appreciation relied on the supposition of design; natural beauty depends on grasping order where a designer is absent. Their central premise remains that "appreciation is directed towards an aesthetic object."[74] Berleant holds that premise is questionable. He prefers to emphasize that the history of modern arts is more a history of perception than of objects. Moreover, he contends that perception itself, far from being a simple visual act, is a "somatic engagement in the aesthetic field."[75] In the appreciation of nature, the premise seems even more restrictive since nature generally refuses discrete boundaries.

Instead, for Berleant, engagement supports a mutual determination by the object and the subject of their meaning and interrelation. His alternative account not only rejects the distinction between art objects and natural objects, but also construes aesthetic experience as an engagement. The distinction seems unacceptably naive: "nature" is itself a cultural product, emerging historically in various forms in diverse cultures, and bearing traces of those variations in any single culture. The essays earlier in this collection evince that a monological conception of nature is a problem to be solved. Kant's conception of the sublime may guide an alternative conception because it embodies a sense of nature escaping beyond the control implicit in any frame. This excess can be the model for the aesthetic experience of nature. Human beings appear in concert with their environment, rather than being separated from it or having to control it by their reason. Their unity is also an assimilation into nature, which cannot simply measure or judge from some external vantage point. Instead nature elicits awe because of its power and continuing mysteriousness.

The aesthetic pleasure possible in this engagement turns on "sensory acuteness...a perceptual unity of nature and human...a congruity of awareness, understanding, and involvement mixed with awe and humility, in which the focus is on the immediacy of the ocean of experience."[76] Nature is something human beings live in "as participants, not observers." These responses are appropriate as much in the usual instance of sublimity, in storms, say, or by mountains, as they are in quieter engagements with "the natural world: canoeing a serpentine river when the quiet evening water reflects the trees and rocks along the banks so vividly as to allure the paddler into the center of a six-dimensional world."[77] In these instances subjects do not contemplate but become immersed in an experience of unity – a unity available also in natural beauty.

By this account, "somatic engagement in the aesthetic field" joins "perceiver and object into a perceptual unity. It establishes a coherence that displays at least three related characteristics: continuity, perceptual integration, and participation. Continuity contributes to this unity by the inseparability (although not the indistinguishability) of the factors and forces that join to give an identity to aesthetic experience. Perceptual integration occurs in synaesthesia, the experiential fusion of the senses, as they join in a resonance of meaning and significance. And the appreciator participates in the aesthetic process by activating the unity of the factors that compose it."[78]

It is worth citing a longer exposition of Berleant's claims about engagement.

The notion of continuity reflects the understanding that art is not separate from other human pursuits but is assimilated into the full scope of individual and cultural experience without sacrificing its identity as a mode of experience. Art objects share a common origin in human activity and in productive technology with other objects that do not ordinarily work in an aesthetic context. In addition, social, historical, and cultural factors influence the kind of work artists do and the uses that are made of their art. Aesthetic perception is bound up with the range of meanings, associations, memories, and imagination that permeate all perception, while aesthetic experience is part of the entire spectrum of human experience. There is a mutuality here, too, for our dwelling in the aesthetic situation affects the broader social and personal uses of art, and these uses, in turn, influence the character of appreciation...

Perceptual integration, the second trait of aesthetic engagement, is the means by which we grasp the continuities in aesthetic experience, the ways in which all the elements in the aesthetic situation join in the procession of a unified experience. Not only have the conventional distinctions become obscured between the creator of art, the aesthetic perceiver, the art object, and the performer; their functions have tended to overlap and merge as well, and they are experienced as continuous. In art, as in modern society, traditional roles have blurred...

Engagement, finally, the central feature of the new aesthetic, stresses the active nature of aesthetic experience and its essential participatory quality. This involvement occurs in many different orders of activity – sensory, conscious, physical, and social – but it is most pronounced in aesthetic experience. The way the arts actually function, in the past as well as the present, reflects such involvement. For aesthetic engagement is grounded on a tradition far older and stronger than any to which the theory of aesthetic disinterestedness can appeal. Indeed, the principle of engagement reflects most of the history of the arts as they have functioned in diverse societies...

All this suggests the importance of a participatory model that recognizes the aesthetic reciprocity of both perceiver and object in the aesthetic situation. The notion of experiential unity is central here, for art does not consist of objects but of situations in which experiences occur. A unified field of interacting forces involves perceivers, objects or events, creative initiative, and some kind of performance or activation. Its principal factors – appreciative, material, creative, and performative – delineate the various dimensions of an integrated and unified experience.[79]

This aesthetic of engagement implies that the aesthetics of nature can be a model for appreciating art, since continuity and perceptual immersion occur in both. Environmental art, for example, unites art and nature by engaging works with their site. It breaks with the possibility of a disinterested separation of a work from its context, or of natural objects from human action, and provides a single experience. Both nature and art exhibit order, and both may exploit disarray; both "function reciprocally with the appreciator, enticing the participant to join in a unified perceptual situation."[80]

Berleant proposes that engagement also resolves some difficulties faced by the disinterested tradition. Appreciating a lover's beauty becomes possible rather than a misnomer for sexual interest alone, for example, and nature can "reveal the transcendent" rather than, at best, as with a disinterested experience, remaining a vehicle that is left behind in a "higher" communion. It allows reflection on the wider contemporary notion of art while extending "nature" into its cultural base.

Even though Berleant and Carlson differ over the distinctiveness of art and nature appreciation their essays join in developing the issues raised by the preceding essays.[81] Both imply criteria for a serious appreciation of nature – an issue Diffey raised at the end of his essay and Hepburn developed in his. Both also set out in more detail the kind of vocabulary appropriate to appreciating nature.

Carlson's turn to a scientific understanding may seem paradoxical at first sight but, as his essay makes clear, is an important tool for grasping the nature of the object that generates response. An inadequate grasp of the object results in a superficial and inarticulate aesthetic experience. However, there may be reasons for questioning the primacy of this grasp of nature. While it provides a powerful vocabulary, it seems to underemphasize the subjectivization of nature that Hepburn proposed as a partner to a determinate explanatory principle. In his essay, "On Being Moved By Nature: Between

Religion and Natural History," Noël Carroll seeks to redress the balance in favor of the "less intellective, more visceral" emotional responses to nature which are rooted in cognitions other than natural historical ones.

Carroll does not intend to deny Carlson's argument for a scientific understanding of nature in appreciations of natural beauty. He does, however, want to reaffirm that we may also be moved emotionally by nature and that this practice "need not be abandoned in the face of Carlson's natural environmental model."[82] The latter proposed in part that nature appreciation depended on being able to establish which aspects of nature are relevant; and natural science provided the most powerful mechanism for that task. By contrast, Carroll proposes that "the cognitive component of our emotional response does the job of fixing the aspects that are relevant to appreciation."[83] People can appreciate waterfalls, for example, by relying on an unsystematic grasp of their operation.

But Carlson has other reasons for advocating a scientific understanding of nature. He can argue that the aesthetic appreciation of nature can be objective – that people will usually falsely say that the Tentons are paltry. The consensus that sees this appreciation as false seems to borrow its bases from art appreciation. Kendall Walton argues that viewers may falsely reject a work because they misconstrue its nature, perhaps looking for a realist and perspectival representation in a Cubist work. Similarly, in natural beauty, where a creator's choice of style or genres is absent, a sound understanding of nature will still guide appreciation, and science or natural history provide the soundest grasp.

For an emotional response to coexist with that natural scientific model, it must be able to claim a similar objectivity. Carroll argues that is possible. Emotional states are appropriate to objects: fear of chicken soup will not sit well with the supposition that chicken soup is not dangerous, and so will be inappropriate to the latter belief. Beliefs, in turn, are reasonable or not; and this allows for the assessment that the emotion in question is objective because it depends on a reasonable belief. Being excited by "the grandeur of a towering waterfall," which "one believes to be of a large scale," is, surely, "an appropriate emotional response," and "if the belief in the large scale of the cascade is one that is true for others as well, then the emotional response of being excited by the grandeur of the waterfall is an objective one."[84] Yet, this sense of scale, appropriateness, and objectivity does not depend on, and is immune to correction by scientific categories.

A critic may condemn this proposal as leading at best to a superficial response to nature. The emotional arousal plays itself out once the viewer grows out of or removed from that feeling of awe. By contrast, a scientific grasp usually grows and deepens the subjects' appreciation. Yet that condemnation cannot be satisfactory. It relies on an unspoken sense of depth and superficiality, speculating without warrant that a greater knowledge will deepen appreciation rather than destroy it, and that emotional arousal is transitory and therefore less than objective.

Arguing for the possibility of appropriate emotional arousal in response to nature invites consideration of this talk of emotions: is it displaced religious feeling, as Diffey suggests? A delusional state that needs to be diagnosed? A susceptibility to philomythia that could stand debunking? Carroll goes for a secular basis for emotional arousal. Citing the work of Jay Appleton, he points to broadly evolutionary "interests that we take in the landscape." Being the kinds of creatures human beings are, they take an interest, for example, in prospects and refuges. The first keep "open the channels of perception," and allow subjects to see that no threat is approaching, while the second reassure subjects that there are places in which to hide. These exemplify a general regard for the environment as "a potential theatre of survival."[85] An interest in the visual appreciation of nature may denote a more immediately somatic interaction with those natural elements. The feeling subjects have in response to nature, then, is instinctual rather than religious.

But does this return Carroll to Carlson's claim about the need for naturalistic explanations, even if these now explain the viewer rather than the object alone? Carroll argues that it does not: that reference to naturalistic explanations shows what causes emotional response. "And when I appreciate a natural expanse by being emotionally aroused by it, the object of my emotional state need not be the recognition of my instinctual responses to, for example, prospects."[86] Carlson might doubt this possibility, however. An appreciation of nature needs a purchase on its object and on its subject, a critic of Carroll might argue, and finds this in a natural scientific grasp of both. If Carroll argues that subjects can appreciate an object without having to know what causes their appreciation, then the meanings, etc., that make up the subjects' appreciation of nature will be neither confirmed nor disconfirmed by the truth or falsity of their claims about their nature. The meaning of nature can be distinct from explanations of its objects and events. If so, then Carroll's claim, that subjects can have appropriate emotional responses to nature, cannot simply coexist with Carlson's, but must also disallow the latter's supposition that a fuller explanation of an object more fully grounds its appreciation. That may also serve to remind us that a scientific understanding of nature has not been monolithic and can be seen as itself a cultural product.

Be that as it may, with Carroll's essay the volume brings its issues to a resolution. The volume does not provide incontrovertible answers: nor did we expect it to. We chose instead to show the structure of the debate about these matters and, through the company of these essays, to set out the parameters for thinking about landscape, nature, natural beauty, and the arts – for giving importance to their overlaps and interaction and the ways in which work in the arts and the natural sciences participates in our interaction with nature.

Notes

1 "Eodem tempore uenit alius quidam de nations Brettonum, ut ferunt, iter faciens iuxta ipsum locum, in quo praefata erat pugna conpleta; et uidit unius loci spatium cetero campo uiridius ac uenustius; coepitque sagaci animo conicere, quod nulla esset alia causa insolitae illo in loco uiriditatis, nisi quia ibidem santior cetero exercitu uir aliquis fuisset interfectus" (Bede, *Historia Ecclesiastica Gentis Anglorum*, III, 10).

2 See the essays by A. Berleant, A. Carlson, N. Carroll, *et al.*, in this volume.

3 See J. Barrell, "The Public Prospect and the Private View" below.

4 See Michael Baxandall, *Painting and Experience in Fifteenth-century Italy* (Oxford: Clarendon, 1972).

5 See Kenneth Clark, *Landscape into Art* new edn., (New York: Harper and Row, 1976).

6 In *Norm and Form* (London: Phaidon, 1966), pp. 107–121.

7 Cited in Gombrich, "Renaissance Theory," 112; *Treatise on Painting* (Codex Urbanis Latinus 1270). Trans. and annot. A. P. McMahon; introduction by Ludwig H. Heydenreich, II, facsimile, (Princeton University Press, 1956), fo. 5r. Cf. Irma A. Richter's edition of the *Paragone* (London and New York: Oxford University Press, 1949) pp. 51ff.

8 Gombrich, "Renaissance Theory," pp. 116–17.

9 *Ibid.*, p. 120.

10 See Thoreau's use of "dirt" and "soil" to refer to the earth, and the ironies he draws out of it: e.g. "Economy," paragraphs 4 and 5, in Henry D. Thoreau, *Walden Or Life in the Woods*, introduction and notes by Francis H. Allen, (New York: Houghton Mifflin Company, 1910) and *The*

Making of Walden With the Text of the First Version, by J. Lyndon Shanley, (University of Chicago Press, 1957). We are indebted to Professor Doug Anderson for bringing these references to our attention.

11 Diffey, "Natural Beauty without Metaphysics," in this volume, p. 47.

12 *Ibid.*, p. 48.

13 Diffey cites John Lowerson's "Battles for the Countryside," in Gloversmith ed., *Class, Culture and Social Change: A New View of the 1930s* (Brighton: Harvester Press, 1980), that describes the 1930s struggle for access to the countryside.

14 *Ibid.*, p. 57.

15 *Ibid.*, p. 61.

16 Hepburn raises the possibility that agreeable aesthetic encounters may always be superficial because penetrating to any deeper level of understanding may break or make impossible all aesthetic encounters.

17 Hepburn, "Trivial and Serious in Aesthetic Appreciation of Nature," in this volume, p. 70.

18 *Ibid.*, p. 72.

19 *Ibid.*, p. 71.

20 *Ibid.*, p. 73.

21 *Ibid.*, p. 75.

22 *Ibid.*, p. 77.

23 Barrell, "The Public Prospect and the Private View," in this volume, p. 81.

24 *Ibid.*, p. 85.

25 *Ibid.*, p. 97.

26 Cited in Barrell, p. 86.

27 Barrell, *ibid.*, p. 97.

28 See "The Work of Art in the Age of Mechanical Reproduction," in Walter Benjamin, *Illuminations*, ed. and intro. Hannah Arendt, trans. Harry Zohn, (New York: Schocken Books, 1969), pp. 217–52.

29 Sitney, "Landscape in the Cinema," in this volume, p. 107.

30 *Ibid.*, p. 119–20.

31 See *Undercut*, Spring, 1983, cited in Sitney, *ibid.*, p. 124.

32 Sitney, *ibid.*, p. 125.

33 John Barrell, *The Dark Side of the Landscape, The Rural Poor in English Painting, 1730–1840* (Cambridge University Press, 1980), p. 6.

34 *Ibid.*, p. 10.

35 See "Trafficking in History," in *On Living in An Old Country, The National Past in Contemporary Britain*, by Patrick Wright with drawings by Andrej Krauze, (London: Verso, 1985), pp. 33–92.

36 For another interesting approach to the nature and power of visual images, see *History of Bourgeois Perception*, by Donald M. Lowe, (University of Chicago Press, 1982).

37 Tuan, "Desert and ice," in this volume, p. 155.

38 *Ibid.*, pp. 146–7, 152.

39 Cited *ibid.*, pp. 153–4

40 *Ibid.*, p. 150.

41 *Ibid.*, p. 146.
42 *Ibid.*, p. 145.
43 Cited *ibid.*, p. 144.
44 Ross, "Gardens, Earthworks, and Environmental Art," in this volume, p. 164.
45 *Ibid.*, p. 165.
46 *Ibid.*, p. 165.
47 *Ibid.*, p. 175.
48 *Ibid.*, p. 177.
49 *Poetics*, ch. 8.
50 Crawford, "Comparing Natural and Artistic Beauty," in this volume, p. 189.
51 *Ibid.*
52 *Ibid.*, pp. 191–2.
53 *Ibid.*, p. 194.
54 Hepburn, "Trivial and Serious in Aesthetic Appreciation of Nature," in this volume, p. 73.
55 Carlson, "Appreciating Art and Appreciating Nature," in this volume, p. 200; quoted from Stolniz, *Aesthetics and Philosophy of Art Criticism: A Critical Introduction* (Boston: Houghton Mifflin, 1960), p. 35.
56 Carlson, "Appreciating art," p. 203.
57 *Ibid.*, p. 205.
58 *Ibid.*, cited at p. 214.
59 *Ibid.*, p. 208.
60 *Ibid.*, p. 209.
61 *Ibid.*, p. 211.
62 *Ibid.*, p. 213.
63 *Ibid.*
64 *Ibid.*
65 *Ibid.*, p. 219.
66 *Ibid.*, p. 220.
67 *Ibid.*, p. 222.
68 Though, clearly, given that issues in Carlson's essay address matters germane to other earlier essays, the following responses will also, by extension, address the other essays.
69 Berleant, "The Aesthetics of Art and Nature," in this volume, p. 228.
70 *Ibid.*, p. 230.
71 Ronald Blythe, *Akenfield. Portrait of an English Village* (London: Penguin, 1969), p. 112.
72 *Emma*, by Jane Austen, edited by Stephen M. Parrish, (New York: Norton, 1972), p. 246. It is a sensibility shared by Austen's heroines as they strive to give intelligent moral support to the gentry in their hour of need.
73 See Warren Roberts, *Jane Austen and The French Revolution* (New York: St Martin's Press, 1979), chs. 1 and 2, and Marylin Butler, *Jane Austen and the War of Ideas* (Oxford University Press, 1975). We are indebted to Ms. Nancy Kelly for references.
74 Berleant, "Aesthetics of Art," p. 232.

75 *Ibid.*, p. 233.
76 *Ibid.*, p. 236.
77 *Ibid.*, p. 237.
78 Arnold Berleant, *Art and Engagement* (Philadelphia: Temple University Press, 1991), p. 46.
79 *Ibid.*, pp. 46–9.
80 Berleant, "Aesthetics of Art," p. 239.
81 Carlson responds to some issues in footnote 53 of his essay.
82 Noël Carroll, "On Being Moved by Nature," in this volume, p. 246.
83 *Ibid.*, p. 253.
84 *Ibid.*, p. 258.
85 *Ibid.*, p. 263.
86 *Ibid.*, p. 264.

Natural beauty without metaphysics

T. J. DIFFEY

I

The theme of this volume is natural beauty, landscape and the arts.
The first question for a philosopher to ask is what does philosophy
have to say *now* particularly about natural beauty. I emphasize *now*,
because, as is well known, historically philosophers, for example,
Plato and the eighteenth-century British, and especially Scottish,
philosophers, were interested in the topic of beauty. At the present
day there has also been some revival of interest in this subject, but
when it comes to what philosophers past and present have had to say
about beauty, I am doubtful how much relevance it has to the
question of how we should think about *natural* beauty. We must be
careful then in an inquiry into natural beauty not to begin by taking
up some question within the traditional philosophy of beauty – such
as for instance whether beauty is a real quality, or whether judgments
of beauty are subjective or objective – for it is difficult to see what
such metaphysical lucubrations could do for the question in hand,
other than offering, what is not to be underestimated, an innocent
form of academic pleasure.

In any case, the modern world takes a short cut with the question of
beauty: everyone, unless having a distinct reason for believing the
contrary, such as a specific religious faith, unhesitatingly takes it for
granted that an extreme subjectivism and relativism must hold sway.
And no matter if these are incompatible positions, aesthetic subjectivism holding roughly speaking that the beautiful is to be *defined* as
what pleases me, and relativism as *what pleases some particular
social group*, with endless permutations on how and at what level of
generality this group is to be identified – anything from a family to an
epoch.

43

Two things in particular strike me about our rampant contemporary subjectivism. First, it is often associated with a sociological (and perhaps also biological) determinism – my tastes[1] *may be my* tastes but they, like everything else about me, so it is contended, must be the product of my environment, genes, gender, class, society, education, occupational group, or whatever. Again the permutations are almost endless. Secondly, and contrary to the letter of subjectivism, the liveliest disputes rage over matters of taste (which the popular newspapers almost never distinguish, as philosophers do, from questions of morality). Yet in spite of these debates on all sides it is taken for granted that everyone's tastes are a kind of fixed datum about which nothing by way of change *for the better* can or should be encouraged. For there is held to be no way of getting outside the circle of taste to judge what taste is better. And insofar as any attempt is ever made to evaluate or educate taste, the standard of good taste which is appealed to is assumed to be nothing more than what is pleasing, convenient or in the interests of those with political power or social influence.[2]

II

As soon as the popular position is stated, some sort of debate and commitment within the philosophy of beauty is unavoidable, however antique much of that philosophy may seem. First, the popular idea that beauty lies in the eye of the beholder is itself intended as a *philosophical* answer to the philosophical question, "what is beauty," and as such is not immune from criticism. One only has to state the doctrine for its difficulties, notwithstanding its ubiquity, to become apparent. One objection has already been hinted at, namely how are its range and scope to be defined. *Is* beauty what pleases *me*? How megalomaniacal. Or what pleases the group? But *what* group? The possibilities for dispute about this are endless.

The doctrine that beauty lies in the eye of the beholder appears invincible because in aesthetics above all there seems to be the least space for error; or to put it the other way round, in matters of taste what seems to be the case must be the case, for that is what taste is. If everyone believes that what is beautiful is what pleases him or her, *what possible grounds could there be for denying* that if it pleases then it is beautiful?

Yet, as Hume noticed in the case of the judgment of works of literature, we don't receive all such judgments with equal weight or seriousness.[3] The question arises therefore of how the individual or the group is to be identified whose sentiments are to count. If we apply Hume's analysis to the case of natural beauty, we shall have to ask by *whose* sentiment then is it to be determined that the coastline, say, west of Swanage in Dorset is a beautiful coast, or (since Hume considered comparative judgments) that this is a more beautiful coast than that lying to the east?

Historically, "judgment" was a term used in the appreciation, criticism and connoisseurship of the arts. It may therefore be objected whether there is anything in the case of natural beauty which corresponds to Hume's ideal critics or judges of works of art. Certainly it is doubtful if "judgment," with all its connotations of passing *verdicts*, is the proper term for my response when I behold say the South Downs at Chanctonbury in Sussex, the Wye at Symond's Yat, or indeed the coast at Swanage. And yet, for all the implausibility of the suggestion that natural beauty is *judged* and that some such judgments carry more weight than others, there is a growing *institutionalization* of natural appreciation, which means that in the question of natural beauty there is now some kind of *authority* exercised. For example, in Britain we now have officially designated "areas of outstanding natural beauty," and there is the growing panoply of information offices, tourist trails and the like in established country parks and more generally all the paraphernalia of what is coming to be called "the heritage." Are not the things so classified held out for viewing, for instruction and entertainment, like so many works of art? Indeed some things in "the heritage" *are* works of art, since art is now commonly included under this term along with country houses, tracts of the countryside, etc. This suggests that unbridled subjectivism is already modified by legislative and official fact.

It does not follow from this of course that corners of nature not officially noticed cannot be beautiful. Nevertheless there is widespread public agreement concerning the beauty of certain landscapes.

Subjectivism, in its popular and most extravagant forms (such as Hume rightly sought to qualify), is in a certain sense realist in its assumptions. It assumes, that is, that the perception of beauty is independent of thought or language. For to respond to beauty, so it maintains, all we need are emotions. (And the cruder forms of subjectivism take it for granted that *emotions* are independent of thought and language, so if we were creatures without thought or language, we could still appreciate natural beauty.)

Although such subjectivism is philosophically untenable, it has some attractions, and given its widespread acceptance outside philosophy it would be surprising if it had not. For one thing, beauty, I mean the beauty of some particular thing or place, does not seem to depend for its existence upon our having to *speak* of it. Rather, beauty is to be beheld, enjoyed and cherished, and this we may do, perhaps should do, in silence. Dunster or Castle Combe, both in the west of England, do not depend for their beauty upon our speaking or thinking of them, though they do depend upon this for their *popularity*. So unless *speaking* of beauty is what is central or necessary to the beautiful, we cannot make beauty a subject of philosophy *if* philosophy is concerned with the meaning, rationality and truth of some very general *thoughts* as expressed in what is *said* (or *written*).

But this is to go too quickly. Certainly things do not seem beautiful by intellectual or ratiocinative deliberation or calculation but "immediately" or "instinctively." We do not make an inference or reason to the *conclusion* that something is beautiful. Yet this is not inconsistent with Kant's powerful point that we appreciate the beautiful in virtue of our rationality. It follows that if animals are not rational in Kant's sense they are incapable of appreciating beauty.

Are we justified in restricting the appreciation of beauty to human beings? Have not Darwin and others discussed the awareness of beauty shown by animals and birds? This, however, pertains to sexual reproduction,[4] if we have in mind the attraction the plumage one creature has for another of its species, and this in turn raises some large questions about the relationship between sexual desire and the appreciation of beauty. Burke, it will be recalled, treats beauty as the passion which belongs to generation, as the passion "directed to the multiplication of the species";[5] whereas Kant insists on the *disinterestedness* of *aesthetic* delight, which I take to be incompatible with the supremely "interested" nature of sexual desire and appreciation.

Something curious happened in the history of aesthetics between Burke and Kant. Beauty got desexualized and, though resexualized by Darwin, philosophical aesthetics with its attachments to Kantian doctrines of autonomy and rationality has not taken adequate account of this. If Kant's account of beauty makes it impossible to explain how beauty can be the object of sexual desire,[6] then either his account is wrong or we must conclude that "beauty" is a radically ambiguous notion between beauty as the object of sexual desire on the one hand and beauty as the object of disinterested, spectatorial, not to say voyeuristic, experience on the other.

Collingwood dismissed the beautiful from aesthetics altogether on the grounds that the beautiful belongs to the theory of love, not the theory of art.[7] But this in its implication that aesthetic appreciation is necessarily the appreciation of art is no help at all in an inquiry into natural beauty – unless we argue, which I am reluctant to do, that to appreciate the beauty of some tract of nature is to appreciate it as if it were a work of art. Collingwood's idea that aesthetic is the theory of art is in the Hegelian tradition of downgrading serious philosophical interest in natural beauty by making the beauty of art superior.

We can begin to see now why there has been no philosophical space since the Enlightenment wherein natural beauty may without molestation dwell. The territory has been carved up between three leading ideas: beauty as the object of biological or sexual interest; beauty as disinterested appreciation of a rational mind; and an idealist rating of art above beauty in importance. On the face of it none of these offers any very promising account of natural beauty. It is not surprising therefore that while the public has taken natural beauty to its heart, subject to the crucial qualification hitherto that such beauty must yield where necessary to the needs of industrial and economic development, contemporary philosophy has remained silent on the subject.

If we attempt an account of natural beauty within this unpromising framework of ideas, then since scenery and other objects of natural beauty are not, at any rate in any obvious sense, sexual objects, and since an inquiry into natural beauty can hardly be expected to begin with the premise that the beauty of art is superior to the beauty of nature, we are left with the view that natural beauty is disinterested appreciation by a rational mind. There is this to be said for it: that whatever kind of aesthetic sensibilities animals and birds may or may not possess, we do not attribute to them aesthetic appreciation of their environment *in so far as we do not expect an animal to admire the beauty of its surroundings or a bird to display any aesthetic sense divorced* from practical activities such as nest building.

What is this "divorced" spectatorial attitude, then, which we humans apparently take to landscape? It seems a curiously thin and unanchored stance, but it has to be remembered that disinterested appreciation in its original formulation in Kant is a much "thicker" notion than it now seems, because appreciation of the beautiful on Kant's account also gives us an intimation of the universe as God's handiwork. This is an aspect of Kant's aesthetics which in this secular age we prefer not to notice.

47

I am suggesting then that the stripped down Kantianism of the spectatorial stance of a rational mind towards nature does not offer any very nourishing account of why natural beauty should so attract us. Subjectivism too, however popular, is equally unsatisfactory. What then are we to say about natural beauty?

III

With care, we can cover a little distance in reflecting on the idea of "natural beauty" without falling into traditional metaphysics and losing the present. For one thing, we can all think readily enough of examples of natural beauty: a prospect, say, of the Sussex Downs as viewed along its line from the top of one of its hills is *undoubtedly* beautiful. This is literally true; I have never heard it doubted nor would I understand anybody who did deny it any more than G. E. Moore would understand a person's denying that his hand held in front of his face was his hand.

How "natural" does this so-called beauty have to be? In virtually all instances of natural beauty, certainly in Britain and perhaps in most of the world, it is false to take "natural" as meaning the absence or exclusion of human agency. It has often been noted that particularly in small, heavily populated countries such as Britain today it is very difficult to find "unspoiled" tracts of nature. In what sense of "natural" are the Downs *naturally* beautiful? Even within living memory their look has been much altered by changes in agricultural use and methods and much improved by the addition of such human artifacts as windmills. For a scene to be naturally beautiful is not so much for it to be in an unmanaged state as for it to *look* as if it were. This echoes some of those older accounts of art which required the skill of the artist's craft to be concealed from the spectator of the finished work.

To insist that nature has to be "unspoiled," where this means unaffected by human agency, in order to be regarded as beautiful, indeed in order, in some meaning of the term "nature," to be regarded as nature at all, suggests a sentimental *a priori* thought at work to the effect that nature must be beautiful and cannot be ugly. Natural beauty by definition of course cannot dispense with beauty, but there is much in nature that, in spite of a sentimental temptation to deny it, is not beautiful.

Yet if terrain is unspoilt, that is often taken as an *a priori* proof of its beauty. So the old adage that God made the countryside and man the town lives on in a new guise. Indeed nowadays we are less likely to think that some apparently unspoilt stretch of land is a "horrid and awful waste" (such as our forebears apparently thought the Scottish Highlands) and more likely to doubt if it can *remain* beautiful *after the proposed intrusion of (further) human agency.* Does the building of an atomic power station or the siting of electricity pylons or an oilrig make this once-beautiful landscape now ugly?

In other words, we are inclined to begin with a standing presupposition, sometimes backed by legislation, that a certain area of countryside is beautiful. The belief that the South Downs, say, are beautiful is something which everybody shares. Then any proposed change is regarded as a threat to its established beauty. Natural beauty seems to consist in a general impression, which is no doubt true of a beautiful work of art too (certainly any change to a work of art will be regarded as a threat to its beauty), but, unlike art, natural beauty seems not to require, or at any rate not characteristically to receive, the minute scrutiny we characteristically accord works of art when we take an aesthetic interest in them. Natural beauty seems a good deal more free of connoisseurs and of "close readings" than are works of art.

There is a less bland way of taking these instances of accepted natural beauty, however, which is to say that there is a kind of stock beauty of natural scenery which turns up time and again in calendars and greeting cards. So here in the case of natural beauty is also to be found the same uncritical popular taste as is possible in the case of art, with all the snobberies and class consciousness that go with art but which, in my view, are not essential to it.

Are all the beauties of nature obvious and well known? When a work of art is charged with ugliness or failure in beauty[8] it may be defended on the grounds that it possesses a difficult beauty not readily perceived by those who can respond only to what is conventionally or familiarly beautiful. The same is true in the case of natural beauty. There are those places by shore, by river and in hills which we find immediately beautiful, but much that is obviously beautiful to us was for our ancestors a case of "difficult beauty." The point is often made that it took the poets and painters to make available to us all the aesthetic quality of "horrid wastes" such as, say, mountains. So, on this account, in the past much of the earth would have struck most of our ancestors with the same dismay as an opera by Berg may have struck the average music lover.

For art to continue this traditional task of making nature aesthetically accessible to a wider public, at least three things are necessary:

49

first, nature requires mediation to an audience because that audience cannot appreciate it unaided; secondly, the art which mediates nature must not be relentlessly formal and abstract in its intentions; thirdly, nature must be available to the artist as a subject for study. I doubt if any of these assumptions are as unproblematic as they must have seemed when say Ruskin was promoting Turner, or Constable was "discovering/creating" picturesque Britain.

IV

The attribution of "natural" to beauty prompts the enquiry what other species of beauty there may be and the one most likely to spring to mind is "artistic beauty." Indeed one may doubt whether the concept of natural beauty could make any sense without its trading upon an implicit contrast with the beauty of art. Might it not be that "natural beauty" designates that which is beautiful but which does not fall under the category of "artistic beauty"? Perhaps, more generally, "natural beauty" means any beauty which is not the beauty of art, nor of the human figure[9] nor of virtue nor beauty of any other kind. This makes "natural beauty" look like some sort of remainder category, and perhaps no more than a dumping ground (if this unfortunate figure of speech may be allowed to intrude here) for whatever beauty cannot be fitted under any other species.

This, however, would be too hasty a conclusion, for by parity of reasoning we could subject all other species of beauty to the same arguments. For their distinctiveness, it might be said, they need the implied contrast with natural beauty as much as it depends for its sense on its contrast with them. The idea of natural beauty too, as of any kind of beauty, looks a good deal firmer when we remember that we can agree on some central or core cases. The important questions might rather be *why* anyone should wish to classify kinds of beauty and *what* is there being classified? But this subject has the unlovely look of the "science of the beautiful," so scorned by Wittgenstein.

These reasonable doubts, however, cannot be allowed to impede some philosophical inspection of the nature/art contrast. For one thing are natural and artistic beauty coordinate kinds or species? If land art or earth art look naturally beautiful and are art, then no.

Is the distinction between natural and artistic beauty any longer useful or viable? I have been suggesting that "natural" and "artistic" are correlative terms: each needs the other, just as in the case of the doctrine of primary and secondary qualities "primary" and "secondary" need one another. So, as in the quarrel between Berkeley and Locke over that doctrine, a parallel question arises: namely, whether the distinction between "natural (beauty)" and "artistic (beauty)" is tenable.

So far our mild skepticism has been directed at the notion of "natural beauty" but it is not difficult to cast doubt on the credentials of "artistic beauty" to constitute a rationally cogent species. Thus though we can all think of examples, and no doubt quite central examples, of artistic beauty, say, Donne's "Hymn to God my God, in my Sickness," Matisse's *La Dance* or Mozart's *Ave Verum Corpus*, this still leaves some questions to be answered which are quite as clamorous as in the case of "natural beauty."

First, there is the obvious question whether the beauties of poetry are all beauties of the same kind, to say nothing of whether they are comparable to the beauties of music, of painting, of sculpture, of dance. And is the beauty of one painting the same as that of another?

Then there is the embarrassing fact that the phrase "the beauties of poetry" is thoroughly dated, not to say antiquarian; it has not been heard in living speech since the eighteenth century. Consonant with this is the familiar fact too that, at any rate within Anglo–American aesthetics in the twentieth century, the topic of beauty, with some noble and well-known exceptions,[10] has been monumentally neglected. Consequently in the *philosophy of art* by and large we have been trying to manage by making do merely with the concept of *art*,[11] without placing any reliance on the idea of *beauty*.

Philosophical interest in beauty broadly speaking began to decline from the late eighteenth century onwards, precisely when the distinction between nature and art began to be more assiduously pressed and the superior claim of artistic beauty over nature promoted by Hegel. Conversely philosophical interest in beauty remained alive while neoclassicist ideals in art commanded conviction; then no great chasm or difference in *kind* was felt between the beauty of art and the beauty of nature. But if beauty became outmoded in art and in the philosophy of art, it retains, in the idea of natural beauty, a place in popular culture.

V

What is naturally beautiful? Trivially there is nature to take the predicate "is beautiful" but, notwithstanding the triviality of this, two things are wrong with it. First, "beauty," I hold, is an attributive and not predicative adjective; I reject Plato's view of Beauty as something standing apart from beautiful things, perfect and complete in itself, in favor of the (Lockean) view that to speak of beauty must always be taken as referring to something or other that is beautiful; so beauty must mean regarding something under a certain mode or manner.

Secondly the famous, not to say notorious, discovery, which we owe to Lovejoy,[12] namely that "nature" is an ambiguous term, implies that when we speak of the *naturally* beautiful or the beautiful *in nature*, we have no unequivocally identifiable subject of attribution. The moral, I believe, is that we cannot understand the idea of natural beauty without considering certain concepts more restricted in scope such as *landscape*, *view* or *prospect*. The concept of landscape is particularly interesting here for its double membership of the language of art and the aesthetics of nature and there is a lot of coming and going between the two in such popular phrases as "the poetry of place."

To identify *something* more determinately than as "nature," as for example a "view," "prospect," "landscape," or whatever, is to conceptualize it in such a way as to imply that the terrain in question *has already been recognized aesthetically*. To ask if a *prospect* is beautiful, or of any aesthetic interest, is as odd as asking whether murder or lying are wrong.[13] These subject-terms are already aesthetic in meaning, whereas the nondescript territory that I may motor through on my way to the beach or office is neither prospect nor view nor landscape. It does not have the status of landscape,[14] either informally in our conceptualization of it or formally as a "beauty spot" or whatever.

It will be observed that these concepts are pretty mixed. Some, such as "prospect" are antiquarian. It is interesting that such aesthetic subject-terms should have an eventful history. Other subject-terms, such as "view," are bland and unnotable (a view may be remarkable but the concept of a view is not – any controversy for example about perspectives concerns, say, Nietzsche's critique of *truth* and not the vantage point on the Downs I select from which to view the Weald below). And yet other aesthetic subject-terms, such as "wilderness," may be the subject of political controversy.

When we have identified adequate subjects of aesthetic attribution in nature, there is still the question implied by the popular theory of beauty as personal preference, namely whether there is any more to the beauty of a landscape, say, than that we find ourselves to possess an apparently instinctive or immediate liking or preference for it? One of the reasons I suspect why the aesthetic defence of a territory against the builders of power stations, motorways, and the like, has often failed is the *widespread philosophical* belief that beauty is merely a matter of personal liking. How then can my mere liking for the pastoral look of the fields by my home be *reasonably* allowed to stand in the way of new roads and factories? It must also be noted, however, that an aesthetic viewpoint does *not a priori* entail that the road or factory should *not* be built.

It is a consequence of our lack of an adequate philosophy of natural beauty that so many disputes about land use hitherto have been conducted within the tacit assumptions of utilitarian preference theory. Then of course *my preference* for heathland can make me seem foolish and quixotic when the forces of progress are mustering to build an atomic power station there. It is hard luck but no credible loss if *I* have to go without my ice cream for the greater good of progress, economic well-being or industrial profit. One of the effects, however, of the recent movements in the west for heightening ecological and environmental awareness is to find more respectable, because more general, utilitarian reasons for the conservation of a landscape. It is no longer so commonly represented that I like the heathland as I like ice cream, which is asking for the swift response, so what and who (except you) cares, but that its preservation may have something to do with the survival of the planet Earth and plenty of people besides myself have an interest in that.

VI

If the popular belief that beauty is in the eye of the beholder is taken reductively to mean that beauty is nothing but personal fancy, this is inconsistent with other popular beliefs such as that natural beauty is a source of spiritual sustenance. Of course there are degrees of popularity and the idea that beauty is in the eye of the beholder is more popular than the idea of beauty as something spiritual. The idea is indeed ubiquitous in the modern world and so is to be found as firmly lodged in official minds as in the minds of the people. Indeed the mind of officialdom, aided and abetted in this matter by the intelligentsia, is, unlike many ordinary people, hostile to the idea of beauty as spiritual sustenance, for how can this be quantified or filed in government records or pleaded for at official committees and tribunals?

The philosophical issue here is what does it mean to think of natural beauty as a source of spiritual sustenance. This is a more important question than any in the traditional metaphysics of beauty but it goes undiscussed because of the hostility it provokes in intellectuals. It has a desperately old-fashioned (Wordsworthian) look about it, an undertow of philistinism in the implication that beauty has a use, albeit a spiritual use, and a murkiness of conception betrayed in the temptation to slip and slide between terms; as if people who believe in natural beauty as spiritual cannot say exactly how it is spiritual or what "spiritual" means: does natural beauty confer "spiritual refreshment," "spiritual strength," "spiritual renewal," "spiritual sustenance" or what? Nevertheless, belief in this, whatever *this* is (and saying what it is is part of the problem) has been one reason why people have sought out the countryside (here taken as synonymous with "nature"). Materialists of many stripes, Marxist and unMarxist alike, can be expected to oppose such belief.

Yet take a subject as historically specific, and in the Marxist sense as unidealist, as you could wish, for example John Lowerson's "Battles for the Countryside,"[15] which movingly describes some political struggles of the working classes in the north of England in the 1930s for access to the countryside. Certainly the spiritual aspect of this struggle does not loom in large in Lowerson's account but it is there. In a reference to Edwin Royce, the President of the Manchester and District Ramblers Association, we learn that: "The real goals of a spiritual communion with the wilderness were blocked by class property rights";[16] and a contributor to *The Countryman* observed that "In the country...You make up your spiritual losses whenever you have time to 'stand and stare'."[17]

Not only materialists, however, dispute this kind of talk. More surprisingly, at least one Christian has denounced the spiritualization of nature on the grounds that it makes an idolatry of the earth, for heaven, not earth, is divine.[18] However, it is one thing to say that nature is a source of spiritual sustenance, another to say that this spirituality consists in the access which nature permits to some sort of transcendent truth. What if this so-called spiritual sustenance means no more than relief to the senses offered by a temporary escape from a bleak urban environment? Yet this assumes a too easy, and in Britain increasingly dated, contrast between the beautiful countryside and the ugly city. As the city becomes postindustrial will the belief weaken in the spiritual power of the countryside?

One reason why intellectuals, particularly philosophers (though not poets and artists), are generally suspicious of this "spiritual appeal" is, I suggest, that modern philosophy, impressed by a materialist interpretation of the science of nature, is hostile to religion. There is a lot of confusion here: for example in how science is to be philosophized, but above all in the fact that Enlightenment atheism,[19] to which modern philosophy, *and with it aesthetics*, subscribes, confuses the rejection of Christianity with the rejection of religion as such. In a secular society it is not surprising that there will be hostility towards any religious veneration of natural beauty *and* at the same time nature will become a refuge for displaced religious emotions.

Our contemporary philosophical atheism, however, affects not only how we regard natural beauty but also our attitudes to art. In most societies art has had an intimate, perhaps inextricable, connection with religion. I conjecture that our situation in the modern western democracies, in which art has broken away from religion, is unusual in this respect. Art now finds itself on its own. The history of this breakaway, enshrined in such doctrines as the autonomy of art, is the history of modern aesthetics though this is rarely recognized in its proper light for what it is. Since most of the world's art has been under the patronage of religion, the historically unprecedented secularization of modern western society is a major question for aesthetics no less than for other branches of learning, and one hitherto inadequately addressed by aesthetics.

VII

It is not only post-Enlightenment atheism that has made belief in the spiritual in nature untenable. More widely, the *philosophical* cherishing of beauty has been undermined in that the rejection of beauty as a foundation for *art* has left beauty beneath the notice of the intellectual classes who, given the repudiation by art, and particularly by modernism, of beauty, and being attached to art, find themselves necessarily enrolled in a battle against beauty. But for the great philosophers of beauty, beauty had a high place within a wider vision: for Plato its place in his devotion to the good, for Kant its task to protect the Christian moral life from misconceptions engendered by the Newtonian science to which he was equally devoted. But since Kant's time it has not been *intellectually* respectable to take beauty seriously. So it comes to seem that beauty goes unvalued. This is well expressed in Milan Kundera's *Book of Laughter and Forgetting*:

55

(Yes, I know. You haven't the slightest idea what I'm talking about. Beauty has long since disappeared. It has slipped beneath the surface of the noise – the noise of words, the noise of cars, the noise of music, the noise of signs – we live in constantly. It has sunk as deep as Atlantis. The only thing left of it is the word, whose meaning loses clarity from year to year.)[20]

But has beauty disappeared? Well the modern world is a big place, and it is nearer the truth I think to say not that beauty has disappeared but that it has disappeared *for intellectuals*. Beauty of course has not disappeared, not the word nor the idea nor the phenomenon. On the contrary, the love of beauty is ubiquitous: in, to take just a few examples, mass tourism, kitsch,[21] the growing concern for the environment (a significant qualification to the generalization that beauty is disregarded by the intellectual classes – though as I implied earlier, environmental movements are not purely aesthetic in their concerns), and, not least, sexual beauty.

To say, however, that beauty has disappeared for intellectuals is to mean that it is not taken as having any intellectual relevance, that it does not figure in our *understanding* of anything. Beauty, *pace* Schiller, is not commonly perceived as having any explanatory or theoretical or practical significance in, say, politics, or economics, or morality; and in a secular state, religion is thought of as the haphazard outcome of birth and upbringing and a matter for private conscience. Otherwise the demands which the state makes upon religion, to be an agent of social solidarity, to provide the ritual for state occasions and to act as a further instrument of law and order, do not, if we keep in mind the popular view of beauty as personal preference, seem to leave much authority or scope for beauty. So in the western world beauty has no acknowledged place in our contemporary ideologies and no longer any philosophical prestige. In this respect popular opinion agrees with the intellectuals. Beauty explains nothing. It is only a matter of appearances; it lies only in the eye of the beholder.

VIII

If it is the fate of beauty both popularly and at the level of intellectual and philosophical reflection to have been reduced to the status merely of what is personally pleasing, the fate of art has been more complex. For one thing art has been largely freed from service to the ideal of beauty. We can trace this to many sources: one is the determined campaign mounted in aesthetics in the nineteenth century to drive out beauty as the criterion of art. Another, and not unconnected, is the intuition held by the modernist *avant-garde* that to think of art primarily in terms of beauty is seriously to understate our sense of the possibilities of art, of what art is or can achieve.[22]

It did not come about by chance then that our modern textbooks in aesthetics are silent about beauty, though the story of how it did happen is complex and cannot be told here.[23] Thus beauty now seems to be a contestable ideal for art whereas there is nothing controversial in finding a particular landscape beautiful. Indeed such I suggested earlier is virtually truistic.

On the other hand, the arts, no less than natural beauty, are seen by many people, though not I think by many contemporary philosophers, at least not in their professional writings, as a source of spiritual sustenance. For some art (perhaps much but *not* all) can seem to give intimation of the transcendent.[24] In a secular society art, like natural beauty, remains a last refuge for religious and noumenal truth and it retains something of this power even for the secularly and atheistically minded and not merely for those who remain religiously inclined.[25] But though art and nature may for many both retain a noumenous dimension, a possible difference between them may be that the claims of *art* to be revelatory of the transcendent seem more plausible today than the claims of nature. For the early Romantics it was the other way round. One of the legacies of Romanticism has been to make a religion of art seem more credible than a religion of nature. And yet is it not an incredibly old-fashioned view that art is revelatory of the transcendent, not heard since the days when Matthew Arnold claimed that: "More and more mankind will discover that we have to turn to poetry to interpret life for us, to console us, to sustain us"?[26] But though Arnold seems to have thought that poetry (not art more generally) would "replace" "most of what now passes with us for religion and philosophy," because there "is not a creed which is not shaken, not an accredited dogma which is not shown to be questionable," he seems to have been more interested in the bearing of Christianity, on conduct, in its ethical dimensions, than in its transcendent claims.

The claim that art is revelatory of the transcendent, *if it is avowed,* is apt to be embarrassing but this does not mean that the noumenal in art, or in another word, the sublime – for example Rothko in painting, Mahler in music – has lost its power to excite otherwise secular minds. Things which in our enlightenment atheism, or more precisely, anti-Christianity, have ceased to be intellectually tenable survive in art. It is not only as Adorno thought that art provides a space against bureaucratic or instrumentalist reason in the modern world. One has to inquire what avails itself of that space. And part of the answer is: among other things, intellectually disowned religious truth.

IX

Can nature too give intimation of the transcendent? Is this what makes spiritual communion with nature, which many have felt, possible, the sense that in nature and through the senses paradoxically one is in the presence of something supersensible? As we have seen, there seems to have been something of this sense of the ineffable in popular feeling towards the countryside, even though it would probably not be expressed nowadays in these terms. Such feeling was prefigured in philosophy and in literature, notably in Kant and in Wordsworth. Thus Wordsworth, moved by the sight of the River Wye above Tintern Abbey:

> Nor less, I trust,
> To them I may have owed another gift,
> Of aspect more sublime; that blessed mood,
> In which the burthen of the mystery,
> In which the heavy and the weary weight
> Of all this unintelligible world,
> Is lightened: – that serene and blessed mood,
> In which the affections gently lead us on, –
> Until, the breath of this corporeal frame
> And even the motion of our human blood
> Almost suspended, we are laid asleep
> In body, and become a living soul:
> While with an eye made quiet by the power
> Of harmony, and the deep power of joy,
> We see into the life of things.
> ......
>   And I have felt
> A presence that disturbs me with the joy
> Of elevated thoughts; a sense sublime
> Of something far more deeply interfused,
> Whose dwelling is the light of setting suns,
> And the round ocean and the living air,
> And the blue sky, and in the mind of man;
> A motion and a spirit, that impels
> All thinking things, all objects of all thought,
> And rolls through all things.[27]

Natural beauty without metaphysics

Of course something grander than the beautiful, namely the wild and the sublime, seem to have provoked this sense of the transcendent in nature. Just as Wittgenstein spoke of the tremendous in art,[28] so too there is the tremendous in nature. Nevertheless there is something curiously fleeting and impermanent about this sense of nature pointing to a reality beyond or other than itself. Is it something which may vary with age and other factors such as class or gender? Wordsworth himself was insecure in his sense of it; for the first passage I quoted above continues:

> If this
> Be but a vain belief...

And the second passage I quoted goes on to bring us back to *this* world:

> Therefore am I still
> A lover of the meadows and the woods,
> And mountains; and of all that we behold
> From this green earth; of all the mighty world
> Of eye, and ear...

For Wordsworth, it seems clear that however his attitude to the transcendent is to be finally judged, his feeling for nature at any rate was not, or was not primarily, an aesthetic matter, where this means responding with pleasure to the look of things and their effects on the other senses, without the assurance of any kind of belief that these appearances are supervenient upon some deeper reality.

The sense we may share with Wordsworth in the excitement of reading his poem that he faithfully recounts an encounter with the transcendent, which we too might experience in similar circumstances, must alas in our more critical, that is, rationally cool, moments seem only an illusion, though a beautiful one. If only it were true, but what reason is there to believe that it is? The modern world, I suggest, does not permit us a Wordsworthian faith in the divinity of nature. Indeed the *beauty* of the landscape now has in some degree to *compensate* those of us who cannot, or who can no longer, believe that in nature we are in the presence of some kind of noumenal meaning.

It is easy to slip inattentively from a consideration of beauty to a consideration of *natural* beauty; and now, in these references to Wordsworth, we seem to have slipped from the subject of natural beauty into that of the sublime without noticing the difference. That is careless but also I suggest instructive in what it may indicate: first,

59

that *natural* beauty is for us, excepting sexual beauty, *the* paradigm of beauty (much more so for example than art); and secondly, that in spite of a recent revival of interest in the sublime in literary criticism, so far as nature goes we do not nowadays pay much attention to any significant distinction between the beautiful and the sublime. The sublime in nature is a species of the beautiful, the beauty of wild and grand places, but is no further significant.

Howsoever the distinction between the beautiful and the sublime was understood by Kant and by the Romantics, and however we are to understand it now, it seems clear that art, by contrast with nature, can manage without beauty, at least beauty of the more obvious sorts. Take *avant-garde* art for example; or the fascination many novels have for us where, though we may *not deny* that they were beautiful, we would *not assert* this either as the most important reason for their hold on our attention.

When I consider, then, not so much the differences between natural and artistic *beauty* as more generally seek to understand the fault line, which became so prominent through the nineteenth century, between art and nature,[29] it seems to me that *truth*, although we ill understand it in relation to art, does at least have more initial purchase in connection with art than with nature. I am more willing, that is, to consider what the expression, a *truthful work of art*, might mean, than what a *truthful landscape* or *prospect*, say, might mean or be.

X

The upshot of this inquiry into natural beauty is that we appreciate nature, *when* this is more determinately identified through such aesthetic categories as "landscape," for its beauty but not for its truthfulness. In the case of nature, if we cannot fall back on the Wordsworthian transcendent or the Kantian noumenal, there is only its beauty to contemplate and enjoy. In the case of art, however, we may consider the work of art under the category of the true as well as of the beautiful. Another way of putting this contentious point is to say that we find the idea of some sort of analogy between art and language much more attractive than the idea that nature is a language. Indeed, essentially related to the marginalization of interest in beauty in aesthetic theory in the nineteenth century was the growing dominance of the notion of art as language to be found in the burgeoning expression and communication theories of art. Art *speaks,* is or is like a *language,* whereas beauty, and therefore natural beauty, is *dumb.* Historically the idea that nature is a language or a book that we can read has been particularly powerful in the development of western science but to my mind is now no more than an archaic and merely beautiful figure. Many philosophical inquiries end with the most important questions, even if broached, unanswered; and this essay is no exception. The most important unanswered question concerning natural beauty is to explain what is now to ground our interest in it *or* how such interest, if self-justifying, requires no ground or foundation. I have been critical of certain traditional answers but have offered no contemporary solution. Is this because the idea of natural beauty is untenable and so as philosophical interest in beauty weakened it made no provision for the idea of natural beauty or is it that we have been blind to the problem? I prefer to believe the latter.[30]

Notes

1 If, as is doubtful, it is permissible to use the term "taste" here. Contemporary usage sanctions nothing more than personal liking; the term "taste" is often rejected for having so-called elitist connotations.
2 I am concerned here to articulate rather than endorse what I take to be a widespread attitude, at any rate in the West today, to the idea of the beautiful. No matter that there are many arguments in philosophy against this subjectivist position; they are not widely known or believed, *intellectually* cogent though many of them are.
3 See David Hume's essay "Of the Standard of Taste."
4 Charles Darwin, *The Origin of Species by Means of Natural Selection* (1859; reprinted, Harmondsworth: Penguin, 1968), ch. 4, "Natural Selection," especially p. 137.
5 Edmund Burke, *A Philosophical Enquiry into the Origin of Our Ideas of the Sublime and Beautiful* (second edn. London 1759, Scolar Press Reprint, 1970), part 1, IX, X, pp. 63–5.
6 Appreciation of the beauty of the beloved in sexual desire seems to be incompatible with disinterested appreciation of that beauty, precisely because this is beauty which we desire to possess and its existence is the object of our passion. Kant of course never discusses this objection to his account of the beautiful. Apart from the implausibility of expecting Kant to inquire too closely into sexual matters, he would perhaps claim that disinterestedness *is not necessarily incompatible* with desire. The beauty of the sexually beloved I can still appreciate for its own sake, and indeed it might be argued, have to, if I am going to admire this beauty in the first place. To deny this is to say that beauty *consists* in the mere fact that sight

61

of the beloved causes sexual arousal (back to subjectivism) rather than that it is this beauty which is the object of my desire. Notice the similarity between the objection that because beauty is the object of sexual desire there cannot be disinterested love of beauty, and the charge often made against Kant's *ethics*, and just as often denied, that acting for the sake of duty means that in acting ethically I cannot act out of friendship, compassion, love or any other "interested" motive.

7 R. G. Collingwood, *The Principles of Art* (Oxford: Clarendon Press, 1938), p. 38.

8 Not necessarily the same thing. There is a lot of discussion traditionally in aesthetics about the differences in meaning between the beautiful, the not-beautiful and the ugly.

9 I notice my assumption that the human figure is not *naturally* beautiful. Ruskin would disagree: *The Seven Lamps of Architecture* (London: J. M. Dent, Everyman Library, n.d.), preface to second edition, p. xxviii.

10 See R. W. Hepburn, "Contemporary aesthetics and the neglect of natural beauty," in Bernard Williams and Alan Montefiore eds., *British Analytical Philosophy* (London: Routledge and Kegan Paul, 1966) pp. 285–310; Guy Sircello, *A New Theory of Beauty* (Princeton University Press, 1975). The study of beauty, however, is now less neglected in aesthetics than it recently was – this volume being one and not the only testament to the change. Conspicuous here of course, and deservedly so, is Mary Mothersill's *Beauty Restored* (Oxford: Clarendon Press, 1984).

11 Although the problematic nature of the concept of art is exceedingly well known, we still seem much less wary in speaking about art than about nature. Or is this confidence disappearing in the face of Marxist and post-structuralist attacks on the concept of fine art, together with a good deal of embarrassment about how to theorize the distinction between fine art and popular culture? Whether there is any embarrassment or reluctance to operate with the concept of art, obviously depends upon whom we are talking about, and the same, I shall suggest later, may be said of the concept of nature.

12 Arthur O. Lovejoy, "'Nature' as Aesthetic Norm," reprinted in his *Essays in the History of Ideas* (Baltimore: Johns Hopkins University Press, 1948). Lovejoy is of course primarily concerned with the use of the term "nature" in aesthetic theory, but there is sufficient overlap between its uses in this and what for example children study when they take "nature study" courses, and in any case Lovejoy says enough about the "meanings of the multivocal terms 'nature' and 'natural'" (p. 76) to alert us to the possible multiple meanings of "natural beauty." If there are n meanings of "nature," are there n species of natural beauty?

13 See the treatment of moral concepts by Julius Kovesi in his *Moral Notions* (London: Routledge and Kegan Paul, 1967). I am suggesting Kovesi's arguments be applied to the concepts under which we find things naturally beautiful.

14 Collingwood makes quite the contrary point in connection with art. "If we call a work of art sublime, or idyllic, or lyrical, or romantic, or

graceful, we mean to call attention to something in the character of the work itself, and what we say about it amounts to praise or blame of the artist as such. On the other hand, if we call it a seascape or a villanelle or a fugue we are attaching to it a predicate with no aesthetic significance whatever...", R. G. Collingwood, *Outlines of a Philosophy of Art* (London: Oxford University Press, 1925), p. 31. Collingwood (and Croce) are well known for their attack on art genres. I make the contrary point, that so far as natural beauty is concerned, we are already responding aesthetically when we identify some segment of nature *as a landscape*.

15 In Frank Gloversmith, ed., *Class, Culture and Social Change: A New View of the 1930s* (Brighton: Harvester Press, 1980), pp. 258–80.

16 Lowerson in Gloversmith, *ibid.*, p. 272.

17 Quoted by Lowerson, *ibid.*, p. 262.

18 J. A. Walter, *The Human Home: The Myth of the Sacred Environment* (Tring: Lion Publishing, 1982).

19 And, for what the personal comment is worth, I share.

20 Milan Kundera, *The Book of Laughter and Forgetting* (Harmondsworth: Penguin, 1983), pp. 103–4.

21 See Tomas Kulka, "Kitsch," *British Journal of Aesthetics*, 28.1 (winter 1988).

22 See for example Roger Fry, *Vision and Design* (London: Chatto and Windus, 1923), pp. 292–3.

23 For a critique of beauty in the philosophy of art see Tolstoy's *What Is Art?* I think too that Hegel is an important figure in the story. He did not of course deny that art was beautiful; on the contrary he prized the beauty of art above that of nature. The long term consequence of this, however, was that with the degrading of natural beauty in philosophy it became "natural" to focus on art without needing to focus too on beauty.

24 I at once concede that without philosophical analysis this means very little. On the necessity for such an analysis, not to be attempted here, see the review in the *British Journal of Aesthetics*, 29.2 (spring 1989) by Anthony Savile of José Luis Zalabardo's translation into Spanish of Kant's *Critique of Judgement*, p. 182.

25 I am seeking to avoid stating the issue in terms of *Christianity* versus *atheism* where *this* means *disbelieving*, as I do, *the claims of Christianity*. Christianity versus atheism was how the issue was fought out in Britain in the nineteenth century, but in Britain today many more religious faiths than Christianity, and not merely competing versions of Christianity, claim our several allegiances.

26 Matthew Arnold, "The Study of Poetry," *Essays in Criticism, Second Series* (London: Macmillan, 1895), pp. 1–3.

27 William Wordsworth, "Lines Composed a Few Miles Above Tintern Abbey."

28 L. Wittgenstein, *Lectures & Conversations on Aesthetics, Psychology and Religious Belief*, ed. Cyril Barrett (Oxford: Basil Blackwell, 1970), I, 23 (p. 8); see also Roger Shiner, "Wittgenstein on the Beautiful, the Good and the Tremendous," *British Journal of Aesthetics*, 14.3 (summer 1974).

29 A huge topic to document, but see for example Baudelaire's protest: "Art, the beautiful, the useful, morality. A grand scrimmage is in progress, in which, owing to a lack of philosophical wisdom, each contestant grabs half the flag and says the other half is valueless." Charles-Pierre Baudelaire, *Selected Writings on Art and Artists* (Harmondsworth: Penguin, 1972), p. 111.

30 I am grateful to Graham McFee for his most helpful criticisms of an earlier draft and to the University of Sussex Philosophy Society for its illuminating discussion of this essay. I have made revisions and incorporated suggestions accordingly but am responsible for any undetected errors that may remain.

3

Trivial and serious in aesthetic appreciation of nature

RONALD W. HEPBURN

The aesthetic appreciation of both art and nature is often, in fact, judged to be more – and less – serious. For instance, both natural objects and art objects can be hastily and unthinkingly perceived, and they can be perceived with full and thoughtful attention. In the case of art, we are better equipped to sift the trivial from the serious appreciation; for the existence of a corpus, and a continuing practice, of criticism (and philosophical study) of the arts – for all their internal disputatiousness – furnishes us with relevant criteria. In the case of nature, we have far less guidance. Yet it must matter, there too, to distinguish trivial from serious encounters. When we seek to defend areas of "outstanding natural beauty" against depredations, it matters greatly what account we can give of the appreciation of that beauty: how its value can be set alongside competing and vociferously promoted values involved in industry, commerce and urban expansion. If we wish to attach very high value to the appreciation of natural beauty, we must be able to show that more is involved in such appreciation than the pleasant, unfocused enjoyment of a picnic place, or a fleeting and distanced impression of countryside through a touring-coach window, or obligatory visits to standard viewpoints or (should I say) snapshot-points.

That there is much work to be done on this subject is of course due to the comparative neglect of natural beauty in recent and fairly recent aesthetics. Although it was the very center of concern for a great deal of eighteenth-century aesthetics and for many of the greatest Romantic poets and painters, subsequent movements such as Symbolism and Modernism tended to see the natural world in a very different light. Darwinian ideas of nature were problematic and disturbing compared with theistic and pantheistic perspectives. Some later aesthetic theories made sense when applied to art, but little or none applied to natural beauty. Formalist theories require a determinate, bounded and shaped artifact; expression theories pre-suppose an artist behind an art-work.

What, first of all, do we mean by "aesthetic appreciation of nature"? By "nature" we must mean not just gentle pastoral landscape, but also tropical forest, tundra, ice floes, deserts, and objects (and events) made perceptible only by way of microscope or telescope. If nature's materials are vast, so too is the freedom of the percipient. We have endless choice of scale, freedom to choose the boundary of attention, choice between the *moving* – whether natural objects or the spectator or both – and the *static*. Our choice of viewpoint can range from that of the underwater diver to the view of the upper surface of clouds from an aircraft or an astronaut's view of the planet as a sphere.

What sort of aesthetic responses and judgments occur in our encounter with nature? We may speak of "beautiful" objects in nature, where "beauty" is used in a narrower sense, when we respond with delight, with love and with wonderment to objects before us. In that sense we may see beauty in the gradations of sky- and cloud-colors, yellow-orange evening light transfiguring a summer landscape, early morning sun-rays seen through mist in woodland, water calm in a lake, or turbulent or cascading in the mountain stream that emerges from the lake. The *feel* of moss or rock. Sounds – curlew, oystercatcher, lark – and where a single bird's cry makes the surrounding silence the more vividly appre-hensible. We may see beauty in formal qualities: flower-patterns, snow- and wind-shapes, the balancing of masses at the sides of a valley: in animal forms and in the grace of animal movement.

"Beauty" is, however, also used more widely. It may cover the aes-thetically arresting, the rewarding-to-contemplation, a great range of emotional qualities, without necessarily being pleasurable or lovable or suggestive of some ideal. Tree branches twisted with age or by wind, a towering thundercloud, black water beneath a steep rocky hillside.

We need to acknowledge a duality in much aesthetic appreciation of nature, a *sensuous component* and a *thought-component*. First, sensuous immediacy: in the purest cases one is taken aback by, for instance, a sky color-effect, or by the rolling away of cloud or mist from a landscape. Most often, however, an element of thought is present, as we implicitly compare and contrast *here* with *elsewhere*, *actual* with *possible*, *present* with *past*. I say, "implicit"; there may be no verbalizing or self-conscious complexity in the experience.

We cannot deny the thought-element, and it cannot reasonably be held (as such and in general) to fight with the aesthetic character of an experience. Consider that paradigm case of aesthetic experience of nature – the fall of an autumn leaf.[1] If we simply watch it fall, without any thought, it may or may not be a moving or exciting aesthetic object, but it must be robbed of its poignancy, its mute message of summer gone, its symbolizing *all* falling, our own included. Leaf veins suggest blood-vessel veins – symbolizing continuity in the forms of life, and maybe a shared vulnerability. Thus the thought-element may bring analogies to bear on the concrete particulars: this fall with other falls; and temporal links – this autumn with innumerable other autumns: the deep carpet of leaves in forests: the cycle of the seasons.

Or we watch the flight of swifts, wheeling, screaming; and to our present perception is added the thought of their having, in early summer, just returned from Africa – the thought (schematically) of that huge journey, their seeming-frailness, their frantic, restless, frightening burning up of energy, in their nearly ceaseless motion. All that is directed to (and fused with the perception of) the tiny, never-still bird-forms themselves. Maybe we think of a wider context still, in relation to the particular animal-form (or rock-form) under our gaze – awareness of the wide evolutionary procession of forms: or one may even be aware of the broadest metaphysical or religious background of all – the world as divinely created – or as uncreated, enigmatically *there*. Not even in the latter sort of case is the thought extraneously or externally juxtaposed to the perception of the natural object or scene. The union, or fusion, is much closer. There is an overall modification of awareness, in which the feeling and thought elements and the perception all interact.

Although analogies with art suggest themselves often enough about how to "frame" the objects of our aesthetic interest, where to establish the momentary bounds of our attention, on other occasions the objects we attend to seem to repudiate any such bounding – to present themselves as essentially illimitable, unframable, or to be in a way surrogates for the unbounded. This is particularly the domain of elemental experience, of the awesome and the sublime. There is an essential, though contested and variable, thought-element here again: it is particularly obvious in the Kantian versions of sublimity, where imagination aspires, but is unable, to cope with a great magnitude or energy of nature. It recoils, but its defeat is compensated for by the realization of moral and intellectual capabilities which are not daunted at all, but whose supreme worth is vividly brought home to the subject. Coleridge descending Sca Fell enacted that Kantian reflective content of sublime experience:

The sight of the Crags above me on each side, and the tempestuous clouds just over them ... overawed me. I lay in a state of ... Trance and Delight and blessed God aloud for the powers of Reason and the Will, which remaining, no danger can overpower us.[2]

Other theories, Schopenhauer's, for instance, saw the moment of ascendancy in our proving able to take a contemplative attitude towards hostile nature.[3]

Without an adequate thought-element, particularly self-image, counterbalancing the daunting external powers, the experience of the sublime may shrivel, or never establish itself in a subject. To some – Mikel Dufrenne, for one – it remains the chief moment in the aesthetic experience of nature: whereas others, for instance Adorno, see the sublime as a historically ephemeral and by now faded mode of sensibility.[4]

To chronicle the effects rather than the components of aesthetic experience of nature would require a much longer story than can be attempted here. Among the most general of these, clichéd though it is, must be the "life-enhancing" effect of beauty, release from the stress and anxiety of practical, manipulatory, causally engaged relations with nature into the calmly contemplative. These work together, I suggest, in the case of natural beauty with a lasting, or always renewable, sense of mystery or wonder that it should be there at all.

Can we then make any reasoned case for distinguishing trivial from serious in this field? If it is a form of perception-and-reflection that we are considering, then as I said at the start, we know that perception (taking that first) can be attentive or inattentive, can be discriminating or undiscriminating, lively or lazy: that the doors of perception can need cleansing, the conventions and the simplifications of popular perception can need resisting. The reflective component, likewise, can be feeble or stereotyped, individual, original or exploratory. It can be immature or confused. And indeed we may secretly be anxious that the thought which sustains our valued experience of nature is in the end metaphysically untenable. To *discard* these issues, to narrow down on a minimally reflective, passive perception, would seem to trivialize in another way. Adorno suspected that our very concept of nature is "idyllic, provincial, insular."[5] I would argue that it is not always so: but it can be, and from comfortable selectivity comes trivialization by another route.

Some of these points, then, suggest the following first approximation: that an aesthetic approach to nature is trivial to the extent that it distorts, ignores, suppresses truth about its objects, feels and thinks about them in ways that falsify how nature really is. All this may be coupled with a fear that if there is to be some agreeable aesthetic encounter with nature, call it trivial if you will, one had better not look too attentively nor think too hard about the presuppositions (the thought-components) on which one's experience rests. To break open the parcel might dissipate the aesthetic delight and set one an over-arduous task to regain at some deeper, more serious level what one had possessed at a more superficial one.

If it trivializes to see nature in terms of ready-made, standard "views," so does it also to see oneself merely as the detached viewer – or indeed as a noumenally free and rational ego. There is a deepening of seriousness when I realize that I am myself one with, part of, the nature over-against me. So, I want to say, an aesthetic appreciation of nature, if serious, is necessarily a self-exploration also; for the energies, regularities, contingencies of nature are the energies, principles and contingencies that sustain my own embodied life and my own awareness. Nature may be "other" to us, but we are no less connatural with it. We do not simply look out upon nature as we look at the sea's drama from a safe shore: the shore is no less nature, and so too is the one who looks.

On a superficial reading of nature, objects tend to have an invariable, univocal expressive quality. Fused, however, with less conventional thoughts, considered in wider or less standard contexts, these qualities admit of endless modification. It is reasonable, then, to include among the trivializing factors bland unawareness of that potential variability, and among factors making for serious aesthetic appreciation of nature must be a background realization of it.

Anticipating later discussion, I need to say here that "seriousness" or "depth" in aesthetic experience of nature cannot be correlated in any simple way with intensity or fullness of thought-content. Some thoughts (perhaps of causal explanation of the phenomena at the level of particle physics) might not enrich but neutralize the experience, or at least fight and fail to fuse with its perceptual content. Or they might trivialize. Other thought-contents again, and in contrast, relate to quite fundamental features of the lived human state, and bear directly upon the perceptual, phenomenal dimension, which their presence cannot fail to solemnize and deepen. Think, for instance, of that realization (thought and sense experience in fusion) of the whole earth's motion, in Wordsworth's skating episode in *The Prelude*, as he suddenly stopped in his tracks while skating in the dark:

> So through the darkness and the cold we flew,
> And not a voice was idle; with the din
> Smitten, the precipices rang aloud;
> The leafless trees and every icy crag
> Tinkled like iron; while far distant hills
> Into the tumult sent an alien sound
> Of melancholy not unnoticed, while the stars
> Eastward were sparkling clear, and in the west
> The orange sky of evening died away.
> Not seldom from the uproar I retired
> Into a silent bay, or sportively
> Glanced sideway, leaving the tumultuous throng,
> To cut across the reflex of a star
> That fled, and, flying still before me, gleamed
> Upon the glassy plain; and oftentimes,
> When we had given our bodies to the wind,
> And all the shadowy banks on either side
> Came sweeping through the darkness, spinning still
> The rapid line of motion, then at once
> Have I, reclining back upon my heels,
> Stopped short; yet still the solitary cliffs
> Wheeled by me – even as if the earth had rolled
> With visible motion her diurnal round![6]

A second important duality characterizes an aesthetic concern with nature. On the one hand, it is nature, nature's own forms, structures, sequences, that we seek to contemplate; and the more serious our engagement, the more earnest will be our regard for, and our respect for, the integrity and the proper modes of being of the objects in nature themselves, inanimate and animate. We see sentimentality, for instance, as trivializing in its tendency, because it may falsely posit human feelings and human attitudes in the nonhuman – or more likely posit *failed* human life and human attitudes instead of *successfully* attained nonhuman life. To put it very schematically, a serious aesthetic approach to nature is close to a Spinozistic intellectual love of God-or-Nature in its totality. It rejects Kant's invitation to accord unconditional value only to the bearers of freedom and reason, and to downgrade phenomenal nature save as it hints at a supersensible, an earnest of which is furnished in nature's amenability to be perceived, its purposiveness without purpose. It rejects, likewise, Hegel's downplaying of natural beauty in favor of the spirit-manifesting practice of art.

But there is another side: even when we discard the excesses of anthropomorphism, to admit no more than this other-respecting concern is to exclude too much. The human inner life has been nourished by images from the natural world: its self-articulation and development could hardly proceed without annexing or appropriating forms from the phenomenal world. They are annexed not in a systematic, calculating, craftsmanlike fashion, but rather through our being imaginatively seized by them, and coming to cherish their expressive aptness, and to rely upon them in our efforts to understand ourselves. Not all of this can be categorized as strictly *aesthetic* encounter or *aesthetic* contemplation: some of it can, and the lines of connection are obvious and important.

That may serve us as a sketch of the duality within our commerce with nature – a respect for its own structures and the celebrating of those, and the annexation of natural forms. Though divergent, those approaches are not opposed: nature need not be misperceived in order to furnish symbols for our inwardness. But their focus and their intention are distinct. Each presents some problems in relation to the spectrum between trivial and serious.

First then we are to consider and contemplate nature in its own terms. This is an aim that sets one serious goal for aesthetic appreciation. What *problems* come with it?

One interpretation of the phrase "in its own terms" would prompt us towards supplying a scientific thought-component. Now, it may well enrich our perception of a U-valley to "think-in" its readily imaginable glacial origins. But, as I claimed earlier, one could not have an obligation to think-in *perception-transcending* ideas or explanations. These might be explanations in physical theory of transformations at the molecular and atomic level that produced the rock of which the valley is made. We cannot oblige ourselves to think-in what must fragment or overwhelm or dissolve the aesthetic perception, instead of enriching it. Aesthetic experience must be human experience – episodic, phenomenal. To destroy it can hardly be to *deepen* it!

We spoke of "respect" for natural objects, and particularly for living beings. But a further and different problem arises when we recall that nature itself shows only a very limited respect for its individuals. For me to respect something is to perceive it as intrinsically valuable. I affirm, even rejoice in, its being and in its manner of being. Suppose, however, I do that with (say) a zebra or a brilliantly colored butterfly newly emerged from its chrysalis. I am going to be hurt and saddened when a lion tears the zebra to pieces, and a bird snaps up the butterfly when it has scarcely tried out its wings. That bleak thought of the vulnerability and brevity of individual life can easily attach itself also to perceptions of *flourishing* living beings, and there is no doubt that to perceive them so is to be closer to the truth of things than not to. Does it follow that in the interest of "depth" one must cancel or at least qualify every response of simple delight at beast or bird? There is conflict here. On the one hand, to seek depth or seriousness seems to rule out optimistic falsifications: but on the other hand, since we are *also* trying to attend in a differentiating and appreciative mode, we surely cannot claim that an undifferentiated consciousness of nature's dysteleology must always predominate in any aesthetic experience.

There is poignancy, too, in the thought that some of the most animated, zestful and aesthetically arresting movements of living beings are directed at the destruction of other living beings – the ballet of swifts feeding on the wing, lithe and rapid movements of panthers or leopards. If we are tempted to abstract from, or attenuate or mute the disturbing thought-content in any such case, is that not to move some way towards the trivial end of our scale? Nature, that is, can be made aesthetically contemplatable only by a sentimentalizing, falsifying selectivity, that turns away from the real work of beak, tooth and claw. That would indeed be to move, and very significantly, in the trivializing direction, and to shirk the challenge to the would-be appreciator's own creativity.

In some situations at least aesthetic appreciation of nature may be made sustainable – without falsification – through fashioning less simplistic (and less inappropriately moralized) concepts of nature's processes and energies. If, for instance, we can celebrate nature's overall animation, vitality – *creative and destructive* in indissoluble unity – we may reach a reflective, or contemplative equilibrium, that is neither unqualified by melancholy nor disillusioned and repelled.

Rather than follow that strenuous route, we may be tempted, as some aestheticians have been, once more to deny that we are properly concerned, in aesthetic experience, with how things actually are; but we should be concerned only with their immediately given perceptual qualities, the sensuous surface. To accept such a limitation, however, though it would lead us thankfully past a great many puzzles and problems, would leave us with a quite unacceptably *thin* version of aesthetic experience of nature. The falling autumn leaf becomes a small, fluttering, reddish-brown material object – and no more: the swifts only rapidly flitting shapes. The extreme here is to purify away, regressively and evasively, all but the merest sensuous show: nature dissolving, fragmenting to kaleidoscopic splinters.

We are working here, implicitly, with a scale. Near one end of it aesthetic experience attenuates towards the perception-transcending substructure of its objects. We do not have an obligation to place ourselves there: with the aesthetic, it is on the phenomenal, the *Lebenswelt*, concrete and abstract both, that we must focus attention. At the other end of the scale, as we have just noted, we exclude all thought, and leave sensuous immediacy only. At both extremes we lose what John Findlay singled out as aesthetic essentials, the poignant and the perspicuous in combination. These opposite dangers are run only when the ready-made stereotyped snapshot appreciatings of nature are transcended, and the subject is actively seeking his or her own synthesis – maximally poignant and perspicuous – with nature's materials perceived and pondered. *Between* the extremes, we might find an acceptable ideal for serious aesthetic perception in encouraging ourselves to enhance the thought-load *almost* to the point, but not *beyond* the point, at which it begins to overwhelm the vivacity of the particular perception.

In my second approach to nature the forms of nature are annexed in imagination, interiorized, the external made internal. Is there in this, in contrast with the previous theme, a suggestion of the solipsistic or at least the narcissistic? Not necessarily: since if we share a common environment, the annexed forms can range from the universally intersubjective, through the shareable though not universal, to the highly individual and personal. *Basic* natural forms are interiorized for the articulating of a common structure of the mind. Through these, the elusively nonspatial is made more readily graspable and communicable. We speak of depths and heights – in relation to moods or feelings or hopes or fears: of soarings and of glooms. We are lifted and dashed, chilled, spiritually frozen, and thawed. We drown, we surface; we suffer dark nights of the soul. Again, there is no simple one-to-one correlation between mental state and natural item. I may interiorize the desert – as bleak emptiness, *néant*: or I may interiorize it as unscripted openness, potentiality ...

As already suggested, metaphor is of the essence in such appropriations. No aestheticizing of natural objects can occur in these ways unless we have discovered metaphor. And that gives us the clue we need in order to apply the distinction between trivial and serious to this area. Many metaphors we use constantly to articulate conscious life are dead metaphors: some are at any time capable of reanimation. But on occasion (and we can let Wordsworth mark for us the extreme point in metaphorical appropriation), a person catches from events in the natural world "a tone, / An image, and a character" so deeply and individually apt that they re-organize or re-center his life. But these too need not be incommunicably private; they may be "fit to be transmitted and made visible / To other eyes." Wordsworth, for instance, saw in the workings and self-transformings of nature on the grand scale (as he narrated in *The Prelude* XIII, on the effects of mist and moonlight on Snowdon) metaphors for the poet's understanding and evaluating of his own imaginative transforming activity, in the fashioning of his own poetry. He explicitly acknowledges the co-presence of perception and thought. "By sensible impressions not enthrall'd, / But quicken'd, rouz'd, and made thereby more fit / To hold communion with the invisible world."

The "invisible world" is the world of spirit, of mind, the spiritual being precisely articulated and modified by its imaginative annexing of the outer world – that is, the sensible impressions derived from it, but also imbued with thought. Our topic is not simply the search for the descriptively apt metaphors from nature for the structure and the ongoings of human inwardness, structures and ongoings that would exist or occur identically and independently whether or not the search is successful: but the annexing is also a molding and making of that inwardness, reflectively or perfunctorily achieved. No doubt some of this can be done by images drawn from domestic or urban life; but there is more than a little suggestion of anxious self-protectiveness in such restriction to the man-made environment. The gain would be that we screen ourselves from the natural immensities that daunt us; the loss that we cut ourselves off from that "renewal of our inner being" which the Romantics saw as derived from meditating on the great permanencies of nature.

A person may find it hard not to take certain natural sequences as generalizable and significant, though enigmatic, "messages" of nature. For instance, the natural sequence of events in a sunrise or the clearing of weather after a storm may seem to carry an optimistic message. Adorno, in *Aesthetic Theory*, writes of the "yearning for

what is promised but never unveiled by beauty" ... "a message seems
to be inscribed" on some aspect of nature, "not all is lost yet." But, he
adds, "the statement that this is how nature speaks is meaningless,
nature's language is not propositional."[7] Analogously, on listening to
a particular piece of music, I may swing between saying (a) What I am
enjoying is simply the emotional quality – a cheering, happy quality –
of *this* sequence of tones and rhythms; and (b) this expresses a
generalizable cheering, a justified hopefulness. Perhaps in both
nature and music, to go to the stronger claim must be to risk illusion.
To be safe, I would have to keep to the cautious, and certainly valid
inference: because this state is actual, this state is at least a human
possibility, and (I may add, still fairly cautiously) a renewable one.

What would trivializing be, here? I think it would be either to be
"fundamentalist," literalist about "messages of nature," or to reject
the whole topic, again in a literalist spirit – that or nothing. More
adequate, and with a claim to seriousness, is to be aware of the
metaphoricality and the enigmatic quality, and to allow that
awareness to characterize the thought-side of the experiences.

The combination of distanced and yet intimate or enigmatically
meaningful, is nowhere more intensely realized than in *dreams*.
Indeed it has been claimed that in any strikingly beautiful landscape
there is an element of the dreamlike. The interiorization seems
half-completed in nature itself, imparting an almost mythological
character to any figures such a scene contains. All are apprehended
with a mysterious sense that the components (or some of them)
deeply *matter* to us, though one cannot say how: the shape of a hill,
the precise placing of a stand of trees, or a solitary rock. To decide that
there is no readable significance is not necessarily to discredit such
an experience or to show it up as illusion. Any discrediting is again
the work of literalism. Naively serious, and *thus* trivial. We seem
invited to "transcend the sheer sensible impressions": we do transcend them, but only into our state of perplexity and wonder. But no
demythologizable message could be more memorable than these
half-perceived, half-dreamed visionary scenes.

Another respect must be noted in which there occur large individual
differences in the aesthetic appreciation of nature. This is in the
degree to which imagination is active in connecting diverse separated
natural forms. I am thinking of the relating of object with object,
structure with structure, searching out analogies between features of
otherwise very remote phenomena. We may see the hills as "lifting

themselves in ridges like the waves of a tumultuous sea." Or we see "high cirrus cloud" as "exactly resembling sea sand ribbed by the tide." (Wordsworth and Ruskin, respectively.)

To be imaginatively alert to such common structures has an obvious unifying, integrating effect – enhancing the sense that we are dealing with a single nature, intelligible in its forms. In at least two ways, however, pursuit of resemblances and analogies can become absurd or one-sided, and so can trivialize aesthetic perception of nature. Some wholly fortuitous, fanciful likeness may be made the object of an excessive wonderment, as when the guide to a system of limestone caves introduces a stalagmite as the Virgin Mary. Again there can result a falsely comforting simplification and idealization of nature. For not *all* is intelligible structure or perspicuous geometry. The veining of rocks, wind-shaping of clouds, undulating of hills – all of these have (as well as their undoubted symmetries) their elements of arbitrariness and opacity, at the phenomenal level. To Kant's important claim that nature looks as if made for our cognitive faculty, we have surely to add the equally important antithetical claim, that in some respects it looks *not at all* as if it were made for us to perceive and to know. Nature's otherness is as real and as aesthetically significant, if we are "serious," as is its readily perceptible chiming forms.

This combination, in our aesthetic perception of nature, of the readily graspable and the opaque, sheerly contingent and alien, merits more than a sentence. The realization that the combination characterizes our aesthetic dealings with nature in general must again count as a mark of seriousness. It is a distinction vital, for instance, to a monotheistic view of nature. If the world of nature were itself divine, then one would expect intelligibility to prevail throughout. If the created world were distinct from God, though the product of his all-rational mind, one would expect a nature with a magnificently intelligible structure, but with signs of the insertion of divine *will* – the contingent, the might-have-been-different. Even if we do not hold a theistic belief-system, there can be a parabolic application of this duality, indicating truthfully enough that the distinction runs very deep in our experience of nature.

What is more, we are able to make aesthetic use, to make a topic of appreciation, of that dichotomy. There would be an aesthetic thinness or emptiness, if the perceptible forms of nature, its skylines and contours and living beings, could all be generated by mathematicians' equations of relatively simple kinds. Perhaps wind-formed sand-dunes and wave-patterns come near, though even there the complexity soon defies our perception of intelligible form. Realizing the duality is one main element in our perceiving of a natural configuration such as one may see on many shores: strata in a rock-face, tilted to an arch, but crumbling and weathered, supporting grasses and the nests of seagulls on its ledges and shelves.

So far, the aspects of aesthetic appreciation of nature which we have considered have sustained our intuition that appreciation can be more, or less superficial, more or less serious. It is possible, however, to be moved by skeptical thoughts which suggest that the *whole* of this area of experience is nothing other than trivial, that aesthetic experience of nature – being founded on a variety of illusions – can never really be serious.

Aesthetic experiences of nature, it may be said, are fugitive and unstable, wholly dependent upon anthropocentric factors such as scale, viewpoint, perspective. The mountain that we appreciate for its majesty and stability is, on a different time-scale, as fluid as the ripples on the lake at its foot. Set any distinctive natural object in its wider context in the environment of which it is a part, and the particular aesthetic quality you are enjoying is likely to vanish. You shudder with awe at the base of your cliff towering above you. But look at the cliff again (if you can identify it in time) from an aircraft at thirty thousand feet, and does not the awe strike you as having been misplaced, as somewhat theatrical and exaggerated, childish even? Can an experience be serious, if it can so readily be undermined?

First of all, something not very different can be true of art-experience as well. A too-remote viewpoint, or a too-distant listening-point can ruin the impact of a picture or performed music; and without a sympathetically and elaborately prepared mental set, and the appropriate context of attitudes and ideas, many works of high art can strike one as grotesque, fatuous, bathetic, or comically solemn. Yet these familiar facts about the conditions of satisfactory art-experience do *not* seem to undermine its worth when the conditions are in fact happily fulfilled.

It is not quite the same with art as with nature. The appreciators of nature have in one way more to do than the art-appreciators; they play a larger creative role in fashioning their aesthetic object. They have to find their viewpoint, decide on boundaries of attention, generate the thought-content. The experience is more of a cooperative product of natural object and contemplator. But what lurks behind the more comprehensively dismissive and skeptical movements of mind with regard to *nature* is an assumption about what we might call "authority." The view from an aircraft allegedly shows you what the cliff *really* is like and shows that your awe was misplaced. Likewise, in the case of the "majestic" and "stable" mountain, a skeptical critic may appeal to the facts of the oneness, the connectedness of the items of the natural world, and of the universality of change and flux; and these are taken to annul or destroy our serious appreciation of the perceptual qualities of a self-selected fragment, our perceptual snapshot or "still" – artificially isolated (as these qualities are) from the whole and the "becoming" of the whole.

To occupy the discrediting perspective is being understood as entitling the critic to say: "I know (or I see) something you are not aware of! From my distance – or from my height – your awe is shown up as misplaced." Or is there something deeply amiss in that comment? And could not I (at the foot of my cliff) say something very similar? "You in your aircraft, though you can see a great deal, are simply unable to perceive and respond to the perceptual qualities that generate the awe I feel. Your viewpoint has its limitations too." What happens very often, I think, is that the ironical, anti-Romantic, belittling, levelling reaction tends uncritically to be favored today as the authoritative reaction ("You won't put anything over on me"). Why this should be so for many people in our society, would need study in the sociology of religious, moral and aesthetic values in their interconnections. What I should certainly want to say myself is that a readiness to conform to such a social trend can be a factor on the side of trivialization, not the side of seriousness, in aesthetic appreciation. Our aesthetic experience of nature is thoroughly dependent on scale and on individual viewpoint. To fail to realize *how* deeply would surely trivialize. Coming to realize and to think-in to one's aesthetic experience the fact of that perspectivity is certainly a factor in the maturing of this experience. But what is highly contestable is the implicit claim that *one* perspective, *one* view, one set of resultant perceived qualities takes precedence over another, and so can discredit or undermine another – or even all the others: that one of them has, in an aesthetic context, greater authority than another. It is easy enough to deal with the art examples. Generally speaking, the painting we can assume to have been *made* to be viewed from the distance at which its significant detail can be discriminated and its overall structure seen as a unity; and the music to be heard closely enough to occupy our auditory attention with all *its* detail.

But the analogy with art may be developed in a further way, one that carries important implications. In the subject-matter of art there is no "authoritatively appropriate" and "inappropriate." Equally fitting objects of attention are substances, relations, events, the abstract as well as the concrete, the momentary, the minute, the everlasting, the insubstantial, even the perceptually illusory. Any of these may be the subject of, say, a poet's celebration and scrutiny. (A study which argues vigorously for this "ontological parity," as its author calls it, is Justus Buchler's *The Main of Light* – particularly chapter 6, [New York: Oxford University Press, 1974]). Is there any reason why this principle should apply any less plausibly to the aesthetic appreciation of nature? It would legitimize any viewpoint on any subject-matter – substance or shadow, any perceptual quali-ties, physical materials, mica, quartz, sand, or more elusive per-spective-dependent qualities like the blueness of the sky, the colors of the rainbow, the enhancement of distance-perception on an atmos-pherically clear day, or the merging of objects in mist. It would of course follow that if I denied special authority to any perspective whatever, I would have to deny it to the perspective which I (still at the foot of my cliff) would very willingly judge to have some preferred status. That it could not have.

The reader will have been aware, as I have been aware, that two recurrent elements in the account I have been giving exert pressures in different directions, or (if you like) remain in stressful relation with one another. On the one side, one way to seriousness in our aesthetic dealings with nature involved a respect for truth – more accurately, for the objective truth such as the sciences pursue – so long as that path does not carry us beyond what can be incorporated in still essentially *perceptual* experience. The terminus in that direction, then, would be the thinking-in to our perceptual experi-ence of what we know to be objectively the case. Remember the examples of glaciation as once shaping the now green valley, and anxiety coloring our response to sighting the wild animal whose predator is seldom far off. There is a correcting or guiding of our episodic experience through an objectivizing movement of mind.

Nevertheless, we have also felt the attraction of a radically anti-hierarchical, in some respects antiobjectivizing movement, towards acceptance of "ontological parity." And according to *that*, the per-ceptually "corrected" and veridical has no stronger or more serious claim to aesthetic attention than has the illusory.

Ronald W. Hepburn

Is there any way, then, of dealing rationally with these conflicting pressures? Should we say: all this is, ultimately, about a game we play with nature, for enjoyment and the enriching of our lives. In any particular situation follow whichever option promises more reward. We are free to respect, or to ignore, the objectivizing option. To feel bound always to pursue it is not really to show commitment to so-called seriousness, but rather to show a profound misunderstanding of the aesthetic. Or would that be simply and shockingly, at the very end, to capitulate to the trivializers?

It strikes me now that perhaps it should not be any surprise to us, if the attempt to apply the rough and ready categories of "serious" and "trivial" to aesthetic experience of nature should not yield neat and tidy results. It would have been rather extraordinary if it had done so! No doubt, that is a self-consolatory thought for being left with those unresolved strains and tensions.[8]

Notes

1 For a treatment different from my own, see Pepita Haezrahi, The Contemplative Activity (Allen and Unwin 1954), ch. 2.

2 Tour in the Lake Country, 1802. cf. also, David Craig, Native Stones: A Book about Climbing (London: Secker and Warburg, 1987), p. 132.

3 A. Schopenhauer, The World as Will and Representation, trans. E.F.J. Payne, (New York: Dover Books, 1969) I. paragraph 39.

4 M. Dufrenne, Esthétique et philosophie, I, "Expérience esthétique de la nature," p. 45. T.W. Adorno, Aesthetic Theory, 1970 (London: Routledge and Kegan Paul, 1984), p. 103.

5 Adorno, Aesthetic Theory, p. 100.

6 W. Wordsworth, The Prelude, bk. I, lines 438–60.

7 Adorno, Aesthetic Theory, pp. 108–9.

8 Versions of this essay were given as lectures at Lancaster and Boston Universities.

4

The public prospect and the private view: the politics of taste in eighteenth-century Britain

JOHN BARRELL

I

I want to offer a comment on some ideas about landscape that are commonly found among writers on art, on literature, and on various other subjects in the second half of the eighteenth and in the early years of the nineteenth centuries in Britain. The main point of my doing this is to show how a correct taste, here especially for land-scape and landscape art, was used in this period as a means of legitimating political authority, particularly but not exclusively within the terms of the discourse of civic humanism. If we interrogate writers of the polite culture of this period on the question of what legitimates this claim, one answer we repeatedly discover, though it may take very different forms, is that political authority is rightly exercised by those capable of thinking in general terms; which usually means those capable of producing abstract ideas – decomplex ideas – out of the raw data of experience. The inability to do this was usually represented as in part the result of a lack of education, a lack which characterized women and the vulgar; and because women are generally represented in this period as incapable of generalising to any important degree, I shall be in this paper very careful *not* to use a vocabulary purged of sexist reference: when I speak of what men thought, of Man in general, of the spectator as *he*, I am doing so with forethought, and in order to emphasize the point that, in the matter of political authority, legitimated as I have described, women were almost entirely out of the question, and the issue to be determined was which men could pass the test of taste.

To develop the ability to think accurately in abstract terms required more, however, than an appropriate education: one further condition in particular is necessary: a man must occupy a place in the social order where he had no need to devote his life to supporting himself and his dependents, or at least (in some versions of the argument) of supporting them by mechanical labor. For if he does have such a need, three things will follow: first, he will be obliged to follow one, determinate occupation, and will discover an interest in promoting the interests of that occupation, and of his own success in it: and his concern with what is good for himself, or for one interest-group, will prevent him from arriving at an understanding of what is good for man in general, for human nature, for the public interest. Second, the experience that falls in the way of such a man – especially if he follows, not a liberal profession, but a mechanical art – will be too narrow to serve as the basis of ideas general enough to be represented as true for all mankind, or even for all the members of a state. Third, because mechanical arts are concerned with *things*, with material objects, they will not offer an opportunity for the exercise of a generalizing and abstracting rationality: the successful exercise of the mechanical arts requires that material objects be regarded as concrete particulars, and not in terms of the abstract or formal relations among them. The man of independent means, on the other hand, who does not labor to increase them, will be released from private interest and from the occlusions of a narrowed and partial experience of the world, and from an experience of the world as *material*. He will be able to grasp the public interest, and so will be fit to participate in government.

Of this ability, a taste in landscape provides one of various tests. And let me begin my account of that test by saying that it turns on the social and political function of the distinction between panoramic, and ideal landscape, on the one hand, and, on the other, actual portraits of views, and representations of enclosed, occluded land-scapes, with no great depth of field. I had better explain that I am using the word "panoramic," here, simply as a shorthand for the kind of extensive prospect we find typically in a landscape by Claude. But I had better offer some more explanations, because I am aware that I am making a bipartite distinction between a consider-able range of kinds of landscapes, some of which – the topographical panorama, the ideal composition of a woodland glade – exhibit characteristics which seem to belong to the different halves of the distinction.

Let me explain the distinction more clearly. It is between land-scapes which seek to exhibit substantial, representative forms of nature arranged in a wide extent of land, and views which, even if panoramic, exhibit the accidental forms of nature, and even if ideal, exhibit their ideal forms within a restricted terrain. That such a distinction is crucial to an understanding of the various kinds of landscape art is, I think, obvious enough; and it is well known that in eighteenth-century England these different kinds of landscape were often – if not always – assumed to be the productions of, and designed for the entertainment of, two different spheres of life, and even of two different classes of people – what and who they were will be considered shortly. It does seem to me however that we continually overlook the importance of the distinction to the eighteenth century; and that it has been possible to do so for a long time is suggested, for example, by this passage from Hazlitt's essays on Reynolds, published in the *Champion* in 1814, in which he comments on what he calls Reynolds' "learned riddle," whether accidents in nature should be introduced in landscape painting. Accidents in nature, as there is probably no need to explain, are *untypical* natural phenomena: sometimes they are regarded as phenomena rare enough to be the result of a complex conjunction of natural causes: storms and rainbows are accidents. More generally, however, accidents are anything in the prospect of nature which suggests that the prospect is being observed at one particular moment rather than another, and which calls attention to that fact: when the light, for example, strikes objects in such a way as to suggest that it will strike them differently a second later; when the form of a tree is such that it seems to be ruffled by a blast of wind of such or such a particular force, blowing from such or such a direction. Anything, in short, is an accident, which suggests a view of nature as other than abstract, typical, a permanent phenomenon, but particularly untypical effects of light, or untypical forms of objects. The debate about whether accidents in nature should be admitted into landscape was not originated by Reynolds: it was a familiar topic among writers on painting committed to an aesthetic of illusion, as Reynolds of course was not. For, of course, a landscape full of accidents is likely to deceive our eyes more successfully, but in doing so it would attach us to images of nature less elevating than those represented in entirely ideal landscapes. But, as shall be seen, Reynolds' "learned riddle," posed in his fourth discourse, was about much more than this.

Of that riddle, Hazlitt writes:

We should never have seen that fine landscape of his [Rubens] in the Louvre, with a rainbow on one side, the whole face of nature refreshed after the shower, and some shepherds under a group of trees piping to their heedless flock, if instead of painting what he saw and what he felt to be fine, he had set himself to solve the learned riddle proposed by Sir Joshua, whether *accidents in nature* should be introduced in landscape, since Claude has rejected them. It is well that genius gets the start of criticism, for if these two great landscape painters, not being privileged to consult their own taste and inclinations, had been compelled to wait till the rules of criticism had decided the preference between their different styles, instead of having both, we should have had neither. The folly of all such comparisons consists in supposing that we are reduced to a single alternative in our choice of excellence, and the true answer to the question, Which do you like best, Rubens's landscapes or Claude's? is the one which was given on another occasion – both.[1]

Hazlitt, characteristically, cuts a knot that Reynolds had attempted to untie; and it seems likely that he does so, not because he is unaware of the importance to eighteenth-century art of the distinction I have referred to, but because he is hostile to the political basis of a division between kinds of landscape, which could also be a division between the kinds of viewer appropriate to each. But either way, Hazlitt suppresses a distinction important to Reynolds, and succeeds in obscuring its importance to us. In this essay I want to re-tie the knot that Hazlitt has cut.

That Hazlitt's response to Reynolds' "learned riddle" is the result not of a failure to understand the point of the riddle, but of a refusal to accept the assumptions on which it is based, is suggested by the fact that three years later Coleridge, who was not at all antagonistic to the notion that the political republic, and the republic of taste, were constituted on a distinction between two kinds of persons with greater and lesser intellectual capacities, was still able to represent that distinction in terms of a distinction between kinds of landscape. Coleridge describes an allegoric vision, in which a company of men is approached by a woman, tall beyond the stature of mortals, and dressed in white, who announces that her name is Religion.

The more numerous part of our company, affrighted by the very sound, and sore from recent impostures or sorceries, hurried onwards and examined no further. A few of us, struck by the manifest opposition of her form and manners to those of the living Idol, whom we had so recently abjured [SUPERSTITION], agreed to follow her, though with cautious circumspection. She led us to an eminence in the midst of the valley, from the top of which we could command the whole plain, and observe the relations of the different parts, of each to the other, and of all to each. She then gave us an optic glass which assisted without contradicting our natural vision, and enabled us to see far beyond the limits of the Valley of Life: though our eye even thus assisted permitted us only to behold a light and a glory, but *what*, we could not descry, save only that it *was*, and that it was most glorious.[2]

Then "with the rapid transition of a dream," Coleridge finds himself again with the more numerous party, who have come to "the base of a lofty and almost perpendicular rock," which shuts out the view; the "only perforation" in the precipice is "a vast and dusky cave," at the mouth of which sits the figure of Sensuality.

The distinction between a viewpoint from which a vast and panoramic prospect is visible, and low, sunken situations from which only the nearest objects are visible, only in close-up, is a repeated motif of Coleridge's poems. In "Reflections on Having Left a Place of Retirement," for example, composed in 1795, the year also of the composition of the first version of the Allegoric Vision, Coleridge compares the low and humble position of his cottage with the view available by climbing from that low dell up the stony mount nearby: "the whole World," he writes, "seem'd *imag'd*" in the "vast circumference" of the horizon: the images in that extensive prospect seem representative and substantial, so that the prospect becomes a microcosm of the world. One theme of "This Lime-Tree Bower My Prison" (1797) is to consider how objects within the occluded prospect of the bower may be seen, as can the objects in the "wide landscape" described earlier in the poem, in terms of the relations of things, rather than as things in themselves. In "Fears in Solitude" (1798), the "burst of prospect" seen from the hill "seems like society," in opposition to the "silent dell" in which Coleridge has considered his fears, in solitude, and in opposition also to his own "lowly cottage." There are numerous poems based on the same pattern of opposition, and the meaning of each component – panorama, and occluded view – is complex, and changes from poem to poem. It is possible, however, to abstract and collocate a number of the significances attached to each image: and to notice that, among the meanings attached to the panoramic view may be the notion of a wider society, and the notion of the ability to grasp objects in the form of their relations to each other; among the meanings attached to the occluded view, from a low viewpoint, are seclusion, of course, and privacy as something opposed to the social in its more extended sense, and also sensuality, which for Coleridge (and also for numerous writers, including Reynolds, before him) was particularly characterized by a tendency to see objects not in terms of their relations, or their common relation to a general, and representative term, but in and for themselves, as objects of consumption and possession.

II

Let me focus first on the opposition between different landscapes as appealing to two different classes of people, and therefore between the ability to grasp things in terms of their relations – of "the different parts of each to the other, and of all to each" – and the inability to do so, which leaves us focusing, myopically, on the objects themselves, on, as Coleridge puts it elsewhere, "an immense heap of *little* things,"[3] the world as perceived by the sensual eye unilluminated by imagination, or the ideal. For a version of that opposition is of course crucial also to Reynolds' theory of art, and in particular to the doctrine of the central form, which is arrived at by the ability to abstract substance from accident, "to get above all singular forms, local customs, particularities, and details of every kind."[4] True taste, for Reynolds, is the ability to form and to recognize representative general ideas, by referring all the objects of a class to the essential character by which a class is constituted; the lack of true taste is the inability to perform this operation, so that we take pleasure not in the ideal representation of objects in terms of their generic classes, but in the unpurged, accidental forms of objects, minutely delineated. For the Coleridge of 1817 that distinction is grounded, of course, in an idealist philosophy: to grasp the relations among objects is to grasp them in terms of the idea which is at once the ground of their existence and the end for which they exist. For Reynolds, and for almost all writers in the eighteenth century in England, the distinction is founded on a distinction between those who can, and those who cannot form general ideas, normally by the processes of abstraction; between those who can compose details into a whole, or compose a whole by the elimination of detail, and, on the other hand, the ignorant who, as Reynolds explains, "cannot comprehend a whole, nor even what it means."

The critic Thomas Tickell, or it may be Richard Steele, makes the same distinction in the context of pastoral poetry in an unsigned essay of 1713:

Men, who by long study and experience have reduced their ideas to certain classes, and consider the general nature of things abstracted from particulars, express their thoughts after a more concise, lively, surprising manner. Those who have little experience, or cannot abstract, deliver their sentiments in plain descriptions, by circumstances, and those observations which either strike the senses, or are the first motions of the mind.[5]

For that reason, he argues, the shepherds of pastoral "are not allowed to make deep reflections," and for that reason too, one of the main pleasures that sophisticated readers take in pastoral is that it exhibits a state of mind which is delightfully simple in itself, at the same time as it promotes the delightful reflection that we are emancipated from its bondage, from the tyranny of external impressions which we cannot control and organize. That is also a reason why pastoral is the lowest of the genres of poetry – because it imitates the motions of the minds of the least rational, the most ignorant, members of society.

Thus, if pastoral or landscape art – however lowly its position in the hierarchy of genres – is to be of value, is to be an object worth the attention of men who *can* abstract, then it must be defended either as Tickell has defended it – so that the pleasure we take in the genre derives from the contrast between the perception of those who are merely in the landscape, and those who are outside it, and observe it – or it must be defended as an art capable of *calling forth* the ability to abstract substance from accident, the general from the particular.

James Harris defends it in this second way. In his *Philological Inquiries*, he considers the cause of the pleasure we derive from natural beauty. "The vulgar," he notes "look no further than to the scenes of culture, because all their views merely terminate in utility." They are "merged in sense from their earlier infancy, never once dreaming anything to be worthy of pursuit, but what either pampers their appetite, or fills their purse"; they "imagine nothing to be real, but what may be touched or tasted." These dwellers in the cave of sensuality thus "only remark, that it is fine barley; that it is rich clover; as an ox or an ass, if they could speak, would inform us. But the liberal have nobler views; and though they give to culture its due praise, they can be delighted with natural beauties, where culture was never known."

But what are the pleasures that the liberal find in natural beauty, which are unknown to the vulgar, the ox and the ass? Harris makes a poor job of explaining what they are – he mostly attempts, simply, to prove that they exist, by adducing those classical authorities who have affirmed their existence. But he *exemplifies* those pleasures with precision; for example, when he writes, "the great elements of this species of beauty are water, wood, and uneven ground; to which may be added a fourth, that is to say, lawn."[6] That is the pleasure: the enjoyment of the ability to abstract from the labyrinth of nature, from the infinite varieties of accidental and circumstantial appearances, the general classes of natural beauty whose combinations please only when, on analysis, they can be resolved again into their components. It is the same pleasure that William Gilpin experienced when he announced that "few views, at least few good views, consist of more than a foreground, and two distances": the pleasure, that is, of abstracting the essential from its confusing particulars, and reducing those particulars to order.[7]

As Harris makes clear, the pleasures of nature are different, according to whether we are among the company of the liberal, or the vulgar; and it is worth reminding ourselves that in the eighteenth century the word liberal still has its primary meaning: it is the adjective that describes the free man, and the liberal arts are still remembered to be the arts which are worthy of the attention of free men. Free men are opposed to the vulgar or – for the terms are in most contexts virtually indistinguishable – the servile. In the civic humanist theory of art that Harris and Reynolds are heirs to, the word servile most usually occurs as the qualifier of "imitation" the "mere" imitation of every-day nature, unabstracted, with all its accidental deformities and details upon its head, is "servile" imitation, unworthy of the attention of a free man. The imitation of the ideal; of nature, in Opie's phrase, "as meaning the general principles of things rather than the things themselves";[8] of the object as freed from the tyranny of sense or need, and represented thus not as a thing, but as idea, and so as incapable of being possessed – this is what makes art a liberal art. It is such an idea of imitation that is the basis of the hostility evinced by Reynolds, for example, against the notion that it is the job of an artist to deceive the eye, to make us believe that a painted object is really there, could be touched as well as seen.

The kind of landscape that can most fully offer this pleasure is panoramic and it is so for various reasons, some of which I shall consider in a moment, but for now it will be enough to point out that the panoramic landscape offers a wide range and variety of objects to abstract from: it is like the "wide experience" which is, according to Tickell, denied to the shepherd, which is not only a more sure basis for accurate generalization, because it minimizes the distorting effect of extreme departures from generic form, but is also capable of offering the most gratifying test of our ability to reduce it to classes and structures. As Fuseli explains, it offers "characteristic groups" of "rich congenial objects." The groups are characteristic, not individual; they are rich, for there is a profusion of them; they are congenial, because organized into reciprocity by the abstracting power of the mind. On the other hand, argues Fuseli, those who imitate the landscape of the Dutch school are worthy of admiration only as they "learn to give an air of choice to necessity"[9] – by which he means, that imitations of Dutch landscape remain merely servile imitations so long as the eye is determined in what it represents by necessity, by the mere fact of an object's being there; or is determined by that servile and sensual vassalage to objects as capable of being possessed, which is never far from characterizations of Dutch art as, *par excellence*, the art of a commercial nation. The more such art rises above the determination of necessity, and learns to represent landscape in terms of a will free from the tyranny of sense, the more it becomes free itself, a liberal art.

By the time Fuseli was appealing to the distinction that I have drawn, it had become so familiar and so general that the distinction between the learned and the ignorant – the polite and the vulgar, the liberal and the servile – was repeatedly and regularly represented in terms of the ability of the former group to apprehend the structure and extent of panoramic landscape. This, for example, is the rhetorician George Campbell, describing the progress of knowledge:

in all sciences, we rise from the individual to the species, from the species to the genus, and thence to the most extensive orders and classes [and] arrive...at the knowledge of general truths...In this progress we are like people, who, from a low and confined bottom, where the view is confined to a few acres, gradually ascend a lofty peak or promontory. The prospect is perpetually enlarging at every moment, and when we reach the summit, the boundless horizon, comprehending all the variety of sea and land, hill and valley, town and country, arable and desert, lies under the eyes at once.[10]

Notice how Campbell, like Harris, though his list is longer, is concerned to produce from his eminence an account of all the classes of objects the landscape contains: the knowledge he arrives at is a general knowledge, in that it is all there is – the whole world imaged in the circumference of the horizon – and it is general knowledge, too, in that all the various objects of sight and knowledge are named by singular nouns, and so reduced to their various classes; when we see the sea and land, hill and valley, town and country, arable and desert, we see all there is to see. It will follow, of course, that those who remain imprisoned within their few acres at the bottom of the eminence will have nothing like the same range of objects to examine, and will have no possibility, therefore, of deriving accurate, general classes from them. They will remain, indeed, as objects in the landscape: they will not be observers, but observed. The point is well exemplified by Aaron Hill, writing to congratulate Pope on his poetry and to apologize for earlier attacks upon him: "Tis a noble triumph you now exercise, by the Superiority of your Nature; and while I see you looking down upon the Distance of my Frailty, I am forc'd to own a Glory, which I envy you; and am quite asham'd of the poor Figure I am making, in the bottom of the Prospect."[11] Those who can comprehend the order of society and nature are the observers of a prospect, in which others are merely objects. Some comprehend, others are comprehended; some are fit to survey the extensive panorama, some are confined within one or other of the micro-prospects which, to the comprehensive observer, are parts of a wider landscape, but which, to those confined within them, are all they see.

It is appropriate that Hill should be addressing Pope, who was shortly to be the author of a poem, the *Essay on Man*, which attempts to describe the "scene of man" as a prospect, which can be observed, and comprehended categorically, from a single viewpoint; and it is appropriate too that Pope, at the opening of his poem, should have identified that point of view as the station occupied by the independent landed gentleman:

> Awake, my ST. JOHN! leave all meaner things
> To low ambition and the pride of Kings.
> Let us (since Life can little more supply
> Than just to look about us and to die)
> Expatiate free o'er all this scene of Man;
> A mightly maze! but not without plan...
> Together let us beat this ample field,
> Try what the open, what the covert yield;
> The latent tracts, the giddy heights explore
> Of all who blindly creep, or sightless soar;
> Eye Nature's walks, shoot Folly as it flies,
> And catch the Manners living as they rise...[12]

In its migration from renaissance Italy to seventeenth- and eighteenth-century Britain, a crucial mutation had occurred in the discourse of civic humanism, a mutation whose origin is identified in the writings of James Harrington, but which was soon eagerly adopted by the range of eighteenth-century spokesmen, including Bolingbroke, Thomson, and Pope himself, for the ideals of those groups which we lump together under the title of the country party, and whose writings are, more than those of any other grouping in early and mid eighteenth-century Britain, concerned with the definition and defense of public virtue. When Florentine republican theory was transplanted to Britain, the ability of the disinterested citizen to grasp the true interests of society had come to be identified as a function of his ownership of landed property.

This was the result of a number of considerations: of the fact that the franchise, the title of citizenship, was attached to a property qualification; of the fact that a substantial landed property produced a sufficient unearned income for its owner to have the time, the leisure, to devote himself to political life; of the fact that he was therefore a member of no profession, and thus could be assumed to favor no particular occupational interest; but most particularly, of the fact that landed property was fixed property, and therefore its survival was involved (it was believed) in the ability of the state itself to survive the corruptions of accident. The owner of fixed property, even when conscious (according to some theorists) of consulting only his own interests, would also necessarily be consulting the true, the permanent interests of the country in which his family had a permanent stake. Whether, therefore, his independence and his leisure actually enabled him to see the public interest, or whether he was conscious only of consulting his own, made little difference: inasmuch as his own interests were those of the public at large, he was, to all intents and purposes, disinterested in a way that others, more dependent for their income on the fluctuating value of movable property, and thus of property which, like *argent liquide*, circulated instead of remaining rooted in one spot, could not be. It is then as a man of landed property that Bolingbroke (and with him, by association, Pope) can "expatiate free o'er all this scene of man" – can grasp the "plan," the design of the wide prospect, which remains simply a maze to those who, situated in one partial position or another, "latent tract" or "giddy height," can only "blindly creep" or "sightless soar." And it is thoroughly appropriate that, as Bolingbroke and Pope range freely over the landscape, they do so as sportsmen: they "beat" the field, and "catch" the Manners, they thus put up. Only the lords of manors, or those possessed of an annual income of £100 or more from a freehold estate, were permitted to shoot game.

III

Let me expand at this point on my introductory remarks on the relation between the ability to generalize, a correct taste in landscape, and the claim to be capable of exercizing political authority. Insofar as the representation of panoramic prospects serves as an instantiation of the ability of the man of "liberal mind" to abstract the general from the particular, it was also understood to be an instantiation of his ability to abstract the true interests of humanity, the public interest, from the labyrinth of private interests which were imagined to be represented by mere unorganized detail. It was precisely the ability of the liberal mind of the free citizen to do this which constituted his claim to be a citizen, a free man, or, as he was often described (though the phrase has a range of meanings) a "public man." A citizen, a public man in this sense, had long been distinguished in republican political theory by the fact that this ability was a function of his reason; whereas private men, men who were not citizens, who were servile, who were mechanics, had been understood, from Aristotle onwards, to have no ability to understand reason, or to follow anything but their own immediate instincts. That is why Harris can compare them with oxen and asses. And because the civic humanist aesthetic of which such men as Harris, Campbell, Reynolds and Fuseli are the inheritors, is based in the language of republican political theory, their own implied definition of who is properly a citizen of the republic of taste is based on the same distinction. The power to abstract, as metaphorized everywhere in the power to comprehend and organize an extensive prospect, is a testimony of the ability to prefer and to promote an art which itself promotes the public interest, as opposed to ministering to the private appetites and interests of particular men.

The relation between these various concerns is clear, for example, in Reynolds' preface to his "Ironic Discourse," a work dedicated to pointing out the congruence of the principles of politics and art. According to Reynolds:

A hundred thousand near-sighted men, that see only what is just before them, make no equivalent to one man whose view extends to the whole horizon around him, though we may safely acknowledge at the same time that like the real near-sighted men they see and comprehend as distinctly what is within the focus of their sight as accurately (I will allow sometimes more accurately) than the others. Though a man may see his way in the management of his own affairs, within his own little circle, with the greatest acuteness and sagacity, such habits give him no pretensions to set up for a politician[13]

– or, of course, as a man of taste; for the function of both is to grasp the relation of particular to general which is the same thing as the relation of private to public; and the function of both is to promote, whether in art or politics, the public over the private interest. It was exactly the inability to do this that, in his *Reflections on the Revolution in France*, Burke had claimed to be necessarily a characteristic of the revolutionary assemblies – composed as they were of tailors and carpenters, men accustomed to considering their own interests as in competition with those of others;[14] and that Reynolds, Blake and Fuseli point out in the Dutch and Venetians, the tradesmen, the mechanics of the republic of taste, not its free gentlemen-citizens. And the binary by which "gentlemen" are opposed not only by "mechanics" but by "tradesmen," together with the civic notion that it is particularly or exclusively the independent owner of a substantial freehold in land who is capable of exercising political authority, often though not always produces an account of the man of liberal taste as one who is not simply a gentleman, but a landed gentleman; and that connection between the public man, the disinterested citizen, the freeholder, and the man of taste, remains available, though it is increasingly challenged, well into the next century. It is evident in the work of Pope, Thomson, and Richard Wilson, and is more than merely vestigial in the writings of Burke, Wordsworth, and Coleridge.

Sometimes however, by some writers, the ability to comprehend the structure of relations within a panoramic prospect is attributed to a rather wider group of potential spectators than we have so far encountered, though this may not always involve attributing a comprehension of the public interest in its widest sense. In *The Wealth of Nations*, Adam Smith encounters the problem that within a complex, commercial society, there may be no viewing-position from which the organization of society or the public good can possibly be grasped: if the philosopher is as much implicated in the division of labor, is as much defined by the propensity to truck and barter, and so as much blinded by his own interests as is any other man, then he has as little access as anyone else to the general view which would seem to legitimate a claim to a general social knowledge. He is reduced to inventing a fictitious and disembodied social spectator, the "philosophic eye," whose viewpoint and whose breadth of vision no individual can be imagined as possessing, unless, as Rameau's nephew puts it, he can "perch on the epicycle of Mercury."[15] But in *The Theory of Moral Sentiments*, where the public interest is conceived of more often in narrower terms – the propensity to place the interests of another before our own, private interests – the viewing-position necessary to make that choice is imagined as accessible to everyone, and it is precisely a viewing-position, from which the interests of ourselves and of another are visible as if within a landscape. Consider this passage, for example, where Smith seems to be reworking an argument from Berkeley from his *Discourse of Passive Obedience*:

In my present situation an immense landscape of lawns, and woods, and distant mountain, seems to do no more than cover the little window which I write by, and to be out of all proportion less than the chamber in which I am sitting. I can form a just comparison between those great objects and the little objects around me, in no other way, than by transporting myself, at least in fancy, to a different situation, from which I can survey both at nearly equal distances, and thereby form some judgment of their real proportions. Habit and experience have taught me to do this easily and so readily, that I am scarce sensible that I do it; and a man must be, in some measure, acquainted with the philosophy of vision, before he can be thoroughly convinced, how little those distant objects would appear to the eye, if the imagination, from a knowledge of their real magnitudes, did not swell and dilate them.

In the same manner, to the selfish and original passions of human nature, the loss or gain of a very small interest of our own, appears to be of vastly more importance, excites a much more passionate joy or sorrow, a much more ardent desire or aversion, than the greatest concern of another with whom we have no particular connection. His interests, as long as they are surveyed from this station, can never be put into the balance with our own, can never restrain us from doing whatever may tend to promote our own, how ruinous soever to him. Before we can make any proper comparison of those opposite interests, we must change our position. We must view them, neither from our own place, nor yet from his, neither with our own eyes nor yet with his, but from the place and with the eyes of a third person, who has no particular connection with either, and who judges impartially between us.[16]

The third person who occupies the position from which the relation of one person's interest and another's can be apprehended is a version of the fictional character whom Smith terms (among other things) the "*impartial spectator*," the imagined arbiter among different interests. And he is outside the landscape, and not as we are in our private capacities, within it, unable to grasp its structure of relations. But unlike most of the other passages I have referred to, Smith seems to suggest that if anyone can attain the viewing-position of this spectator of the moral landscape, we all can. The corollary of that concession, however, is that the extensive prospect cannot be used as an image of a wider society than the one in which most of us make our private determinations on moral questions.

Or consider this record of spoken observation by Reynolds, on the nature of happiness:

It is not the man who looks around him from the top of a high mountain at a beautiful prospect on the first moment of opening his eyes, who has the true enjoyment of that noble sight: it is he who ascends the mountain from a miry meadow, or a ploughed field, or a barren waste; and who works his way up to it step by step;—it is he, my lords, who enjoys the beauties that suddenly blaze upon him. They cause an expansion of ideas in harmony with the expansion of the view. He glories in its glory; and the mind opens to conscious exaltation; such as the man who was born and bred upon that commanding height...can never know; can have no idea of; at least, not till he come near some precipice, in a boisterous wind, that hurls him from the top to the bottom, and gives him some taste of what he had possessed, by its loss; and some pleasure in its recovery, by the pain and difficulty of scrambling back to it.[17]

We can read this passage simply as a more than usually eloquent rehearsal of a moral commonplace, that a happiness achieved after suffering and effort is a good deal more worth having than a happiness which, because its possessor has never known suffering, is the less grateful to him on that account. But if we read it, as surely it invites to be read, in the context of the assumed connection between an ability to comprehend the order of society, and the ownership of heritable property in land, it becomes an impassioned outburst, the more impassioned because this account of how a "noble sight" may truly be enjoyed is addressed to a noble company, "my lords," who claim to enjoy it simply because "born and bred on that commanding height," from which they seem to observe and *command* the view below. In order to distinguish between the kind of enjoyment that they derive from the prospect, and the kind enjoyed by those who have to toil up to that eminence, Reynolds suggests that to the "lords" the prospect is not really a metaphor at all: they may presume that the "expansion of the view" produces a similar "expansion" of their "ideas," but it does not; and if to them the prospect has any metaphorical application, it is simply as a figure for the "eminence" they enjoy as a result of the nature and quantity of their inherited fortunes. The figure achieves its full significance only – as the geography of the passage suggests – for whoever can appropriately be represented as a laborer, who "works his way up" to the eminence "from a miry meadow, or a ploughed field, or a barren waste." The passage suggests that the image of the panoramic landscape could be appropriated from the "lords" whose political authority it has been used to justify; but it suggests too that a struggle to appropriate the viewing-position usually attributed to the landed aristocracy can simply result, whoever comes out on top, the lords or a meritocratic bourgeoisie, in a continuation of the division of society into the observers and the observed, the rulers and the ruled.

IV

Let me now collect up the various characteristics we have so far seen attributed to the two kinds of landscape that I distinguished at the start of this essay. On the one hand is the ideal, panoramic prospect, the analogue of the social and the universal, which is surveyed, organized, and understood by disinterested public men, who regard the objects in the landscape always as representative ideas, intended to categorize rather than deceptively to imitate their originals in nature, and so who study, not the objects themselves – not for example the individuals in a society, or their individual occupations – but their relations. They are enabled to do this by their ability to abstract, and by their ability to comprehend and classify the totality of human experience.[18]

On the other hand is the occluded landscape, which has so far been treated as representing the "confined views" of the private man, whose experience is too narrow to permit him to abstract. Such landscapes conceal the general view by concealing the distance: and Fuseli, appropriately, uses an image derived from such landscapes to figure, more generally, the detrimental effect which a profusion of detail has on the "breadth" of composition he admires: "the discrepance," he writes, "of obtruding parts in the works of the infant Florentine, Venetian, and German schools distracts our eye like the numberless breakers of a shallow river, or as the brambles and creepers that entangle the paths of a wood, and instead of showing us our road, perplex us only with themselves."[19] The characteristic imagery of occluded landscapes – a cottage, for example, embosomed in trees which permit the distance to appear only as spots or slices of light, is emblematic of a situation in life from which no wider prospect is visible.

On this other hand, also, is topographical landscape, which did not represent objects as classified and comprehended. Topographical landscape seems to become more despised – in the theory, though not in the practice of landscape painting – as the century grows older; not just because of the hostility of the academy, or of that hostility taken as something internal to a theory of art disjoined from social and political change. Towards the end of the century it had become increasingly clear that landed property was not as fixed as it had by some been claimed to be earlier in the century: it was involved in an economy of credit, and was not in itself a guarantee of disinterestedness, except perhaps insofar as it permitted its owners the leisure necessary for a career in public life. The hostility to topographical landscape thus comes to be based not only in its un-idealized, un-intellectual character, but on the connection, also, between sensuality as the failure to abstract from the data of sensation, and of sensuality as a desire to possess objects which could only be re-deemed, as objects worthy of the attention of a free man, by elevating them into representative types which could not be possessed. Thus for James Barry, who described the property-market in late eighteenth-century England as anything but stable, more like "a game of chance,"[20] topographical landscape was simply a portrait of our possessions, or of land as inviting possession; and for Fuseli, such landscapes may "delight the owner of the acres they enclose," but delight and interest him therefore only in his private capacity.[21]

That last point suggests a distinction between two kinds of land-scapes I have been considering that is more complex than the one I have largely been making so far, by which the different landscapes appeal to different classes of people, to citizens and to the rest. For they can also be understood as appealing to two different spheres of life of the citizen: the public sphere, where he is enjoined to consult only the public interest, and the private sphere, where he is tempo-rarily released from his obligations as a citizen. This distinction has already been suggested, perhaps, by my remarks on Coleridge's conversation-poems. The distinction made in these terms is not a simple one, and in attempting to understand why it is not, we can approach an understanding of Reynolds' learned riddle, with which Hazlitt expressed such impatience; and we can approach, also, an understanding of Hazlitt's impatience. For if ideal panoramic land-scape is constructed as public, in opposition to various different kinds of landscapes constructed as private, the fact remains that, within the terms of the doctrine of the hierarchy of genres, landscape art, of whatever kind, is constructed as private, in opposition to the public art of history painting.

Reynolds, for example, makes it quite clear – as who does not? – that one function (perhaps it is no longer for him the main function) of history paintings in the grand style, is that their subject "ought to be either some eminent instance of heroick action, or heroick suffer-ing. There must be something either in the action, or in the object, in which men are universally concerned, and which powerfully strikes upon the publick sympathy."[22] We should always remember, when we encounter the term "public" in civic humanist criticism, that it is never a simple shorthand for the audience, or for anyone. It is the audience, it is everyone, only in their public character: history painting must appeal to whatever concerns us universally; with what concerns us as universal men, as men considered in the light of what is common to all of them, their substantial nature, and not what is of concern to their private and accidental identities. Landscape painting, on the other hand, is, as Reynolds and Barry suggest, concerned with the representation of quietness and repose, with what were understood to be private feelings, and with what were described as *private virtues*: the only virtues open to be exhibited by those who were not public men, but open to them, also, when in retirement, or for some other reason not acting upon the public stage. It is this function of landscape painting that justified its existence, but which, in doing so, depresses it to the lower reaches of the hierarchy of genres, as it similarly depresses pastoral poetry below the epic and the tragic. It may be, as Barry points out, that in a society threatened by the forces of corruption, the private virtues are the only secure values left, and that landscape will come to seem preferable even to the subject-matter which history painting exhibits, in an age without public heroes;[23] but in such an age, it is equally true that the public virtues of history painting are more urgently in demand, or should be, and the supremacy of the genre, as the only genre capable of effecting a reform of public life, must be more urgently insisted upon.

It is at the interface of these two classifications of ideal panoramic landscape that Reynolds' learned riddle is engendered. According to one system of classification, the representation of such landscapes is an instantiation of the political capability of the public man, perhaps especially of value in an age in which the sphere of action of such a man was steadily being confined, as I have argued elsewhere,[24] to the *comprehension* of the social order, rather than its reformation; to the vindication of social structure as ordained by providence, or by the market, rather than to the creation of a social order other than that created by commerce, by the forces of private interest. On the other hand, according to the system of classification of the hierarchy of genres, landscape art is the instantiation of private virtues, often as a muted criticism of the values of that parody of a truly public, civic life which is the actuality of affairs in courts and cities. How then should landscape be represented? If as a public genre, it is essential that it should eliminate accident, and should exhibit ideas, as George Campbell puts it, "not in their private, but, as it were, in their representative capacity."[25] If on the other hand it is a private genre, it seems that the representation of accident is appropriate to it: and that Reynolds, for all his seeming decision in his fourth discourse in favor of Claude's landscape, purged of accident, over the accidental forms of Rubens, is nevertheless impressed by the argument from the privacy of the genre, is clear from the terms in which he poses his riddle. He does not ask, as Hazlitt suggests, simply whether the landscape painter should "introduce" the accidents of nature. His terms are far more specific than that. He asks whether "landscape painting has a *right* to *aspire so far* as to reject what the painters call Accidents of Nature" (my emphasis).[26] His meaning is, that an artist who, like Claude, does so reject them, may be aspiring above his station, and presuming to give to a private genre the universal and public status of history painting. To answer, no it shouldn't thus "aspire," is to deny the power of images of panoramic landscape to instantiate the intellectual abilities and talents of public men, of the disinterested citizens of the republic of taste and of the political republic alike. To answer, yes it should, risks threatening the public status of history painting, by encroaching upon it, and by suggesting, perhaps too openly, that public virtue is now indeed rather a matter of seeing than of doing. The riddle could not be solved, and though in his fourth discourse Reynolds appears to decide, as Hazlitt suggests, in favor of Claude, in his later discourses he shows considerable approval of the representation of the accidental forms of nature by the happy accidents of technique. This is a concession he makes only to landscape painters, and only to them on the understanding that they work in a private genre, one addressed to our privacy, in which we may therefore take pleasure in the accidental forms of nature unideal-ized into generic form.

V

We can sum up the problem which generated Reynolds' "learned riddle" in some such way as this: for Reynolds, although history painting is still unchallengeably at the top of the hierarchy of genres, its position there is no longer easily justifiable in terms of a *rhetorical* aesthetic, and an aesthetic of illusion, by which it deceives us into a sympathy with its actors which can move us to desire to perform the acts of public virtue which they perform. Reynolds justifies its preeminence, instead, as a genre which casts the spectator in the role, less of potential agent than of observer, the observer of common humanity, represented by general forms. As far as landscape painting is concerned, then, as long as it is considered as a private genre – as occluded landscapes always, but as ideal landscapes only sometimes are – it is still imagined to be governed by a rhetorical aesthetic: it moves us to delight in, and to wish for, tranquillity and repose; and, as such, it can be enjoyed by all, for it is a law constitutive of a

99

rhetorical aesthetic that *all* can feel the effects of art, if all cannot determine the principles on which those effects are produced.

But when ideal panoramic landscape is treated as a public genre – as I hope I have shown it continually but not invariably was, in Britain in the period I have been considering – it was not accorded that status by means of a rhetorical, but of what may be called a philosophical aesthetic: the best landscape painters, and those best equipped to appreciate them, are those few who can successfully reduce concrete particulars to abstract categories, the signs of which are less natural and more arbitrary than those employed in occluded landscapes, and are absolutely not intended to deceive the eye. If landscape can appeal to its audience in this way, however, and no longer simply rhetorically, then there are good reasons why it should be treated, as for rather different reasons Ruskin would treat it, as a genre as important, and as public, as history painting; for it is now the aim of both to enable the exercise of that broad and comprehensive vision and that ability to abstract representative from actual nature that are now more clearly the qualifications for citizenship than a disposition to perform acts of public virtue. In short, it is by Reynolds' philosophical aesthetic that landscape has a claim to be regarded as a genre with a public function, which it does not have in terms of a rhetorical aesthetic.

Why then should Hazlitt, who is unlikely to have been unaware of the implications of the riddle, choose to ignore them? One reason is that he clearly considers it one of his tasks as a writer to abolish the distinctions between public and private – in politics, as a distinction between who can and who cannot participate in government; in painting, as a distinction between one kind of picture that appeals to us as citizens, another that appeals to us as private individuals. If Hazlitt succeeds in collapsing this distinction in his writings on art, it is largely by denying that painting has any public function at all, and by treating it as an art which offers private satisfactions to private individuals. But still his impatience with the distinction is a political impatience, insofar as it is related in particular to a distaste for the habit of addressing the politer part of that audience as "the public," whether they acted as a public or simply as the acquisitive purchasers of pictures as private property. Anything that perpetuated this flattery, and the political division on which it was based, was an object of his attack; and he was especially hostile to the notional connection between the ownership of landed property and the claim to political disinterestedness.

The public prospect and the private view

For these reasons, I cannot help admiring Hazlitt for treating Reynolds' "learned riddle" as a knot to be cut; but nor can I help regretting that he could do so, as it seems to me, only by denying the connection between art and politics, or rather between art and the public sphere, which had given such explanatory power to the writings of Reynolds, Barry, Blake, and Fuseli, and had insisted on the interdependency of the republic of taste and the political republic, which Hazlitt was determined to dissolve.[27]

Notes

1 Hazlitt, "On Genius and Originality," *The Champion*, December 4, 1814, reprinted in Robert R. Wark, ed., *Sir Joshua Reynolds: Discourses on Art*, 2nd edn., (New Haven and London: Yale University Press, 1975), p. 324.

2 S. T. Coleridge, *Lay Sermons* (1817), ed. R. J. White, (London: Routledge, Kegan and Paul and Princeton University Press, 1972), p. 136.

3 *Collected Letters of S. T. Coleridge*, ed. E. L. Griggs, (Oxford: Clarendon Press and New York: Oxford University Press, 1956–71), vol. 1, p. 349.

4 Wark, ed., *Discourses*, p. 44.

5 *The Guardian*, no. 23, April 7, 1713.

6 Harris, *Philological Inquiries* (1780–1), and *Hermes* (1751), in *The Works of James Harris* (Oxford, 1841), pp. 525–6, 218.

7 Gilpin to William Mason, quoted in C. P. Barbier, *William Gilpin* (Oxford: Clarendon Press, 1963), p. 50.

8 John Opie, *Lectures on Painting* (London, 1809), p. 13.

9 *The Life and Writings of Henry Fuseli*, ed. John Knowles, (London, 1831), vol. 2, pp. 217–8.

10 Campbell, *The Philosophy of Rhetoric* (London, 1776), vol. 1, p. 5.

11 A. Hill, "Preface to Mr. Pope" (preface to *The Creation*, 1720), series 4, no. 2, (Ann Arbor, Michigan: Augustan Reprint Society, 1949 and Los Angeles: William Andrews Clark Memorial Library, University of California, 1950), p. 1.

12 Alexander Pope, *An Essay on Man*, Epistle I (1733), lines 1–6, 9–14; my remarks on Pope in this essay are adapted from my *English Literature in History, 1730–1780: An Equal, Wide Survey* (London: Hutchinson, 1983), pp. 35–6.

13 Reynolds, "preface" to the "Ironical Discourse", in Frederick W. Hilles, ed., *Portraits by Sir Joshua Reynolds* (London: Heinemann, 1952), p. 129.

14 Edmund Burke, *Works* (London, 1815), vol. 5, p. 104.

15 D. Diderot, *Le Neveu de Rameau*, ed. Jean Fabre (Geneva, 1963), p. 103. The phrase is borrowed from Montaigne: see n. 312, p. 236.

16 A. Smith, *The Theory of Moral Sentiments* (1759), eds. D. D. Raphael and A. L. MacFie, (Oxford: Clarendon Press, 1976), p. 135. Raphael and

MacFie suggest a source for this passage in Berkeley's *New Theory of Vision*, section 54; to me it seems closer to his *Discourse of Passive Obedience*, section 28.

> ...if we have a mind to take a fair prospect of the order and general well-being, which the inflexible laws of nature and morality derive on the world, we must, if I may so say, go out of it, and imagine ourselves to be distant spectators of all that is transacted and contained in it; otherwise we are sure to be deceived by the too neat view of the little present interest of ourselves, our friends, or our country.

17 Spoken observation of Reynolds, recorded in Madame D'Arblay, *Memories of Dr. Burney* (London, 1832), vol. 2, pp. 281–2; quoted in Lawrence Lipking, *The Ordering of the Arts in Eighteenth-Century England* (Princeton University Press, 1970), pp. 204–5.

18 I can make this point more clearly to those who have read David Solkin's recent essay. "The Battle of the Ciceros: Richard Wilson and the Politics of Landscape in the Age of John Wilkes" (*Art History*, 6.4 December 1983), in which Solkin discusses Wilson's *Cicero and his two friends at his Villa at Arpinum* (1770). Solkin's brilliant account of the painting might be strengthened by pointing out that the image of Cicero as the guardian of the public interest is further defined by his being represented in an ideal, extensive prospect, and not in the kind of occluded landscape depicted, for example, in Wilson's *Solitude* of eight years earlier.

19 Knowles, ed., *Fuseli*, vol. 2, p. 251.

20 J. Barry, *An Inquiry into the Real and Imaginary Obstructions to the Acquisition of the Arts in England* (London, 1775), p. 207.

21 Knowles, ed., *Fuseli*, vol. 2, p. 217.

22 Wark, ed., *Discourses*, p. 57.

23 *Ibid.*, p. 70; Barry, *Works* (London, 1809), vol. 2, p. 405.

24 Barrell, *English Literature in History*, "Introduction."

25 Campbell, *Philosophy of Rhetoric*, vol. 2, p. 104.

26 Wark, ed., *Discourses*, p. 70.

27 When this essay was submitted for publication, it was imagined that it would be published before my book, *The Political Theory of Painting from Reynolds to Hazlitt: "The Body of the Public,"* (London, New Haven: Yale University Press, 1986). A number of passages in that book are repeated from this essay. The first chapter of the book contains a more detailed account of the "rhetorical" and the "philosophical" aesthetic, and of Reynolds' thinking about the principles and place of landscape painting. The essay has previously been published in Simon Pugh, ed., *Reading Landscape: Country–City–Capital* (Manchester University Press, 1990), and in my *The Birth of Pandora and the Division of Knowledge* (London: Macmillan, 1992 and Philadelphia: University of Pennsylvania Press, 1992).

5

Landscape in the cinema: the rhythms of the world and the camera

P. ADAMS SITNEY

I

Landscape seems to have been granted no place among the topics of argument in the aesthetics of the cinema. There is a vast literature on montage, language, the human face, the city, sound and silence, fiction and truth in film, but almost nothing on natural beauty. Yet from the very beginning films were made outdoors. Some of the first apologists for the cinema as an art made a point of the power and beauty of natural surroundings in film. Sergei Eisenstein, the most ambitious and thorough of film-maker-theoreticians, devoted the culminating essay of his career to "the music of landscape,"[1] but it was the question of cinematic rhythm that really absorbed his attention at that time, as we shall see.

Although theoreticians describe cinematic landscapes in order to exemplify points, the topic itself is virtually an unconscious issue of film theory. In fact, it was not until the late 1960s and throughout the seventies that a genre of landscape cinema was created by European and North American *avant-garde* film-makers, and even then it was not until the 1980s that the aesthetic issues raised by these film-makers were recognized as such. In this essay I shall follow some preliminary remarks with a sketch of the ways in which the historical evolution of cinematic technology called forth changing evocations of landscape beauty. The third part surveys the predominance of meteorological phenomena as a function of the cinema's capability for rendering movement, while the fourth gives some examples of the integration of landscape issues into narrative contexts. Next I shall examine the presence of the idea of landscape in the writings of some significant film-makers and theoreticians, before finally focusing on *avant-garde* landscape films.

103

In one of the rare articles studying the nature of landscape in a film, Gilberto Perez wrote: "Yet landscape has its own demands and its own way of resisting an attempt to press it into unwarranted service. Although generous with appearances in the role of scenery, tolerant of prettification and sentimentalization – doubtless out of indifference to such petty concerns – landscape will seldom countenance an importune display of its features in support of an undeserving story or scheme ... Easily as landscape yields its vistas to the camera, any substantial support it will give to a film's undertaking must be earned."[2]

The wit, and the oddity, of Perez's trope personifying the cinematic landscape as if it were a reticent cowboy or an aloof woman ends up calling attention to the difficulty of articulating the aesthetic issue itself. The pathetic fallacy dominated much of the historical development of landscape imagery in cinema; accordingly, Perez hyperbolically imagines a spirit of the landscape that condescends to play such a role only for the most talented directors. With justification, he dismisses what I take to be the enthusiasm for filmed scenery which advertisers and some reviewers like to call "lavish" by condemning it to the abyss of prettification and sentimentalization. Although Perez tactfully spares his readers an example of this banality, I would suggest that David Lean's color films (The Bridge on the River Kwai [1957], Lawrence of Arabia [1962], Doctor Zhivago [1965], Ryan's Daughter [1970], A Passage to India [1984]) pose the problem of the cinematic picturesque in its most nagging form. The genuine popular appeal of these films and of the myriad of works inspired by their continuing successes attests to the persistence of an idea, a banal fantasy really, that the cinematic equivalent of enduring literature would result from the transportation of the most skilled and talented stage actors into naturally spectacular, "authentic" locations where an impressive variety of meteorological phenomena would provide opportunities for them to demonstrate a histrionic range beyond the spectrum elicited by the theatre's symbolic setting and suggestions of weather.

Most of the movie industry, public television, and the audience that patronizes Academy laureates seem loyal to this ideal. Although this fantasy may not always be as petty as Perez rightly claims it usually is, he is correct in his recognition of a more narrowly construed landscape tradition within cinema as a fine art. This essay is an attempt to outline that tradition, first in terms of the historical evolution of the representation of filmic landscapes, then through a brief survey of some of the most original uses of landscape in narrative and *avant-garde* genres.

I take it to be obvious that the technical means of rendering landscape and objects of natural beauty are nearly identical for the arts of photography and cinema. It would be just as obvious to anyone who has considered these to be arts that, despite their technical congruence, they have taken very different approaches to representing natural beauty in their virtually parallel histories. The landscapes recorded in Eadweard Muybridge's albumen stereoptica and Ansel Adams' silver gelatin prints or the peacock feathers of Sir John Hershel's cyanotype and Edward Weston's mollusk shell image all could have been films, but the traditions of cinema for the most part neglected such options. We seem to be able to account for this with another obvious point: films take control of time, and controlling time, have an affinity for representing movement. On the other hand, it is the radical arrest of movement that gives some of the charge to most powerful photographs.

Most casual film viewers would find it difficult even to imagine watching the film of a single view of a mountain or a series of feathers in negative for, say, ninety minutes, although later in this essay I shall discuss some extraordinary films that actually do something like that. Even in the earliest years of the cinema, before the 1920s when the feature length film assumed its dominance, the programs of short comedies, melodramas, documentaries, and newsreels that made up a typical screening session did not include films devoted solely to a single landscape or a natural object.

The fifty year precedence of photography over cinema had made a decisive difference. The earliest photographs required a long exposure time and an intensity of light, conditions that made static vistas and objects ideal subjects. Even more than that, the viewer's option to study a photograph at leisure, in sustained or repeated viewings, underscored an affinity to paintings (in which, of course, landscapes and static natural objects were commonly represented by the nineteenth century). The more light-sensitive chemicals of the turn-of-the-century helped to make possible the invention of cinema at a moment when photography was exploring the freezing of human and animal movement. Furthermore, the theatrical conditions for the public projection of films, as well as their fixed temporal duration, encouraged the view that cinema was a form of drama.

Photography itself was as much conditioned by the reigning

aesthetics of its moment of invention as it, in turn, helped determine the aesthetic issues of the cinema. When Hegel argued that "the proper subject-matter of poetry is spiritual interests, not the sun, mountains, woods, landscapes ... " because "man's external world ... has essential worth only in relation to man's inner consciousness,"[3] he articulated the primacy of human action in literature that the cinema has massively inherited. His contemporary rival in aesthetic philosophy, Schopenhauer, could have been predicting the triumphs of still photography landscapes when he wrote:

Every modification, even the slightest, which an object receives through its position, foreshortening, concealment, distance, distribution of light and shade, linear and atmospheric perspective, and so on, is unerringly given through its effect on the eye, and is accurately taken into account ... Now if we take into consideration the sight of a beautiful view merely as *brain-phenomenon*, then it is the only one of the complicated brain-phenomena which is always quite regular, methodical, faultless, unexceptionable, and perfect.[4]

Broadly speaking we may say that these two nineteenth-century views of landscape predict, respectively, the tendencies of the dominant narrative cinema even at its best, and the optical intensification of much, but certainly not all, of the *avant-garde* cinema. Nevertheless the ineluctable *temporality* of the medium undermines the objectivity of any photographic image with people in it by foregrounding and dramatizing the human presence in the landscape, and even when there are no human figures in the field of vision, the temporal nature of the image points to the human control of its representation. It is that temporal inflection upon which innovative film-makers have capitalized; I shall examine its consequences more fully after a brief survey of the effects of different film stocks, screen ratios, lenses, and sound on the representation of landscape in films.

II

The first films in open air were depictions of human and mechanical movement: workers leaving the Lumière factory, the arrival of a train and passengers getting off, photographers arriving by boat for a convention, feeding a baby, playing cards outdoors, and some pranks with a garden hose. When these early films were successful and audiences showed an eagerness for more scenes of human action, cameramen from the Lumières' and other companies toured the world collecting both typical and unusual scenes. The first aesthetic challenge of cinema, however, was finding an action that precisely filled and was wholly contained within the two minute exposure of a single roll of film.

Thus landscape entered cinema as one of the arenas of human action. At its most spectacular it was an exotic enhancement to foreground movement. Early in the twentieth century, once the combination of shots into a single edited film had become the standard mode of composition, natural disasters – floods, eruptions, the aftermath of earthquakes – came to constitute adequate subjects for short newsreel films.

Two of the three fundamental modes of emphasizing landscape in cinema appeared in the earliest films, those of the late 1890s: the moving camera and the panoramic sweep. One of the Lumière cameramen mounted his tripod in a gondola in order to record movement through the Grand Canal of Venice, thus opening to cinema the option of penetrating spatial depth. Similarly, the swivel-head tripod allowed the camera to arc laterally while filming. Such sweeping movements were called panoramas insofar as they recalled the popular installations of both painted and photographic vistas on the inner circumferences of specially constructed rooms. This type of shot became so conventional that the analogy to the panoramic exhibition was forgotten and the name reduced to a "pan" shot. Yet unlike the panoramas, the pan shot maintained the filmic frame and thereby reflected in a stylized manner the movement of human eyes over the field of vision; it did not create the illusion of an ambience around the viewer. The filmic pan underlines the ineluctable *potentiality* of offscreen space: the sense of the landscape extending in all directions beyond the edges of the screen contributes to the illusion of the camera's presence in the field of vision. In a sense the conventionally static frame then becomes a special instance of cinematic construction, a pause in the movement of the mechanism. At first the difficulty of making pan shots with crank-driven tripods, because of the problem of coordinating the hands turning of the film and the tripod head with two different cranks, somewhat retarded their frequent use while at the same time drawing attention to their uniqueness.

Exhibitors were quick to exploit the illusions of cinematic movement through space. The Cinéorama of the 1900 Paris Exhibition recreated the experience of a giant balloon ride with ten synchronized projectors and a circular screen. By 1905 Hale's Tours was projecting films shot from trains and boats outside the windows of a static Pullman car for paying customers eager to experience the illusion of what even earlier British exploiters had called "Phantom Rides."[5]

As the popularity of Hale's Tours declined, a third element of the syntax of the cinematic representation of natural beauty began to appear: the long shot including, by 1908, aerial cinematography. This is the most ambiguous and the least unique to cinema of the three key elements. In theory the long shot was in place with the invention of cinema. Photography had picked up from landscape painting a series of pictorial strategies for representing wide views with figures dwarfed in the middle or far background, or enlarged in the foreground of the picture plane with the extensive space behind them. Often painting and photography suggested a subjective view of deep space by including a viewer in the foreground, and even though the cinema quickly found other means of articulating such subjectivity, it never rejected this alternative option. The long shot is long, or distant, in regard to the center of human activity. Thus a long shot often has an "establishing" function, locating an individual, a group, or even a municipality in a wider landscape. While it can emphasize human dominance, such as a city or a fortress capping a hill, or the massing of people and monuments, more frequently it serves to diminish the human scale.

Furthermore, the long shot takes on cinematic meaning in the context of other, closer shots and alternate perspectives. For instance, a long shot becomes an establishing shot when a more detailed view (or series) follows it. Thus the stylistic power of the long shot grew with the refinement of the concept of editing or rhythmical shot alternation in the first twenty years of this century. William K. Everson cites *Land Beyond the Sunset* (1904), an Edison film made for the Fresh Air Fund, as an unusually early exploitation of natural beauty. The film ends with a slum child, inspired by a fairy tale, rowing a boat to his death in "the land beyond the sunset." Everson describes the final shot: "the camera stays in the same position on the sea shore, while in a series of cuts the boat is shown farther and farther out to sea, until it disappears into infinity."[6] Here, as often in the history of the cinema, a sublime topos – the sea – dominates the climax of the film.

Shortly after the First World War the Swedish cinema gained international prominence from its sophisticated deployment of the natural sublime in such films as Victor Sjöström's *The Outlaw and his Wife* (1917) and Mauritz Stiller's *The Treasure of Arne* (1919); the former showed its protagonists' exile in mountainous forests and the latter featured a dash across an ice field.

As the syntax of filmic narrative congealed, genres emerged which were predicated upon dramatizing the situation of individuals in distinctive landscapes. The Western and the Documentary of "the noble savage" are characteristic of these genres. Insofar as city life came to represent modernity in films, the Western made extensive use of uninhabited landscapes as coefficients of historical fiction.

Film artists persistently found ways for utilizing the technological developments of film stocks and equipment to render new landscapes. In *Nanook of the North* (1921) and *Moana* (1926) Robert Flaherty invented narratives of daily life for a Canadian Eskimo and a Samoan adolescent which he presented as anthropological documents as if they were untouched by his presence or imaginative molding. In the former film Flaherty used the standard orthochromatic film stock of the day with its bold contrasts and a greater capability of rendering pure whites and saturated blacks than later black and white negatives. Capitalizing on the graphic dynamics of the tonal range, he emphasized Nanook's continual struggle for shelter and food in an environment of snow and ice.

However, in *Moana*, after he gave up on an experimental color process, he came to use the recently developed panchromatic stock which sacrificed bold blacks and whites to gain subtle tonal nuances in the gray ranges. The gradations of panchromatic film encouraged Flaherty's reversal of the agonistic relationship of man and nature in *Nanook*; *Moana*'s exoticism evokes hyperboles of integration between the human and the natural, of Polynesian bodies and tropical environments, culminating in a ceremony of the tattooing of the adolescent eponymous hero. That the film-maker had to bribe his protagonist to endure the outdated tattooing ordeal is one indication of the graphic centrality of the visual texture of flesh – and of the metaphor of the body as a landscape – in the genesis of the film and in its style.

A comparison of these two films by Flaherty with the orthochromatic contrasts exploited by Weine's *The Cabinet of Dr. Caligari* (1919) and the panochromatic eloquence of physiognomies in Dreyer's *The Passion of Joan of Arc* (1928) dramatizes the contingency of landscape photography to the visual potential of the film stocks. Both films transpire within radically stylized, expressionist sets. In the former bold black and white backdrops create a paranoic cityscape; the latter limits the visual presence of the expressionist castle where

Joan is tried to muted background (it was painted pink to appear off-white on the panchromatic film) except for a periodic moment when it suddenly looms as a sinister fortress.

The international success of sound cinema, firmly established by 1930, gave the landscape a voice: wind, sea, fire, thunder, more often than not artificially produced or doctored for clarity and effect, vitalized landscape images and extended the auditory environment (as did the sounds of birds, animals, traffic, etc.) beyond the visible frame. With much more precision than before, music could emphasize and reflect the images, often banalizing them as in Flaherty's *The Louisiana Story* (1948), but sometimes engendering a striking synthesis, as in the case of Prokofiev's score for Eisenstein's *Alexander Nevsky* (1938). Above all, the inclusion of speech permitted a wide range of strategies for calling attention to the visual landscape: in *Fort Apache* (1948) a Chicano cavalryman toasts the panning overview of an arroyo in Monument Valley, "la tiera di mia madre," at a turning point in the film that marks the domination of the desert by the brutality of the U.S. army; when the heroine of Rossellini's *Stromboli* (1949) calls to God from the smoking heights of the volcano, her acknowledgment of the "beauty" and "mystery" of the island she had until then hated and feared encourages ours as the film's viewers; the speech of an old man to the Sicilian landscape from a balcony early in *Salvatore Giuliano* (1962) fuses the tragic tone of the film to the fatal presence of the island.

After periodic experiments throughout the silent period, the gradual shift from black and white to colour cinematography, which extended from the rare color films of the 1930s to the even rarer black and white films after 1970, abetted the exploitation of picturesque locations. Some of the most sophisticated color films such as Bergman's *Cries and Whispers* (1972), Antonioni's *Il deserto rosso* (1962), and Tarkovsky's *The Mirror* (1974) set up internal antitheses to give meaning to color landscapes; Bergman concentrates most of his film in richly saturated interiors to give three exterior scenes resonant beauty: the initial dawn, a memory of a dead mother in a summer garden, and a final autumnal scene of sisters in the same surroundings; Antonioni uses different color stocks to distinguish the polluted harbor of Ravenna from the heroine's fantasy of a mysterious Mediterranean cove; Tarkovsky alternates between black and white and color in a complex narrative memoir of a childhood country home.

Confronted with the economic challenge of television in the 1950s some producers (led by Americans who felt the competition first) turned to what had been the experimental heritage of widescreen formats to exaggerate the difference between cinema and the small round, oval, and later rectangular cathode tubes of television. The extended lateral range of CinemaScope and the high resolution of large gauges such as Todd-AO and 70mm encouraged more theoretical speculation than practical transformation of film aesthetics. Thorold Dickinson, however, gives the following example of a rare use of the inherent possibilities of the wide screen for landscape cinematography:

In ... *Ride Lonesome* (1959), a Western in CinemaScope by Budd Boetticher, a group of horsemen ride in mid-shot, the camera tracking back across the desert with a high ridge of sand in the background. Some small objects like dead trees come into view on top of the ridge. The conventional audience waits for a close-up that does not come: those objects are not dead trees, for they begin to move. Horses with Indians riding them. And the chase is on. When did you first see the objects? Before or after you saw the leading cowboy stiffen? Here the director is not leading a passive audience by the hand, showing it only what it wants to see. Here the audience is on its own.[7]

More pervasive than widescreen formats or large gauges has been the use of the zoom lens since the 1950s. In addition to providing a range of positions from close-up to long shot from a single camera setup for which it seems to have been developed and as it was initially used, this lens permits "zooming," a virtual movement that can mechanically and smoothly traverse space more rapidly than a camera on a dolly as well as indicate trajectories almost impossible for a conventional camera, such as across mountain peaks. In *Barry Lyndon* (1975) Kubrick repeatedly situates his characters in a pastoral landscape, an eighteenth-century battlefield, or a palatial estate by zooming from a close-up detail to an extremely long shot, often as the punctuation for the beginning of a scene. Going from the human event to the enlarged vista in which it is about to transpire, this repeated gesture unfolds the landscape as a theatre for action, but it occurs so frequently that it calls attention to the mechanics of the lens which foreshortens the close-up extreme as if squeezing the visual space and then gradually draws out the depth while it expands laterally. This gesture is as deliberate and as stylized as the use of specially constructed lenses to film interior scenes by candlelight; for the film's beauty derives from the interaction between advanced cinematic technology and the accurate renderings of eighteenth-century scenes.

111

III

Louis Delluc: "This is without a doubt the most beautiful film in the world. Victor Sjöström has directed it with a supremacy which makes any commentary superfluous. It shows him as a consummate and humane actor, as it does his leading lady and the third unusually expressive member of the cast: nature!"[8]

The leading French apologist for the art of the film, himself a film-maker, was praising the recently released *Outlaw and His Wife* (1917). Sjöström's adaptation of an Icelandic stage melodrama entailed a thorough exploitation of the landscape of the Lapland mountains: the story of Berg-Ejvind, sentenced to ten years in prison for stealing food for his young siblings, is one of flight steadily higher into the mountains. An idyllic wilderness romance of hunting, bathing in hot geysers, and Edenic love collapses when another outlaw finds the hero and the widow who fled to the mountains with him. Exploiting the tropes of verticality around which the film organizes itself, Sjöström shows his hero rescued from a cliff fall by his rival only to have to throw his young daughter to her death in order to escape to an even higher and more remote peak. In the end the embittered couple die together in a blizzard.

Many ambitious films have exploited the topos of the illusion of freedom offered by a mountain ascent: Leni Riefenstahl's *Das Blau Licht* (1932) evokes in black and white an extraordinary "blue light" emanating from a Swiss peak that only an outcast, Italian-speaking woman, played by the director herself, can ascend; a young German falls to his death trying to enter the enormous crystal geode at the summit; Walsh's *High Sierra* (1941) begins with a released convict's need to sit in a park and ends with his futile attempt to hold off the police from a mountain perch; in a more subtle way Mann's *The Naked Spur* (1953) locates itself at the Continental Divide in Colorado to give a topological dimension to the film's erotic and moral problematic: a bounty hunter's determination to bring a thief back to Texas dramatically gives way to his love for the thief's girlfriend and her fantasies of life in California.[9] Naturally such films profit from the depths of space visible from lofty camera positions while inventing modes of dynamizing the vertical dimension of the screen surface.

The use of sublime landscapes often coincides with spectacular meteorological displays. Cinema was the first art that could represent the temporality and rhythm of a storm. The blizzard that ends *The Outlaw and his Wife* is an anticipation of the violent sandstorm that dominates Sjöström's American film, *The Wind* (1928). From *Nanook of the North* to Kurosawa's *Derzu Urzala* (1975) the unique ability of film to capture the movement of snow has been used to emphasize the harshness of the natural world and difficulty of human survival in it. Olmi's *Tempo si e fermato* (1959) eloquently describes the transition from adolescence to maturity as the acquisition of a stoic attitude toward blizzards and snow.

More dramatic even has been the fascination with the breakup of ice fields: the climax of Griffith's *Way Down East* (1920) with its last minute rescue of the heroine before she went over a falls on a slab of ice inspired the strategic center of Eisenstein's *Alexander Nevsky* (1938) where the Russian general lures the Teutonic knights onto an iced-over lake that is about to crack, and less central ice floes in Pudovkin's *Mother* (1925), Adolfas Mekas' *Hallelujah the Hills* (1963), and *Derzu Urzala*.

Sea storms have provided film-makers with opportunities for elaborating upon a traditional painterly topic, particularly in the opposition of water and rock. Flaherty's *Man of Aran* (1934) climaxed in a fierce storm which the film-maker prolonged through montage; the second half of Jean Epstein's filmic career was largely devoted to the Breton seascape, culminating in *La Tempestaire* (1947) in which he used "slow motion sound" to accentuate the voice of the storm. In his beautiful film, *La terra trema* (1948) Visconti, adapting Verga's novel *I Malavoglia*, ascetically avoided any attempt to reproduce the novelist's description of fishing boats in a storm and allowed the image of women anxiously waiting on the stormy rocks of the port to carry the full weight of the episode.

Despite the repeated success of making sublime weather a central factor in many major films, it is in the depiction of gentler meteorological phenomena that cinema has developed a unique capability: the movement of clouds, changes in the intensity of light, the indication of breezes in the vibrations and swaying of flora, and the gradations of rain are natural events which cinema can render with nuances previously the exclusive domain of poetry. Yet the filmic weather can attain an objectivity beyond the scope of poetry or it can function within poetry's connotative realm according to the talent and disposition of the film-maker. In many city-bound films rain instantiates the penetration of natural beauty. Ivens's short film *Regen* (1929) elicited the following enthusiastic description from Erik Barnouw:

With extraordinary beauty and precision, Ivens portrays the patterns made by rain – at first gentle, later of mounting violence – falling in puddles,

113

gutters, canals, rivers, running down windows, umbrellas, wagons, cars, bicycles, dripping from gutters, spouts, umbrella spokes, and limbs of statues. The film starts modestly but develops richness and complexity; we are seeing a great city through the lens of rain. Made under the influence of the painter-as-documentarist genre, *Rain* was perhaps its most perfect product.[10]

Dovzhenko's *Earth* (1930), a great pastoral elegy for a fictional hero of mechanization and collectivization, murdered for bringing a tractor to Ukrainian farms, frames its slow paced and visually rich narrative of georgic passions with opening images of the wind moving through fields of grain and sunflowers and a concluding montage of fruits soaked by rain. Incorporating the Edenic fantasy of human life refracted in vegetative cycles which formed the basis of *Moana* and was to be repeated in a melodramatic mode by Murnau in *Tabu* (1931), his equally lush panchromatic vision of doomed love in the south Pacific, *Earth*, mocks the naivete of that very ideal and inscribes an eroticized myth of socialist labor in the film to bridge the natural beauty of the static landscape and the dynamic rhythms of mechanized productivity and collective celebration.

IV

The most subtle uses of natural beauty in narrative cinema occur when contexts render the landscape and the weather ambiguous. At the climax of Renoir's *Partie de campagne* (shot 1936, edited 1946) two friends make love to a young woman and her mother, whom they have coaxed away from the father and the young man he employs to different parts of a riverbank. The director cuts from the amours to details of a rain shower: ominous clouds, a sudden movement of the wind, rain on the river. The deflection from the lovemaking to the squall is so conventional that viewers must anticipate an eventual return to the scene of human action which in most circumstances would resolve the ambiguity of the natural images, which seem to represent symbolically the erotic tension and release of the young woman while at the same time they could naturalistically indicate an unforseen squelching of the parallel seductions. Renoir prolongs the description of the storm with a richly ambiguous image of the river quickly receding from the camera as the rain intensifies. Furthermore, instead of returning to the lovers, he introduces a title that tells us many years have passed until the concluding epilogue in which the daughter, now unhappily married to the grotesquely dull assistant, wistfully encounters at the same spot her lover. The timing and placement of the storm as metaphor, transition, culmination, or interruption irradiates the sequence with a pathos none of its images alone can sustain, although the greatest stress falls on the receding river.

Perez, whose general observation of cinematic landscape I have quoted from his essay on this film, writes of this climax:

> The rainstorm strikingly frustrates pastoral expectations, not only for the day but for the years that seem to be swiftly passing, and not only for the characters but for all of us who joined them in the sunny arrival and now look upon stormy nature from the departing perspective of a visitor no longer identifiable with them, generalized beyond their circumstances and their century. That uncannily rapid departing motion of the camera – rapid like our passage through the world where we're all mere visitors – evokes the movement of a consciousness that recognizes its own foreignness amid the trees and the river and the rain, its own irremediable separation from the things of nature.[11]

The moral complexity of Dreyer's *Vredens Dag* (1943) derives from the deliberate contradiction the film exhaustively employs between our conditioning by cinematic conventions to sympathize with attractive young lovers in idyllic landscapes and the moral scruples we must suspend in identifying with their pleasure. Dreyer located the rare excursions out of the interiors, where most of his tragedy of sixteenth-century repression and adultery occurs, in a setting where symbolic hints of the fallenness of nature disturb the illicit idylls. Each time the lovers, a young woman and the son of her aged husband, go out of their home the landscape reflects in varying degrees their amorous illusions and their bitter consequences: their first and most innocent excursion ends when they see someone gathering wood to burn a witch. At the turning point of the film, after they have fallen in love, the woman reads the image of a tree and its reflection in water as an image of the fusion of ideal lovers, but the young man sees it as barren narcissism. Despite the storm that accompanies the woman's acknowledgment of the demonic quality of her hatred for her husband, and the dense fog that engulfs them when her son breaks off the relationship after his father's death, Dreyer invests the film with such a thorough moral ambiguity that the unquestionably symbolic landscape sustains two incompatible interpretations, in which the source of the tragedy lies in the reckless will of the young protagonists or the repressive society of the elder representatives of religious order.

In his earlier film, *Vampyr* (1931), Dreyer had used fog and a foglike gel over his lens to visualize a realm between life and death in which bodies and shadows could move independently. Similarly Mizoguchi makes use of the cinema's capacity for articulating the spatial ambiguities of fog at the transitional moment in his *Ugetsu Monogatari* (1953).

Mizoguchi's integration of landscape into narrative, however, might best be illustrated by his *Sancho Dayu* (1954) where the geographical trope of exile permeates the film. The wife, son and daughter of a just governor in medieval Japan are kidnapped and enslaved trying to follow him into exile on a remote island. Brother and sister gathering branches and reeds for a shelter for a fellow slave abandoned to die are reminded of a parallel act the last evening before they were taken from their mother; this memory stirs them to escape. The son's eventual success allows him to make a tour of sites: his father's shrine on an island hill overlooking the sea, the forest pool where his sister drowned herself, and his mother's beach hut, where he unexpectedly finds her alive, but blind. In striking compositions of forests, mountains, and island coasts, filmed with the director's characteristic long takes from a sinuously gliding camera, the plot of the film invests the landscape with intimations of the human brutality and loss its natural beauty hides.

A number of fundamental geographical strategies have been invented by film-makers to give landscape meaning. Ford's Westerns repeatedly call upon the eroded monoliths of Monument Valley as backdrops as if to put into perspective the heroics and savagery of his cavalry and Indians in a geological time indifferent to the conflict of civilizations. Rossellini's six-part episodic film of the liberation of Italy from Fascism, *Paisà* (1946) moves from the verticality of Sicilian cliffs from which the Germans throw the bodies of an American soldier and the young Italian woman helping him, to the flat marshes of the Po valley where the body of an executed Partisan floats. In *Aguirre, Der Zorn Gottes* (1972) Herzog takes over and inflates this very trope, opening his film with distant shots of the antlike procession of Pisarro's army down an Andean mountain as a contrast to the sustained flatness of the movement through Amazon tributaries in the rest of the film.

V

Uniquely among the film-makers who have produced theory Eisenstein raised the issue of landscape as factor in the poetics of film. He claimed that the silent cinema depended upon "landscape sequences" to express "emotionally what only music is able to express completely."[12] Yet in his lengthy essay ostensibly devoted to "the music of landscape and the fate of montage counterpoint at a new stage" he has very little to say about natural beauty in cinema. Elaborating on analogies from Chinese scroll painting, El Greco's "View of Toledo," and Van Gogh's landscapes in a meditation so sinuous it threatens its coherence, he recasts the pathetic fallacy as "nonindifferent nature," before turning to his central topic of cinematic rhythm:

Thus, having begun with the question about the music of landscape, about "nonindifferent nature" in the narrow sense of the word, we imperceptibly moved into whole performance complexes into which the landscape grows and toward which it develops. (p. 354)

In the most general terms, "Landscape can serve as a concrete image of the embodiment of whole cosmic conceptions, whole philosophic systems" (p. 355).

With orthodox encouragement from the travel meditations of the young Engels on the relationship of landscapes to the religious ideas of their inhabitants, he draws the conclusion that the task of cinema is to articulate the sense of becoming immanent in landscapes, especially the "social becoming" of the Soviet Union. So the examination of the musicality of landscape in cinema quickly shifts to a discussion of the musicality and the ideology of montage. This corresponds to the persistent pattern in film theory in which questions of rhythm slip into arguments about ideology or meaning. Cinematic rhythm, it would seem, is a matter of postponing or rushing meaning.

Throughout the volume which culminates in the chapter on landscape, Eisenstein insists on the principle of montage as the fundamental tool for expressing and organizing cinematically the music of landscape. Some forty years later, Andrey Tarkovsky, sharing similar goals, challenged Eisenstein's principles:

Cinema ... is able to record time in outward and visible signs, recognizable to the feelings. And so time becomes the very foundation of cinema as sound in music, colour in painting, character in drama.

Rhythm, then, is not the metrical sequence of pieces; what makes it is the time-thrust within the frames. And I am convinced that it is rhythm, and not editing, as people tend to think, that is the main formative element of cinema.[13]

Tarkovsky gives an impression of a Bergman film to illustrate the rhythmical pressure of natural beauty – the ellipses are his:

... in The Virgin Spring [1960] I have always been stunned by one shot of the dying heroine, the girl who has been monstrously raped. The spring sun is shining through the trees, and through the branches we see her face – she may be dying or she may be already dead, but in any case she clearly no longer feels pain ... Our foreboding seems to hang in the air, suspended like a sound ... All seems clear enough and yet we feel a hiatus.... There's something missing.... Snow starts to fall, freak spring snow ... which is the piercing scintilla we needed to bring our feeling to a kind of consummation: we gasp, transfixed. The snow catches on her eyelashes and stays there: again, time is leaving its tracks in the shot.... But how, by what right, could one talk about the meaning of that falling snow, even though within the span and rhythm of the shot it is the thing that brings our emotional awareness to a climax? Of course one can't. All we know in this scene is the form the artist found to convey precisely what happened. On no account must artistic purpose be confused with ideology, or we shall lose the means of perceiving art immediately and exactly with the whole of our being....[14]

Tarkovsky suspends this sympathetic account of Bergman's use of snow between the repudiations of symbolic meaning in his own use of natural beauty – "Rain, fire, water, snow, dew, the driving ground wind – all are part of the material setting in which we dwell; I would even say of the truth of our lives," (p. 212) – and the metaphoric dimension of the spectacular image that concludes his film Nostalghia (1982): a Russian country house situated within the walls of a ruined and roofless Tuscan cathedral. It is the final moment in a film about the pathos of exile in which the beauties of the Italian landscape cannot quite compensate for the nostalgia for a lost homeland. In Wild Strawberries (1957) Bergman too had used images of natural beauty as signs for the losses of childhood and youth, as does Jonas Mekas in Diaries, Notes & Sketches (Walden) (1968) and Reminiscences of a Journey to Lithuania (1971).

Pasolini cites the use of landscape in another Bergman film, The Devil's Eye (1960) in his central theoretical essay, "The Cinema of Poetry," as an example of the power of cinematic "prose:"

... when Don Giovani and Pablo leave [Hell] after three hundred years, and we see the world once again, the appreciation of the world – something so extraordinary – is presented by Bergman as a "long shot" of the two protagonists in a somewhat wild stretch of springtime country landscape, one or two extremely ordinary "close-ups," and a great "establishing shot" of a Swedish panorama of disturbing beauty in its transparent and humble insignificance. The camera was still; it framed those images in an absolutely normal manner. It was not felt.[15]

Scorsese achieves a parallel effect in *The Last Temptation of Christ* (1988) a film much indebted to Pasolini, with a long shot of a landscape more verdant than those to which the film had accustomed us through which Jesus passes as soon as the "Angel" rescues or tempts him from the Cross. Language supports and sustains the subtle chromatic intensification as the Angel explains that the landscape he sees is not Heaven but the earth which even angels often envy, and that the kingdom of heaven is actually "harmony between the earth and the heart."

Here again the observation of cinematic landscape is an illustration, not a theme, of theoretical speculation. In his own *Notes for an African Oresteia* (1969) Pasolini comments with a voice-over on images he has gathered in preparation for a future film (never made). While his commentary encourages us to see the archaic heroism of African faces and to think of their transformation from mythopoeic societies to constitutional republics as parallels to the dynamic transitions at work in the world of Aeschylus' Athens, the pressure of his language gives an animistic cast to his remarkable long shots of the African landscape and his details of massive, often gnarled, trees, as he describes how he would use them to represent the Furies becoming the Eumenides.

VI

By the time Pasolini announced the transformation of a cinema of prose into a "cinema of poetry" within the domain of the advanced narrative film, that is in 1965, landscape had begun to play a new and vital role in the *avant-garde* cinema of North America and Europe. The international emergence of a cinema of landscape resulted from the confluences of numerous causes. Relatively inexpensive 16mm equipment was widely available; viewers had been educated to recognize the personal styles of a number of directors, an incipient crisis in the world of painting encouraged painters to try their hands at cinema and students in art school to consider the option of film-making; and the growth of color cinematography fostered the search for new subjects.

The most prolific and protean of *avant-garde* film-makers, Stan Brakhage had published his theoretical essay *Metaphors on Vision* at the end of 1963. He argued that cinema was the first and only art that could render the temporality of vision: the shift of focus, reactions to peripheral vision, superimposed memory scenes, and eye movements, while maintaining a sense of the body's movement in space. In *Sirius Remembered* (1959) he returned again and again to the carcass of a dog in the woods, filming the dissolution of the body through winter and spring. In *Mothlight* (1963) he assembled fragments of the natural world, moth wings, seeds, leaves, grasses, between sprocketed strips of transparent film editing tape to make a film in which we see the light passing through rather than bouncing off objects. In 8mm he filmed Arapahoe Peak, the most prominent mountain visible from his home in the Rockies through four seasons to make *Song 27: My Mountain* (1968). *Angels'* (1971) looks at a distant snow covered landscape from the window of an airplane; *The Machine of Eden* (1970) adopts the perspective of a sick child to organize images of the Colorado landscape as if they were coefficients in the Biblical myth of origin, a theme he takes up again in *Creation* (1979) in the sublime landscape of Alaskan glaciers where he repeats the Romantic topos of a river in the sky by showing upside-down shots made from a boat moving through ice floes.

The primary distinction of Brakhage's landscapes are their complexity and sophistication. Technically the filming of *Creation*, for example, may owe something to that of Flaherty's *Louisiana Story*. Flaherty reverts again and again to gliding shots as if from the pirogue of the boy he has selected as his protagonist, and those gliding movements are matched by the telephoto shots closely following the swimming alligator that pursues his pet racoon. Brakhage never reverts to the sentimentality of the story of the boy and his pet, nor does he make his films as covert commercials as Flaherty did here for Standard Oil. But even more important is the continual attention to shifting qualities of light and image that makes Brakhage's landscapes as unpredictable as Flaherty's are conventional. Brakhage generally eschews sound to make the eye more attentive to microsecond nuances, while the soundtrack of *Louisiana Story* tutors the viewer to feel tense or carefree according to the needs of the unconvincingly imposed plot.

The enormous ascesis involved in taking the mediating figure, the actor or the documentary subject, as well as the narrating or commenting voice, out of the film and making the images bear the full weight of emotional articulation entails a sacrifice of both the dramatic and the epistemological organization of the film; we lose the ground from which the unrolling of images can be assimilated into a system that anticipates them, allowing us to experience fear, hope and the achievement or frustration of desire. In a Brakhage work the presence behind the camera and in charge of the editing decisions is the unseen subjectivity at the heart of hundreds of films that represent what he sees without giving us his attendant knowledge or expectations of those sights. The compensation for this sacrifice is the inheritance of a rich tradition of landscape painting and photography susceptible to reconception in terms of cinematic rhythm.

In the dreamlike movements amid the glaciers of *Creation* the viewer may simply share the film-maker's wonder at the dynamics of light bouncing off the water, light, and minimal vegetation. But, cued by the film's title, he or she may come to notice that the reversal of shots (so that some glaciers seem to float in the sky) alludes to a "dividing of the waters from the waters." Such a hermeneutic leap would be rewarded by a recognition of the paced introductions of land, grass, trees, birds, and even eventually a woman into the images of the moving landscape. Nothing could be farther from Brakhage's aesthetic than the dramatization of Adam's sleep and the emergence of a naked woman from his rib. In his film all the elements of the creation drama appear already in place: they are the flora and fauna we would expect and which anyone would see from a boat trip in Alaska; the woman is mature, dressed, outside of a dramatic context. The point of the analogy to Genesis seems to be that an honest and fresh encounter with the presence of a sublime landscape has the power of a moment of origin. In this respect, and in many others, Brakhage brings to cinema a rich Romantic heritage, mediated by poetry and his long study of Frederick Church and other landscape painters.

Brakhage learned the elements of landscape cinema from the much simpler films of Marie Menken, several of which are collected in the *Notebook* she kept from the early 1940s until her death in the 1970s. The fragment *Raindrops* alternates the imposed rhythms of a rapidly panning camera over a pool needled by rain with the immanent tension of moisture building up enough mass on a leaf to fall as a drop. The freewheeling handheld camera of *A Glimpse of a Garden* (1957) calls attention to the offscreen movements of Menken's body as she tours a large flower garden. Brakhage expanded and refined Menken's visual rhetoric and he redefined her concept of a subject, radically turning away from the exterior authority of a predetermined topic – rain, or a garden – to center his films in a complex field of his perceptions and emotions in whatever situation he films.

By contrast, when Tarkovsky writes that he uses rain "to create a particular aesthetic setting in which to steep the action of the film,"

(p. 212), his choice of terms indicates the hierarchical distinction between human action and natural setting. So even though the slow camera movements away from the protagonists and along moss-covered boards to the flooded foundation of an old house or from a farm into the surrounding woods, images which end *The Mirror*, have much in common with Brakhage's investment in landscape (but not with his filmic style), the emotional resonance of such shots extends metonymically from the dreamy narrative in which they occur. Conversely, Tarkovsky's story, however elliptical, informs us how to view those shots of the iconography of lost childhood.

Montage plays a crucial role in Brakhage's landscape films as it does in the diary film genre which has been largely influenced by his work. Even the titles of two such films, Hutton's *Images of Asian Music* (1974) and Kobland's *Landscape and Desire* (1981), draw attention to the fundamental issues at stake: the former marks the continuation of Eisenstein's linking of landscape and music in Hutton's diary of travel in Southeast Asia, while the latter points out a Brakhagean distinction between the concrete and the immanent aspects of the images Kobland retained from a trip across America.

Another montage tradition in the *avant-garde* cinema stems from Vertov's Whitmanesque assemblage of contrasting visions of the diversity of the Soviet Union, *One Sixth of the World* (1926). The auditory and visual collisions of Kubelka's *Unsere Afrikareise* (1966) and the pyrotechnics of Warren Sonbert's largely silent films depend upon the sudden juxtapositions of discontinuous and diverse terrains. As Brakhage's landscapes bring to the fore the network of eye and body movements that constitute the inscription of his consciousness in the films he makes, these films use landscape as a foil to point to the synthetic authority of editing.

Many of the most original landscape films of the late sixties and early seventies drew their power from the repudiation of both montage and the rhetoric Brakhage had painstakingly developed for the articulation of subjectivity. Whereas Brakhage used a variety of ways of registering camera movement to map the scanning of his eyes, the presence of his breathing body, and the "stream of [his] thoughts" (to use William James' metaphor), a number of film-makers in his wake tried to disengage such devouring subjectivity and utilize the mechanical automatism of the camera to emphasize the independence and the transcendence of the exterior world. By limiting themselves to a monomorphic technical strategy – one zoom movement, a single panning shot, a fixed camera position, etc. – these film-makers could emphasize the convergence of two poles, the natural world, and the mechanical system of representation. Jacobs' *Soft Rain* (1968) is actually a cityscape: as the same unbudging shot of a street from a window is repeated three times, the rain of the title sometimes fuses and sometimes can be distinguished from the grain of the color emulsion. Gehr's *Untitled* film (1977) shares Jacobs' use of slight retardation (filming at 24 frames per second and projecting at 18 frames per second) for aesthetic effect, as well as his choice of a dull urban setting to emphasize the beauty and rhythm of precipitation; from a single camera position he very slowly shifts focus or zooms (they are virtually the same when no fixed object anchors the field of view) through snow flurries until a brick wall gradually comes into focus. In the course of the film a number of images are suggested, including a pool of water lilies. Baillie's *All My Life* (1968) explores the power of a single pan, from a fixed tripod, to linearize and temporalize the elements of an urban garden: three rose bushes, a broken wooden fence, and power lines against a clear sky.

The British film-maker Welsby and the Canadian Snow invented unique methods of filming landscape. Welsby has rigorously explored ways of harnessing natural rhythms to control the rhythms of filming, from the elemental idea of using time lapse techniques he progressed to mounting cameras on branches in the wind or in boats that would allow the tides to determine the direction of the lens while the current and surface turbulence affected camera movement. He also built tripods with windmill projections that would spin a mirror before the camera, interrupting the otherwise fixed view of a park with a countershot of the camera and the area "behind" it with increasing frequency as it becomes more windy.

Snow had an elaborate tripod constructed with remote control and capability for programming in advance in order to make *La Region Centrale* (1971), a three hour and ten minute long exploration of a barren track of northern wilderness. The camera can trace baroque spirals, circles, and erratic movements of the land and sky without encountering a sign of human presence through a variety of times, including the dawn, and a moonlit night. Snow's film, like Welsby's, can be seen as an adjustment to the near solipsism of Brakhage's vision; a number of its topoi – the shadow of the tripod, the synthetic "dance" of the moon, the prolonged dawn – can even be traced to sources in Brakhage's influential *Anticipation of the Night* (1958). The mechanical functions operating in Welsby's and Snow's landscape films resist his metaphoric humanization of the filmic apparatus, and by extension, the landscape it records.

When *Undercut* devoted its spring 1983 issue to landscape in photography, film, and video, A.L. Rees, one of the issue's coeditors, stressed the historicity of landscape films: "[Landscape] is already coded for us, not only by the technique and material we use, but also by the sheer volume of images which precede us and which we know." His coeditor, Michael O'Pray, revealed the polemical thrust of the issue when he wrote:

Reducing the representation of landscape to Romanticism or an aesthetic form of political conservatism seems inadequate as explanation, particularly in the light of its use by such film-makers as Eisenstein, Snow, and Straub-Huillet.[16]

In fact, the Straub-Huillet film, *Too Early, Too Late* (1981) plays a significant role in the volume. It is the paradigmatic instance of the representation of landscape as an historical palimpsest. In two parts, the film presents a series of long-held, static or panning shots of peopled landscapes, first in France over which a letter from Engels is read, then in Egypt to the accompaniment of texts from Mahmoud Hussein's *Class Conflict in Egypt 1945–1973*. There is both a critical essay on the film and an interview with the film-makers, who in ignorance of the *avant-garde* cinema claim, "no one has ever shot landscapes in a film and then held and, as it were, caressed them. As if they were precisely characters."[17] Consistent with the political claims of the editorial, Mildred Budney and Yehuda Safran identify the ubiquitous wind in the film as "the 'terrible wind' blowing 'across Europe,' let loose upon the opening page of the *Communist Manifesto*." They conclude: "Like the spirit of revolution, the wind itself cannot be seen: only in those things, those bodies, animated by it can its action be shown, and known."[18]

In another effort to extend the topic beyond the *avant-garde* cinema, the editors include an essay by Simon Whatney on Greenaway's *The Draughtsman's Contract* (1982) an allegory of the "distinction between 'seeing' and 'knowing.'" Brakhage himself contributed a brief letter claiming that imageless films or light and color variations he had made and titled with arabic or roman numerals were landscapes as well: "Thus my 'landscapes' of these last several years have been possibly near equivalents of innerscape upon which all seen, with the eyes opened, must be imprinted."[19] And in an interview, Welsby offered an Hegelian definition of the topic: "Landscape is a subdivision of nature as a whole. The degree to which we call it landscape is the degree to which the mind has had an effect on it, the degree to which it is structured and modified by ideas and concepts."[20]

The opinions and perspectives gathered by Rees and O'Pray were too diverse to allow a consensus. The *Undercut* contributors could not even agree about what their topic was. Above all, one cannot say that a theory of the landscape film or a theory of landscape in film emerged from that unique collection of essays and interviews. However, it is just as clear that "landscape" had, at least at that moment, become a term in the epistemology of cinema, essentially because *avant-garde* film-making in a number of different modes had conjoined the representation of natural beauty with explorations of how the film-making tools "see" and "know" their subjects.

The primary achievement of the *avant-garde* cinema in this area has been to force a contemplation of the natural world in different mediations by the cinematic apparatus. The landscapes of the narrative cinema, as Eisenstein and Bazin suggest, are latent expressionistic theatres, confronting or echoing the minds of the human figures within them. The aleatoric magic Tarkovsky describes in Bergman's *The Virgin Spring* (1960) ultimately confirms this version of the pathetic fallacy. But there is a fundamental change of aesthetic orientation when there is no actress in the scene, no body on which the snowflake can land. Snow, Brakhage, Welsby and other landscape film-makers have used cinema to look at the natural beauty of the world, and in watching their films we share their surprise and excitement at the disjunctions and the meshings of the rhythms of the world and the temporality of the medium.

Notes

1 Sergei Eisenstein, *The Nonindifferent Nature*, trans. Herbert Marshall, (Cambridge University Press, 1987), pp. 216–383.
2 Gilberto Perez, "Landscape and Fiction: Jean Renoir's Country Excursion," *Hudson Review*, 42.2 (summer 1989): 342–3.
3 G.W.P.F. Hegel, *Aesthetics: Lectures on Fine Art*, trans. T.M. Knox, (Oxford University Press, 1975), p. 972.
4 Arthur Schopenhauer, *The World as Will and Representation*, trans. E.F.J. Payne, (New York: Dover, 1966), vol. 2, p. 403.
5 John L. Fell, ed., *Film Before Griffith* (Berkeley: University of California Press, 1983). Raymond Fielding, "Hale's Tours: Ultrarealism in the Pre-1910 Motion Picture," pp. 116–30.

P. Adams Sitney

6 William K. Everson, *American Silent Film* (New York: Oxford University Press, 1978), p. 35.
7 Thorold Dickinson, *A Discovery of Cinema* (London: Oxford University Press, 1971).
8 Bengt Forslund, *Victor Sjöström: His Life and Work*, trans. Peter Cowie, (New York: Zoetrope, 1988).
9 André Bazin made the following observations in "Beauty of a Western": "And so for the director of *The Naked Spur* man is barely separate from nature ... For Anthony Mann landscape is always stripped of its picturesque effects ... Grass is mixed up with rocks, trees with desert, snow with pastures and clouds with the blue of the sky. This blending of elements and colors is like a token of the secret tenderness nature holds for man, even in the most arduous trials of its seasons.

In most Westerns, even in the best ones like Ford's, the landscape is an expressionist framework where human trajectories come to make their mark. In Anthony Mann it is an atmosphere." Trans. Liz Heron in *Cahiers du cinéma: The 1950s: New-Realism, Hollywood, New Wave*, ed. Jim Hillier, (Cambridge: Harvard University Press, 1985), p. 167.
10 Erik Barnouw, *Documentary: A History of the Non-Fiction Film*, (New York: Oxford University Press, 1974), pp. 78–80.
11 Perez, "Landscape and Fiction," p. 256.
12 Eisenstein, *Nonindifferent Nature*, p. 218.
13 Andrey Tarkovsky, *Sculpting in Time: Reflections on the Cinema*, trans. Kitty Hunter-Blair, (New York: Knopf, 1987), p. 119.
14 Tarkovsky, *Sculpting in Time*, p. 213.
15 Pier Paolo Pasolini, *Heretical Empiricism*, ed. Louise K. Barnett, trans. Ben Lawton and Louise K. Barnett, (Bloomington: Indiana University Press, 1988), pp. 183–4.
16 *Undercut*, (London: London Film-makers' Co-op.), no. 7/8, spring 1983, p. 3.
17 *Ibid.*, p. 29.
18 *Ibid.*, p. 36.
19 *Ibid.*, p. 16.
20 *Ibid.*, p. 77.

6

The touch of landscape

DON GIFFORD

In transit to these shores, convoyed by Thomas Jefferson and George Washington among others, the Pastoral and Picturesque of the English Garden underwent something of a sea change. The Pastoral was drained of its literary allusions to Virgil and Horace in favor of real (if prosaic) countryside. The Picturesque lacked the reinforcement of the portfolios of prints and the picture galleries which were standard features in English great houses. The English Garden left a landscape in which the thumbprint of the hand of man was everywhere in evidence; it left the relatively tame wildernesses of the Wye Valley and the Lake District to confront the hundreds of thousands of square miles worth of wilderness, that always seemed to be lying in wait just beyond the horizon.

And wilderness came into the eighteenth century in America with something of a spin on it. In New England the Puritans had confronted the wilderness by demonizing it and its aboriginal inhabitants and challenging both to mortal combat – the object: to tame both so that they looked and behaved like the landscape and inhabitants the Colonists had left behind in the English countryside. The Reverend John Eliot's converts, the "Praying Indians," were dressed as English yeoman farmers and settled in model (English) farm villages on the outskirts of Massachusetts Bay Colony. By the late eighteenth century, central and southern New England and most of the East Coast within easy reach of water transport were on their way to being as thumbprinted as the mother country, but the demonic, unexplored wilderness still lurked beyond the western horizon just as it had lurked beyond the villages of the Praying Indians over a century before.

Jefferson's eye and hand when he laid out the gardens at Monticello were informed by his 1786 tour of a number of gardens in England

127

(part of the time in company with John Adams). The notes that he took during that tour repeatedly complain that this or that garden "shews still too much of art," and he determined for Monticello, in addition to a *ferme ornée* (flower borders and kitchen gardens near the house), "lawns and clumps of Trees, the lawns opening so as to give advantageous catches of prospect."[1] And in those prospects Jefferson would have seen vistas of wilderness in the mountains west of Monticello. And that seeing must have been informed by an insightful concept of wilderness, a concept and grasp of the meaning of wilderness that would culminate in the several months' worth of encyclopedic briefing he gave Meriweather Lewis and William Clark before sending their "Corps of Discovery" into the unknown of wilderness (1804–6).

That sense of the wilderness just beyond the horizon has lingered to inform the American imagination of landscape – though it is frequently the romantic wilderness of Alfred Bierstadt's sweeping Rocky Mountain canvases and John Muir's *The Mountains of California* (1894) rather than the wilderness that speaks, as in Malory's phrase, "with a grimly Voice." Bierstadt urged visitors to his gallery to view the paintings through binoculars so that the visitor would have to move his head to take in the whole scene just as he would have had to move faced by the mountainscape itself. Ironically, that added bit of "realism" only served to emphasize the distance between viewer and the remote Rocky Mountain landscape.

In the benign context of Walden the pond and *Walden* the book Thoreau can assert: "In wilderness is the preservation of the world," but Thoreau heard the "grimly Voice" of wilderness on the slopes of Mount Katahdin when the comfortable surround of Walden Pond gave way to "vast, Titanic, inhuman Nature" that gets man "at a disadvantage ... and pilfers him of some of his divine faculty."[2] That voice also rang in Melville's head as he contemplated what he regarded as the condescending benignity of Emerson's *Nature* in contrast to "the tiger heart that pants beneath" the tranquil surface of the tropical Pacific, and the play of "serene, exasperating sunlight that smiled on, as if at a birth or a bridal,"[3] after a cataclysmic encounter with Moby Dick.

Faulkner implies the essentially aloof (and to the initiate, benign) neutrality of that "grimly Voice" in "The Bear" when Ike McCaslin visits the Great Bottom for the last time just as it is about to be logged off. Ike encounters an enormous rattlesnake in this doomed Eden, and "as it began to glide away from him, moving erect," (as the snake in

Genesis had moved before the Fall), Ike blesses its presence in the Indian language of his spiritual father, Sam Fathers: "'Chief,' he said: 'Grandfather.'"[4] And in so doing he affirms the passing of the wilderness.

Wilderness remains to trouble the American imagination of landscape because we are the heirs to what George Caitlin, the painter of Indian life and of prairie and wilderness landscapes, called the "juggernaut civilization" that has squandered the riches of the wilderness and undertaken to tame it by paving it over. We are Caitlin's heirs too, struggling to slow the onrush of the juggernaut even as we share the prodigal expectations of those who assumed that the plains would never run out of buffalo, that the skies would never run out of passenger pigeons. Part of the ambivalence that haunts our imagination of wilderness as we idealize/exploit it may be our guilty fear of it, or, as Faulkner suggests in *Go Down Moses* our fear of the wilderness within ourselves which matches its counterpart, the wilderness without – and in part because of our growing sense that "the grimly Voice" has found a new venue in the urban worlds just beyond our suburban horizons. But wilderness is still the scale and measure of our sense of landscape, even though the worlds we inhabit are sub-rural, sub-urban.

In the Colonial beginnings the ever-presence of wilderness challenged and at times confused the newcomers' traditional assumptions about how a working landscape should be ordered and gardened. Coming, as even the English settlers did, from different local cultures and contrasting traditions of land use, the Colonists had to compromise and in effect improvise post-Medieval orderings of the land.[5] The Domesday Book was closed; but we are mistaken if we assume the wilderness to have been a clean slate, ready for the newcomers' land-use habits to be imposed at will. The wilderness was a cluttered slate that made its own demands even as it appeared passively to accept Colonial compromise and evolve toward the regional working landscapes that we can sense as the "ordinary countryside" on the periphery and beneath the surfaces of modern development; those ghostly presences, the "typical" New England farm, Virginia plantation, Pennsylvania Dutch landscape, etc. But the historical presence of the wilderness is still there in the background as it never seems to be in the homelands from which the Colonists came.

By the early nineteenth century the working landscapes and gardens of the new republic were regarded as readable moral barometers. As William Cobbett put it in *The American Gardener*,

The sentence of the whole nation is, that he, who is a sloven in his garden, is a sloven indeed.[6]

And many of Cobbett's contemporaries took the even higher moral ground that flowers in gardens (grown for other than medicinal purposes) were a wasteful and frivolous vanity. Those puritanical and utilitarian strictures began to erode towards the middle of the century, but perceptions of landscape continued in a moral vein.

Andrew Jackson Downing, the popular and influential American landscape architect of the mid-nineteenth century, preached the values of the native landscape of this new Eden and promoted a gardening that has its affinities with the English Garden on the one hand and with the painting of the Hudson River School on the other. He pointed out that this was not a country of great estates but that "we are, comparatively, all landlords," and therefore must, as "blest inhabitants of Sion,"[7] accept our democratic responsibility to dress our landscape and keep it. And a chorus of other voices, including Calvert Vaux, Jackson Jarves, and Frederick Law Olmsted, was there in support. When Olmsted and Vaux won the design competition for New York's Central Park, they "originated the rural park movement in the United States."[8] Following the lead of the prematurely dead Downing, their vision was informed by moral and social utility. Their purpose: "to humanize the physical environment of cities and to secure precious scenic regions."[9] At a stroke they were advocating both "rural" city parks and the park-preservation of significant moments of wilderness, and it is of note that when in 1864 President Lincoln ceded the Yosemite Valley to California "for public use, resort and recreation...inalienable for all time,"[10] Olmsted was among the first commissioners. Olmsted and Vaux argued that it was the duty of governments, local, state and federal, to educate the "aesthetic faculties" as well as to encourage the "useful arts."[11] Olmsted's question about the gardens of the English Great Houses has its democratic bearing here as well: "Is it right and best that this should be for the few?"[12]

The democratic and social optimism of that view had its dark (largely unacknowledged at the time) counterpart in Melville's savage caricature of the Pastoral Idyll in the opening chapters of *Pierre: or the Ambiguities*, a novel which was to climax in a profoundly skeptical view of man's role as credible beholder of the natural world:

Say what some poets will, Nature is not so much her own ever-sweet interpreter, as the mere supplier of that cunning alphabet, whereby selecting and combining as he pleases, each man reads his own peculiar lesson according to his own peculiar mind and mood.[13]

But Melville's novel was dismissed under the headline "HERMAN MELVILLE CRAZY"; his darkly antiromantic view of the natural world was shunned in favor of poetic (and frequently sentimental) affirmations of *Nature*.

Wordsworth and Coleridge who had done much to establish that poetic of nature had also reacted against the fixed picture-frame perspectives urged by the "stations" and "prospects" of the English Garden and of Thomas West's *A Guide to the Lakes* (1778). Theirs was an in-touch-with, flow-through experience of landscape. But that too underwent a change as it approached these shores. In part, the close affinity and interchange between nature, landscape and garden which they advocated was dislocated by the proximity of wilderness; in part, it was refracted through the American preoccupation with ideas and passed into a hierarchy that mounts chapter by chapter through Emerson's little book *Nature* from II. "Commodity" through III. "Beauty" up towards poetry and VII. "Spirit" and VIII. "Prospects" (with its anticipation of noumenal monism, the triumph of mind over matter).[14] Wordsworth's emphasis on "the power/ Of harmony and the deep power of joy" ("Tintern Abbey," lines 46–7), engendered by the unconscious presence of the "beauteous forms" (line 22) of the Wye Valley metamorphoses into something close to a religion of transcendental consciousness in Concord:

Standing on the bare ground, – my head bathed by the blithe air and uplifted into infinite space, – all mean egotism vanishes. I become a transparent eyeball; I am nothing; I see all; the currents of the Universal Being circulate through me; I am part or parcel of God. *Nature* (1836) chapter I.

No terrors of nature's wildernesses here; the "grimly Voice" of Mount Katahdin is peacefully remote. Nature is sought for the trancelike occasions of transcendental vision which it can provide. Eight years later, after the onset of a benign skepticism, Emerson's earlier hierarchy shifts towards a balance of opposites in the essay "Experience":

In the morning I awake and find. . .Concord and Boston, the dear old spiritual world and even the dear old devil not far off.

The commute between Boston and Concord crosses the Great Rift in the American landscape, the great divide between the bulldozers of this "juggernaut civilization" and a reasonably, democratically affirmed natural world. Thoreau protested that the commute was

131

tilted in favor of Boston and the juggernaut. Andrew Carnegie, reading Emerson's "Self-Reliance," also found the commute tilted toward Boston, and, finding the tilt in his favor, he was content.

Emerson complained that Thoreau was "the captain of a huckleberry party" when he should have been "engineering for all America."[15] The captains of huckleberry parties are all around us today, armed with the relatively new science of ecology, armed with computers that are increasingly capable of modeling the dynamic flow of the biosphere, and armed with lawyers. The captains of industry have spawned their faceless bureaucracies; they have their banks of computers and skillful programmers, and their lawyers and public relations experts. The Rift widens; it is farther than ever from Concord to Boston. As the computers talk over our heads (global warming or no? wetlands or development? oil or the Alaskan tundra?) we are in danger of losing our sense of the eco-niches of landscape we individually inhabit beneath the wash of global generalities.

As we explore this Great Rift, we realize that we live in a laminate of economic, commercial and political interests that can co-opt things with astonishing rapidity and thoroughness. When the democratic ideal of individual freedom and independence is debased in the direction of unbridled individual or corporate license, license to treat the landscape one owns as one pleases, the social fabric of landscape can all too easily be torn asunder. (If I want to trash my yard, it's mine to trash; if I want to jet ski this lake, it's a free country; if our corporation wants to clear-cut the temperate zone rainforest it owns, it's ours to cut.) Sixty percent of the water consumed in Las Vegas, Nevada is used to impose a stage set of lawns and artificial lakes on a desert landscape. And there is Manhattan, in Whitman's phrase "girdl'd by water," most of it walled off from pedestrians by highways; none of it fishable or swimable, let alone potable.

A corollary to the democratic ideal of individual independence is the ideal of equal opportunity and freedom of access to public places and spaces. The numbers of museum visitors among the tourist hordes started to mount in the 1950s and 1960s. Museums began to proliferate, and all sorts of new museum spaces were being created: museum villages such as Sturbridge and Plimouth Plantation and Jamestown Settlement and hybrids such as Disney Land and Disney World. Marketing techniques were everywhere introduced, and as National and State Parks and public gardens realized themselves as scenery and landscape museums, they adopted those techniques. Their ecosystems have, for the most part, been creditably maintained, but at the same time they have been promoted with considerable, if quiet, marketing panache. The experience of the visitor has been shifted: the emphasis is no longer on the visitor as participant, guided by the muse of landscape or wilderness who presided over that museum but on visitors as spectator-shoppers, consumers who come in search of a "product," who enter and leave through the museum or garden or park shop and are even followed home by the shop's catalogue after they have left.

The situation excites an ambivalent response. The experience of Yosemite or the Adirondacks or Cape Cod or Dumbarton Oaks or the National Arboretum on principle should be democratically available to all. But crowds oppress Yosemite; development threatens the Adirondacks and is suburbanizing the Cape; and while Dumbarton Oaks and the Arboretum seem well-attended but fairly calm, they could easily join the list of endangered landscapes. Within a few miles of my desk there are stretches of the Appalachian Trail so worn by overuse that the footpath fans out from one into many and turns into an eroding morass when it rains, and everywhere in the woods and on the slopes there is the trash of passage.

The demographics of access to the national heritage of wilderness, landscape and garden presents us with a "true dilemma," one that cannot be translated into a "problem" and "solved." To organize Yosemite for full access, for example, would be to destroy the experience for most visitors and to further threaten the already fragile ecology of that apparently rock-ribbed valley. The Grand Canyon is annually swamped by an estimated four million visitors a year. To limit access by lottery or high fees or some other form of rationing would alleviate the overcrowding but deny the experience to the population at large with no real attention to what the public and personal value of that experience ought to be.[16] And there are further questions: does it have to be this or that "special place"? Or can many of the large-scale special landscapes or wildernesses be decentralized, spread out and about? If, as Thoreau suggests, almost any corner of the natural world can offer a day's ration of "poetry," can we redefine "special place" in the interest of what he called "the preservation of the world"?

The pressures on the national heritage of landscape are not limited to the demographics of access which we can see and quantify. We can see and quantify what's happening to the understaffed state parks and forests in Massachusetts; they are being turned into unpoliced land fills, dumping sites for old cars and appliances and tires and asbestos and other forms of waste.[17] We can imagine the trasher's attitude toward landscape though we rarely see it and are wise, when we do, not to object. Nor can we see and irrefutably quantify the acid rain from the coal-fired power plants of the midwest that threatens the forests and lakes of the northeast. In season, smog from the Los Angeles basin makes it impossible to see from one rim to the other of the Grand Canyon. A polluted water supply threatens to turn the Everglades into Neverglades.

There are other discontinuities between the beholding eye and the landscape besides the demographics of tourism and pollution. One discontinuity is embodied in the beholder as conquistador, out to combat and conquer the natural world. The nineteenth century invented and popularized sport as a form of contest with the natural world as adversary – big game hunting and mountain climbing came into vogue, but in retrospect the white hunter's safari and the conquest of the high Alps (1854–65) seems a period of child's play compared to the conquest-preoccupations of this century. There are the obvious high conquests: the North Face of the Eiger in midwinter, Everest without oxygen, the ocean depths, the moon; and there are the everyday instruments of conquest that are all around us: trail-bikes, all-terrain vehicles, beach buggies, outboard motors, jet skis, scuba equipment, snowmobiles (and the trail groomers that clear the trails for them), and ski slopes complete with lifts and snow-making machinery. All these suggest some order of conquest and control of the natural world and modify what it means to be in-touch-with the landscape.

For all of us there is the automobile, which, at speed, profoundly alters the perceptual relation between foreground, middleground, and background; the foreground, a blur; the middle ground, a fleeting glimpse; the background, relatively stable. We school our eyes not to see all three at once (or we get car sick). Many highways thread worlds of trashscape; others are called parkways and designed with some attention to the "circuits" they describe through the landscape, to "prospects" and how they unfold, and fitted with turnouts, "stations" where the traveller could pause for the view. But contemporary highway designers frown on these turnouts as danger points, and many on highways in the northeast are being closed off, locking the traveller in his glass and steel cocoon, urging the eye forward at a steady speed. Few of our so-called "parkways" are what Olmsted and Vaux originally proposed, "parks" more than "ways," ribbons of park that interconnected other parks. In our time the "way" has clearly taken precedence over the "park."

When we arrive at some way station or oasis in the natural world, we are greeted by other discontinuities: commercial developments that crowd in wherever tourists and vacationers converge, concentrations that seem designed to tell us that our attention span in the quietude of landscape or wilderness would be incredibly short, that the mountains or the woods or the river or the lake or the shore cannot be allowed to speak for themselves, but have to be amplified and jacked up by theme parks, amusement galleries, sports facilities, and shopping "opportunities." We can resist those challenges to contemplative experience, but season by season they are becoming harder to avoid.

And the future stands ready to crowd us further. A California company is in the process of constructing complexes of motel, parking lot and special movie theatre near the entrances of several national parks and monuments – in Tusayan, Arizona, for example, near the Grand Canyon National Park which is too rugged for access by many people; and elsewhere – one is proposed for Zion National Park at Springdale, Utah. The film technology the company uses is called Imax, a screen seventy feet wide and fifty feet high, almost a wrap-around that gives the viewer the sense of being in the midst of the scene, in the rush of white water on the Colorado, in the helicopter threading in and out of canyons to surprise us with moments of dramatic prospects. The company explains its motives:

About 80 percent of the visitors at national parks have no opportunity to run the rivers or hike the canyons or camp in a wilderness area...
And [another] part of our motive is to alleviate pressure on the parks themselves by creating an experience that precludes an undue number of people from trampling all over the wildflowers.[18]

All serene. The democratic ideal of access for all is fulfilled; fragile ecosystems are preserved (at six dollars a head). But the gulf between human percipient and landscape yawns; the tactility of wind-air-sun on skin, sight on eye, sound on ear, the kinesthetic melody of the body in motion are all gone. Just outside the park gate, we will be out of the air-conditioned automobile or tour bus into the air-conditioned theatre; once in, we could just as readily be in the Smithsonian in Washington or the American Museum of Natural History in New York as at the Grand Canyon. I first saw the Grand Canyon film at the Museum of Natural History. It is fascinating and exciting as film, exhilarating, really, but film is not landscape. A video-tape tour of

Central Park in Manhattan or of Prospect Park in Brooklyn is not the humanizing experience of roaming and exploring the quietude and gentle mysteries designed to stimulate perception that Olmsted and Vaux had in mind. If it were, we could pave over all that acreage in a splendid burst of real estate feeding frenzy.

Most urban centers in this country are starved for park space, not in the quantitative sense of the percentage relation between park acreage and city acreage but in the qualitative sense of access-to, in-touch-with. Recent studies of urban behavior suggest that the radius of a city-dweller's resort to public space (to landscape) is the three to five minute walk. These studies would suggest a scatter of parks and parkways throughout the city instead of a few big parks. Not that the big "rural" parks like Manhattan's Central Park aren't splendid, but for the average city resident such parks are an expedition away. And urban sprawl plus a surround of expressways with no provision for pedestrians blur the edge between cityscape and countryside, another expedition away.

In the essay "Experience" Emerson complains that, no matter how hard we try to extend our reach, our "souls never touch their objects," and we seem involved in a vast national conspiracy to make sure that "contact" with landscape (to use Emerson's word) never takes place.

Wherever we look, discontinuity and severance are being urged on us, on our bodies by the air-conditioned containers of our homes and cars and work places and public places; on our ears by electronic and mechanical sound though I can have Mozart instead of traffic noise on my morning walk and instead of wind and wave if that walk happens to be on a beach. And separation is urged upon our eyes by the camera lens, the photo-frame, and the glance-and-move-on way we have learned to read photographs on a page and have carried over to the way we read paintings on a gallery wall and the way we read the passing landscape. And the camera offers another insidious possibility: I'll snap a picture of it now and really look at it later.[19] With the advent of the readily portable video camera, further changes in the way we habitually perceive the surround are in the offing. Faced with an interesting landscape, video cameras I have observed all seem to behave in much the same way: a wide angle shot to frame the whole, a zoom in to pan from detail to detail and then the move to another landscape at a different site. The video camera eye is in motion from a single station in contrast to the still photographer's tendency to move from station to station, angle to angle within a given landscape.

Coda: but for all these distractions and discontinuities, this want of contact, there have been positive signs in the last three decades, notably the twin explosions of public interest in art museums and in the practice of gardening. Those interests have, of course, been packaged and promoted by marketing specialists, but the eclectic vigor with which both are being pursued all around us can be accepted as evidence of a residual "hunger" for the in-touch-with that has been an important (if frequently interrupted) strand of our evolving traditions of landscape.

Notes

1 Quoted in *The Genius of the Place*, eds. John Dixon Hunt and Peter Willis (New York: Harper and Row, 1975) p. 333 from Jefferson's manuscript notes of the tour now in the Swem Library of the College of William and Mary.
2 *The Maine Woods* (Boston, 1864), p. 64.
3 *Moby-Dick* (New York, 1851), ch. 41.
4 *Go Down Moses* (New York: Random House, 1942), pp. 329, 330.
5 See Sumner Chilton Powell, *Puritan Village: The Formation of a New England Town* (Middletown, CT: Wesleyan University Press, 1963).
6 (Baltimore, 1823), p. ix.
7 "Rural Architecture" in *Rural Essays* ed. George William Curtis (New York, 1853).
8 Laura Wood Roper, *FLO: A Biography of Frederick Law Olmsted* (Baltimore: Johns Hopkins University Press, 1973) p. ix.
9 *Ibid.*, p. xxi.
10 *Ibid.*, p. 268.
11 *Ibid.*, p. 93.
12 *Ibid.*, p. 69.
13 (1852; reprinted, New York, 1929) p. 476.
14 Emerson, *Nature* (Boston, 1836).
15 In an "address of considerable length," delivered at Thoreau's funeral service, May 9, 1862.
16 The British have sought to control access to the Lake District by severely limiting public parking and by rigorously enforcing laws against illegal parking. Net result: access is limited to those who can afford reservations in lodging places (and who are lucky enough to get them), and to those vigorous enough to come on foot or bicycle (but there are severe restrictions on camping out).
17 *Associated Press*, Boston, reprinted *The North Adams Transcript* (North Adams, MA, May 20, 1991), p. 9.
18 *New York Times News Service*, reprinted *The Berkshire Eagle* (Pittsfield, MA, February 18, 1991) p. A:3.

19 The dilemma of the photographer's eye is beautifully put in Frank Gohlke's *Landscapes from the Middle of the World, Photographs 1972–1987*:

> If I had to choose between having the photographs but no memory of having made them, or enjoying the process without being able to see the photographs, which would it be? The question may go to the heart of the matter, but the answers all seem to lead me away. It began to feel like trying to land a fifty-pound fish on a two-pound line, and at that point wisdom would suggest silence.

7

Desert and ice: ambivalent aesthetics

YI-FU TUAN

The water-scarce (desert) and frigid (ice) regions are among the earth's harshest environments. A glance at any world-population map shows that these are the "empty quarters" which for long have successfully resisted the human imprint. Attitudes to these environments by people who have settled in the more accommodating, kindly parts of the earth have been complex and deeply ambivalent: we find instances of indifference and deliberate neglect, or, at the other extreme, keen interest as potential economic resource and base of political power; we find desert and ice viewed as threatening presences to be conquered in the name of national pride and manhood, or as challenge to the prowess of science; and last, though certainly not least, we find worshipful admiration tinged by fear. It is this last attitude that I should like to explore. To do so, I need a point of departure and conceptual frame. Home is the point of departure for real as well as figurative explorations. I will therefore start with the concept of home.

Love of home is universal, whether this be rain forest, dry boundless plain, or tundra. How is it possible for humans to differ so greatly in the environment they prefer? Although the larger environments differ strikingly in character, the places where people actually spend most of their time, sleep, and eat can have much in common. Home is not a simple entity. It is best seen as a succession of concentric circles, at the center of which is home narrowly defined, or homeplace. This homeplace at the center, wherever it occurs, has two primary physical traits: enclosure and multisensory texture. Homeplace is everywhere a protected – at least partly enclosed – space: that is to say the tent and corral of the nomad and the igloo of the Eskimo. Homeplace is also a variegated world of shapes and colors, sounds and odors, even in the desert. Its appeal – its aesthetic appeal –

139

derives from this complex mix of sensory stimuli. Beyond the homeplace thus understood are broadening, increasingly abstract, rings of "home space." In the measure that their value as shelter declines, their appeal is directed more and more to the eye. The physical characters of the larger homes, or home *spaces*, can differ greatly from each other. At the scale of home space, the environments of the desert nomad and the rain-forest hunter have little in common. Beyond home space is alien space, which is normally perceived as threatening. Few societies in the world (and these are usually materially advanced and self-confident) and few individuals in any society are drawn to it.

Homeplace, which nurtures biological life, commands the strongest attachment and loyalty. The word love is natural to homeplace. So many things in it give passing aesthetic pleasure – a shining copper pot, a handsome rug, cool shadows – that one is hardly aware of them individually; nothing stands out in perception and as experience, but together they engender a diffuse sense of well-being. By contrast, home space commands appreciation at a more conscious level. When describing home space that stretches beyond one's immediate circumambient world, the use of an aesthetic vocabulary, including the key word "beauty" or "beautiful," seems appropriate. As for alien space, it can be life-negating in severity and yet inspiring – overpoweringly beautiful or sublime. Desert and ice have provided Western man with experiences of beauty and, on rare occasions, a sense of the sublime that overcomes the distinction between self and other.

WHAT DESERT? WHAT ICE?

Although both desert and ice have resisted permanent human habitation, they differ in the degree of resistance. No matter how vast and desolate, deserts reveal human traces: oases support permanent or temporary settlements and even the bleakest hamadas have been crossed – at one time or another – by trade caravans. In contrast, the great ice floes and plateaus have repelled all human imprint until modern times.

Western civilization began on the margins of the greatest desert in the world. Yet, the ancient Greeks and the European savants influenced by them have persistently sought, throughout the West's long history, to deny the desert's overpowering and hostile presence. Such a presence posed a threat to fundamental human needs and desires –

the need for water and food, the need for control, and the desire for a harmonious and well-designed earth. The Greeks were curious about foreign places and peoples, but they paid remarkably little attention to the arid belt at their doorstep. Under (in part) the influence of Homer, they tended to see Libya – one of the three fundamental units of the earth – as fertile.[1] From Herodotus to Strabo, geographers repeatedly underestimated the size of Africa, and thereby the size of its great desert. The Greek conception of climatic zones, which has powerfully affected Western thought, was based on temperature, not on precipitation; and until the mid-twentieth century, whether places were hot or cold received far greater scientific attention than whether places were dry or wet.[2] In the centuries when nature was viewed through Christian lenses, there was reluctance to recognize the existence of large deserts because they seemed incompatible with the wisdom of God. A theory of the hydrologic cycle found favor because it supported the idea of a well-designed, providential earth. Even in the late eighteenth century, a scientist of the stature of James Hutton would admit to only two dry areas on the earth's surface, "Lower Egypt and a narrow spot upon the coast of Peru."[3] Empirical evidence on the extent of deserts, gathered over the centuries by traders, missionaries, and explorers who crossed them, was overlooked in the interest of maintaining a reassuring physico-theological theory of the earth.[4]

Natural theologians and philosophers in the Old World were not alone in their cavalier disregard of evidence. Explorers and early settlers of dry lands in North America and Australia also showed a disposition to ignore what they found inconvenient or undesirable. True, in North America the myth of the Great American Desert emerged to capture for a time the imagination of certain Eastern writers.[5] Nevertheless, most Americans in the latter part of the nineteenth century were inclined to see a potential for agricultural wealth far beyond the hundredth meridian; and if the aridity was too obvious to be denied, its effect on farming and human settlement was palliated by the widespread belief that "rain followed the plow," or that the planting of trees would induce rain.[6] Similar hopeful myths developed in the exploration and settlement of Australia. The existence of a forbidding dry core was denied for as long as possible. Rather than sterility and inaccessibility, Australian explorers and writers held on to the view that perhaps a great river crossed the island continent, or a large body of water – an inland sea – occupied its center.[7]

141

How one sees and what one sees are affected by language, including the ordinary geographical terms in use. To English speakers, the word river evokes a distinctive image based largely on the European experience. Whenever an explorer of the great Australian outback encountered a body of moving water, he called it a river even though the Australian namesake bore at best only a rough resemblance to its European model: the one usually petered out in swamp and sand, the other flowed in ever greater volume to the sea. "River" was not the only geographical word that misled. Other common terms such as mountain, pasture, meadow, and wood also did not fit well with the Australian reality; all of them, however, evoked certain images of European provenance that were highly desirable. Sometimes an Australian explorer or settler might more or less deliberately engage in mild self-deception, that is, use words in the hope that reality would conform to them. Thus when a hopeful frontiersman applied the word "parkland" to an Australian scene, he saw deer rather than kangaroos; and the use of the expression "a gentleman's estate" could almost persuade him to see a mansion emerging from beyond the next hillock.[8]

In contrast to deserts, the great polar regions of the earth did not lend themselves to dreams of potential fertility or to the illusion of small size easily conquerable by man. From Greco-Roman to medieval times, most Europeans who gave the matter any thought conceived the region around the North Pole to be one vast, frozen, uninhabitable, and impenetrable waste. However, there were a few exceptions to this negative image, the most important of which was the myth of the Open Polar Sea, nurtured by the longing for a navigable passage across the roof of the world. Belief in it, once established in the minds of explorers eager for glory and the riches of Asia, proved remarkably tenacious. Suggested by an English merchant in 1527, it continued to be upheld until the last quarter of the nineteenth century, and this despite repeated blockages by ice as ships attempted to navigate the Northwest or Northeast Passage.[9] Another example of wishful geographical thinking was the idea that some kind of oasis or even, possibly, an unknown civilization lay in the midst of the frozen world. The idea of an oasis on the ice cap of Greenland was finally abandoned in 1883 when Nils Nordenskjold failed to find it after penetrating some seventy-five miles inland. Economic reward was a primary motive for polar exploration until modern times. The polar regions, which held no promise for agriculture, nevertheless might contain mineral wealth. Coal was eventually found in Antarctica, but the discovery came as a surprise: mineral wealth was not in itself a motivating force for exploration.

DESERT STERILITY

From the viewpoint of people who lived in a fertile oasis or in a city, the desert at their doorstep was laden with negative images of sterility, death, darkness, and evil. Zoroastrianism's moral dualism – the sharp division between followers of truth and followers of lie – derived from the husbandmen's experience of the vivid contrast between their ordered life of agricultural abundance and the violence and predation of migratory desert tribes.[10] In China, a recurrent theme in historical writing is the conflict between sedentary people and nomads, farm and pasture, and – from the Chinese viewpoint – culture and barbarism. Chinese poetry, where it touches the steppe and desert, is filled with a sense of desolation, wind-blown melancholy, and death.[11] In Hebraic-Christian thought, desert wilderness signifies the unsown; it is a howling wasteland, a realm of evil spirits beyond God's presence and even somewhat beyond his control. One explanation of the desert waste is that it was a consequence of God's curse: Adam's Fall brought with it the decay of the earth (Genesis 3:17). In Deuteronomy, Moses warned his people that if they did not heed the commandments of the Lord, "their heaven shall be brass, their earth shall be iron, and their rain shall be powder and dust (28:23)."[12] As late as 1849, Lieutenant J. H. Simpson resorted to this explanation. While crossing northwestern New Mexico he noted the sterile appearance of the land and the abandoned Indian ruins – a melancholic state that he attributed to God's curse. As God had turned "the water springs" of the East into dry ground, so he could also "in His sovereignty, not only have cursed, and for a similar cause, the country in question with the barrenness under which we see it languishing, but by this very means have scattered abroad its inhabitants."[13]

DESERT BEAUTY AND SUBLIMITY

From the earliest times recorded in the Bible, a harsh view of the desert existed simultaneously with its opposite. The opposing views tended to come at first from different sources; later, increasingly, they emerged from the same source: the prophet who recognized the repellent barrenness of the desert also saw it as the condition for spiritual uplift and exaltation, or he might see the desert itself as exhibiting an austere beauty. In the Old Testament, the Sinai wastes stood for death, disorder, and darkness, but also for God's transcendent power and redemptive love. The preexilic prophets, in particular, interpreted the forty years of wandering in the desert as a period when God was especially close to Israel. In the New Testament, Christ was sent into the wilderness to be tempted by Satan (Matthew 4:1), yet he also withdrew from men into a lonely spot so as to pray to his Father (Mark 1:35). Both the temptation and the transfiguration occurred on a high mountain (Matthew 17:1–3). Contradictory attitudes persisted into the early Christian era. From the second to the fourth century, hermits ventured into the Egyptian desert as spiritual athletes: they expected to strengthen their souls by doing battle with Satan in his own desolate realm. Evil spirits and wild beasts, Satan's minions, constantly tried their faith. Yet the hermits also saw themselves as living in Edens of innocence. The wild beasts served Satan, but they were also animals before the Fall who lived in peace under human dominion.[14]

"To me a town is a prison, and the desert loneliness a paradise." Jerome thus vigorously articulated an attitude that was fairly common in his time and later.[15] Prominent was the disillusionment with the worldliness of the world and even of Church institutions once these, following the conversion of Rome, began to imitate secular models and in time could hardly be distinguished from them. There was more than a touch of misanthropy among the desert hermits and the early Church Fathers who sought solitude for themselves or praised it. Human beings were a distraction and a temptation. Their presence destroyed the vast solitudes that enabled one to contemplate God – naked man to naked God – contemplation that lifted one up to "celestial ecstasies" (John Cassian).[16]

At the most general level, we see here a desire for simplicity, and with it, greater intensity. Multiple sensory experience of the kind that one has on the farm or in the city is all very well, but, to some temperaments, they are too diffuse, their impacts cancel each other out, they distract and comfort rather than lead to something overwhelming for which the soul or spirit yearns. In religious terms, this attitude might be taken as a yearning for God. A fairly common metaphor for both the soul and its God is the desert. "Be like a desert as far as self and the things of this world are concerned," preached Meister Eckhart. The soul moves from the multiplicity of the human world to the unity of the Holy Trinity, and then beyond even the Trinity, to the "barren Godhead," to the "desert of the Godhead."[17]

In modern times, from the eighteenth century onward, the religious motivation for seeking the desert has waned or disappeared. Misanthropy remains a reason, however, as also the desire for a crystalline and nonhuman place that challenges normal values, the desire for the secular equivalent of spiritual athleticism, transcendental experience, an impossible perfection, the sublime. The acerbic British writer Norman Douglas, at his first view of the sterile salt depression in Tunisia, expressed relief "at the idea that this little speck of the globe, at least, was irreclaimable for all time; never to be converted into arable land or even pasture, safe from the intrusion of the potato-planters or what not." Douglas noted a certain "charm," in that "picture of eternal, irremediable sterility."[18] The same romantic bias is evident in such well known adventurers and writers as Charles Doughty, T. E. Lawrence, and Wilfred Thesiger. When Thesiger was given the opportunity to traverse the Empty Quarter of Arabia, he rejoiced for he believed that "in those empty wastes I could find the peace that comes from solitude." But to his surprise and disappointment, he found that Bedouin camps and caravans were not only crowded but extremely noisy, as if by noise they could fill the void.[19] Lawrence of Arabia is perhaps the best known of the three Englishmen. In the *Seven Pillars of Wisdom*, a best-seller and minor classic, Lawrence's contempt for the body shows through clearly: "The body was too coarse to feel the utmost of our sorrows and of our joys. Therefore we abandoned it as rubbish..." Of the two poles, "death and life, or less finally, leisure and subsistence, we should shun subsistence (which was the stuff of life) in all save its faintest degree." Not for Lawrence "this jasmine, this violet, this rose;" rather he yearned to drink in, with his Arab friend, "the very sweetest scent of all...the effortless, empty, eddyless wind of the desert."[20]

In North America and Australia, the sweeping spaces of the dry interior have been elevated to mythic status. Frontier and outback have become national symbols of hardy responsible manhood, of individualism in America and camaraderie in Australia, of a clean and genuine way of life inspired by nature and the spirit of place, in contrast to the parochialism and communal stickiness, the unassimilated alien ways of the coastal cities. In both countries the love of the interior was fueled by misogyny, a distaste for the "softness" of culture, for commercialism, and, more generally, mankind in its swarming numbers.

145

G. Edward White has drawn our attention to the importance of Frederic Remington, Owen Wister, and Theodore Roosevelt in converting the West into a prime symbol of essential "Americanness." Biased and arrogant, disdainful of the clannish ways of the new immigrants who flocked to the cities, and vain of their own Anglo–American heritage, these craggy individuals nevertheless showed genuine sensitivity to the harsh grandeurs of the West: witness the panoramic paintings of Remington, Wister's fiction, and Roosevelt's journalism. In 1884, Roosevelt wrote: "Nowhere does a man feel more lonely than when riding over the far-reaching, seemingly never-ending plains; and after a man has lived a little while on or near them, their very vastness and loneliness and their melancholy monotony have a strong fascination for him." In summer, at the hottest times "all objects [on the dusty plains] that are not nearby seem to sway and waver." There are few signs of life, but "now and then the black shadow of a wheeling vulture falls on the sun-scorched ground." In winter, "when the days have dwindled to their shortest...then all the great northern plains are changed into an abode of iron desolation. Sometimes furious gales blow out of the north, driving before them the clouds of blinding snow-dust, wrapping the mantle of death round every being that faces their unshackled anger." Or, "not a breath of wind may stir; and then the still merciless, terrible cold that broods over the earth like the shadow of silent death seems even more dreadful in its gloomy rigor than is the lawless madness of the storms."[21] Note the messages of death; they never seem far from the minds of those who seek the transcendent and the sublime.

Australia's experience of its interior provides certain parallels with the American experience, as several modern scholars, outstandingly H. G. Allen and J. M. Powell, have noted.[22] One parallel is the conversion of the island-continent's bush or outback into a symbol of genuine Australianness and virtue. Tom Collins, author of the novel *Such Is Life* (1903), which has been called the most Australian of all literary works, put it thus: "It is not in our cities or townships, it is not in our agricultural or mining areas, that the Australian attains full consciousness of his own nationality; it is...here [the Riverina district of western New South Wales] as at the centre of the continent. To me the monotonous variety of this interminable scrub has a charm of its own..."[23] The myth of the interior flourished in the late nineteenth century and persisted into the first decade of the twentieth. As in the United States, Australians have come to believe that their quintessential character was not formed in lush meadows or large cities, but in the heartland. Australia's heartland is the "wide brown" country of "beauty and terror" (in the words of the poet Dorothy Mackellar);[24] there, in trials endured alone or with a mate, purification could occur and a unique "Bush ethos" emerge. The beckoning of the interior might, however, have fatal consequences. Death was never far away. The balladist Barcroft Boake, a popular and fervent advocate of the great outback of Queensland and New South Wales, wrote the following grim lines:

> Where brown Summer and Death have mated—
> That's where the dead men lie!
> Loving with fiery lust unsated—
> That's where the dead men lie!
> Out where the grinning skulls bleach whitely
> Under the saltbush sparkling brightly;
> Out where the wild dogs chorus nightly—
> That's where the dead men lie![25]

WHY FARTHEST NORTH AND SOUTH?

Few subtropical and mid-latitude deserts are wholly barren. By contrast, the great ice floes and inland plateaus are implacably hostile to human life. They are the great empty spaces. Why would anyone want to go there? Histories of polar exploration and biographies of explorers show how mixed the motives can be. Before the eighteenth century, the chief driving force appears to have been economic. Explorers wanted to find a way to the land of the spices over the ceiling of the world. The myth of the Open Polar Sea made such attempts seem not unreasonable. However, by the end of the eighteenth century, the idea that a Polar passage of commercial value could exist had to be given up. From then on the most frequently proclaimed reason was science. Geography must be served. So long as there were places unrecorded by man, so long must scientists continue to risk their lives for the sake of gaining new knowledge. The rhetoric was not always convincing even to those who made it. Other forces were clearly at work, including the desire for adventure, to set a record, acquire sufficient income to be independent, test the limit of human endurance, know oneself uncozened by civilization, win glory for self and country. In the desire to plunge into an alien space that severely tested the body there was probably also an unrecognized desire for death.[26]

Yi-Fu Tuan

FRIDTJOF NANSEN (1861–1930)

Of all the polar explorers, the Norwegian Fridtjof Nansen and the American Richard E. Byrd are perhaps the most introspective and philosophical. They have left behind not only scientific observations and records of great adventure and superhuman endurance but also reflections on nature, cosmos, and the meaning of life. Both of them appear to believe that life is more likely to yield its deepest meaning surrounded by the inhuman silence, beauty, and terror of ice than in the quiet of one's study.

Nansen was an accomplished marine biologist, diplomat, and humanitarian. Yet without doubt his claim to lasting fame rests on his achievement as an explorer. Two expeditions were especially notable. The first, undertaken in 1888 with five companions, successfully crossed the ice plateau of Greenland. The second, far more ambitious in scale, was an attempt to reach the North Pole by drifting across the polar basin in his ship the *Fram*. When Nansen realized that the ice floes were not going to carry his ship all the way to the Pole, he abandoned it (March 14, 1895), and with only one companion, F. H. Johansen, sought to walk to their destination. They reached latitude 86° 14′ North, which was then the northernmost point attained by man, but had to give up going further because of the jagged, impassable condition of the ice. Their trip back to civilization was a saga in itself – stuntlike in its boldness: they walked south across the shifting ice, paddled in kayaks over open stretches of water and reached Franz Josef Land, where they wintered (1895–6), and where they were eventually picked up by members of a British team.[27]

Although Nansen failed to reach the North Pole, he won international acclaim for his imaginatively conceived and executed expedition, which must also be counted a success because no member of the team was lost (the *Fram* returned safely under the leadership of Otto Sverdrup) and because the expedition obtained voluminous scientific data on all aspects of Arctic geography and oceanography, including the single most important finding, namely, a frozen sea lay around the Pole and filled the polar basin. Nansen, trained as a zoologist and talented in research, could have led a fruitful and rewarding academic career. But this was not to be. One might even have predicted for him a path of adventure from his boyhood predilection for Viking stories and especially for the scenes and scenery evoked in accounts of English exploration. As a grown

148

man, Nansen was haunted by time and death; he was almost a mystic notwithstanding a natural competence and ease in worldly affairs. And for all his tangible scientific achievements, he must have wondered at times whether science was the real drive behind his expeditions. Nansen and his companions crossed Greenland's ice plateau on skis. To Nansen's annoyance, journalists tended to characterize the crossing as a daring feat or even, because of the use of skis, a sport.[28] He preferred to see it as justified by its results, which were a contribution to science and to humanity insofar as they had practical significance. Yet Nansen himself was not free of doubt. While he was drifting on an ice floe off the coast of Greenland in 1888, and it looked as though he was moving farther and farther away from his goal, "he dreamed that he had returned home after crossing the inland ice, but he was ashamed because he could tell nothing of what they had seen on the way across." Again on January 18, 1894, when the *Fram* was drifting towards the North Pole, he dreamed that he had returned to Norway after successfully completing his trip, but he also dreamed that he "had neglected to take exact observations, so that when people asked where he had been, he could not answer."[29]

THE EXPLORER'S SENTIMENT FOR HOME

Sentiment for home would seem incompatible with a temperament that yearns almost constantly for adventure and to be on the edge of the unknown. Yet this need not be so. Home is of course necessary to the adventurer as a secure base and point of departure; in psychological terms, moreover, its very existence as a world of familiarity and routine devoted to nurture and comfort appears to enhance in some individuals a desire for the alienness of inhospitable space. The sentiment for home is prominent in Nansen's writings. To the modern ear, accounts of home have a mawkish ring that contrasts rather sharply with the cool prose used elsewhere to describe the most extraordinary hardships. "For the last time I left my home and went alone down the garden to the beach, where the *Fram*'s little petroleum launch pitilessly awaited me. Behind me lay all I held dear in life. And what before me? How many years would pass ere I should see it all again? What would I not have given at that moment to be able to turn back; but up at the window little Liv was sitting clapping her hands..."[30] Hibernating with Johansen in their primitive hut on Franz Josef Land, Nansen thought of his wife and daughter at home. He wrote in his diary (December 19, 1895): "There she sits in the winter's evening, sewing by lamplight. Beside her stands a young girl with blue eyes and golden hair playing with a doll. She looks tenderly at the child and strokes her hair. Her eyes grow moist, and heavy tears fall on to her sewing...Here beside me lies Johansen asleep. He is smiling in his sleep. Poor boy, I expect he is at home spending Christmas with those he loves."[31]

Camp is a home-away-from-home, which can seem all the more homelike in the way it caters to and satisfies the body's demand for familiarity and comfort by contrast with the indifference or active hostility of ice-bound nature outside. Thus Nansen wrote of his domestic life on the Greenland plateau: "However hard the day had been, however exhausted we were, and however deadly the cold, all was forgotten as we sat round our cooker, gazing at the faint rays of light which shone from the lamp, and waiting patiently for our supper. Indeed I do not know how many hours in my life on which I look back with greater pleasure than these. And when the soup, or stew, or whatever the preparation might be, was cooked, when the rations were served round, and the little candle-stump lighted that we might see to eat, then rose our happiness to its zenith, and I am sure all agreed with me that life was more than worth living."[32]

Ernest Shackleton, the British explorer of Antarctica, shared Nansen's sentiment for home, though to those who were left behind it could seem baffling if not also a little hypocritical. The launch that awaited "pitilessly" to take Nansen to his ship was there in answer to his own desire and will: no external circumstance dictated his departure. Shackleton would seem to have labored under the same ambivalence or false consciousness. When he left in 1907 for his Antarctic exploration he wrote to his wife, expressing his regret as though he had been ordered by external authority to do so. "My darling wife, Your dear brave face is before me now and I can see you just as you stand on the wharf and are smiling at me my heart was too full to speak and I felt that I wanted just to come ashore and clasp you in my arms and love and care for you..."[33] With Shackleton, as with Nansen, a strong attachment could develop for their home-away-from-home. Leaving camp on October 29, 1908, for the track to the South Pole, Shackleton wrote: "As we left the hut where we had spent so many months in comfort, we had a feeling of real regret...It was dark inside, the acetylene was feeble in comparison with the sun outside, and it was small compared to an ordinary dwelling, yet we were sad at leaving it. Last night as we were sitting at dinner the evening sun entered through the ventilator and a circle of light shone on the picture of the Queen. . ."[34]

ARCTIC BEAUTY AND DEATH

Nansen was deeply responsive to the grander aspects of nature's beauty. This comes through in those passages of the journal where he describes the aurora. "However often we see this weird play of light, we never tire of gazing it; it seems to cast a spell over both sight and sense till it is impossible to tear one's self away." Norse mythology has enhanced the spell. "Is it the fire-giant Surt himself, striking his mighty silver harp, so that the strings tremble and sparkle in the glow of the flames of Muspellsheim?"[35] But perhaps even stronger evidence of Nansen's romantic temperament and love of nature occurs in those passages where he does not try to describe a beautiful scene but is simply noting an event, which is itself full of drama and unearthly beauty. Crossing the ice plateau of Greenland by sail and under moonlight is an example. Nansen notes: "It was rapidly getting dark, but the full moon was now rising, and she gave us light enough to see and avoid the worst crevasses. It was a curious sight for me to see the two vessels coming rushing along behind me, with their square viking-like sails showing dark against the white snowfield and the big round disc of the moon behind."[36]

Nansen at one time called himself an atheist; later this was moderated into agnostic. He did not believe in the existence of God, nor in afterlife. If life had a purpose it was to use one's faculties and exploit one's opportunities for the benefit of future generations. This noble sentiment was predictably translated into effective humanitarian action. Outwardly successful in every way, Nansen nevertheless suffered from depression in those periods when he was unharnessed to the strenuous exercise of polar expedition; and even in his own world of Arctic ice, where he saw beauty and splendor he almost always saw death. It is striking how often he coupled ice with death. The first sentence of his two-volume work *Farthest North* reads: "Unseen and untrodden under their spotless mantle of ice the rigid polar regions slept the profound sleep of death from the earliest dawn of time."[37] The polar region was, for Nansen, the "kingdom" or "realm" of death. Time itself seems frozen. "Years come and go unnoticed in this world of ice. . .In this silent nature no events ever happen. . .There is nothing in view save the twinkling stars, immeasurably far away in the freezing night, and the flickering sheen of the

aurora borealis. I can just discern close by the vague outline of the
Fram, dimly standing out in the desolate gloom...Like an infinitesi-
mal speck, the vessel seems lost amidst the boundless expanse of this
realm of death."[38] On Franz Josef Land where Nansen wintered in
boredom and discomfort, his morbid thoughts are reflected in images
of whiteness, coldness, marble, and silence. His journal entry for
December 1, 1895, reads: "A weird beauty, without feeling, as though
of a dead planet, built of shining white marble. Just so must the
mountains stand there, frozen and icy cold; just so must the lakes lie
congealed beneath their snowy covering; and now as ever the moon
sails silently and slowly on her endless course through lifeless space.
And everything so still, so awfully still, with the silence that shall one
day reign when the earth again becomes desolate and empty..."[39]

RICHARD E. BYRD (1888–1957)

The year Richard Byrd was born was the year Fridtjof Nansen sailed
across the inland ice of Greenland. The American and the Norwegian
are thus a generation apart: the one rose to be an admiral, the other an
ambassador and a statesman. Both were successful men of the world
as well as great polar explorers. What distinguished them from their
peers in their own time and in the past was a characteristically
modern desire to make their voyages into the geographical unknown
also voyages of self-discovery. Both wrote books, but Byrd wrote the
book entitled *Alone*, which has the timelessness of literature. It is a
record of his four-and-a-half months spent alone (in 1934) on the Ross
Shelf Ice of Antarctica. Why was he there? What were the reasons for
wintering at latitude 80° 08′ South? There were good scientific
reasons for the mission. The one that really mattered to him was,
however, personal – the extraordinary experience itself. He wanted
"to be by himself for a while and to taste peace and quiet and solitude
to find out how good they really are."[40] Physical desolation at the
Advance Base was absolute: "In whatever direction I looked, north,
east, south, or west, the vista was the same, a spread of ice fanning to
meet the horizon. The shack itself faced west for no particular
reason..."[41] Harrowing experiences occurred. But the worst was an
attack of despair that followed a period of sickness. Self-doubt
assailed him. "I had gone there looking for peace and enlightenment...[and] I had also gone armed with the justification of a
scientific mission. Now I saw both for what they really were: the first
as a delusion, the second as a dead-end street." His thoughts drifted

to his family and he was led to conclude that, "At the end only two things really matter to a man, regardless of who he is; and they are the affection and understanding of his family. Anything and everything else he creates are insubstantial; they are ships given over to the mercy of the winds and tides of prejudice. But the family is an everlasting anchorage, a quiet harbor where a man's ship can be left to swing to the moorings of pride and loyalty."[42]

I have noted that Nansen's thoughts in the Arctic drifted periodically to death, not in moments of despair or danger but rather in moments when he could pause and confront the ice-bound world's dominion. Byrd was more sanguine. Only rarely did his prose carry a funereal tone. Describing icebergs enveloped in fog was one such occasion: "Everywhere those stricken fleets of ice, bigger by far than all the navies in the world, [wandered] hopelessly through a smoking gloom." Another was a commentary on the disappearing of the sun at Advance Base. "Even at midday the sun is only several times its diameter above the horizon. It is cold and dull. At its brightest it scarcely gives light enough to throw a shadow. A funereal gloom hangs in the twilight sky. This is the period between life and death. This is the way the world will look to the last man when it dies."[43]

For Nansen, polar beauty did not necessarily console; for Byrd, by contrast, it was the portal to a sense of oneness with the cosmos. Repeatedly in Byrd's diary, the message of peace and harmony came through. "The day was dying, the night being born – but with great peace. Here were the imponderable processes and forces of the cosmos, harmonious and soundless. Harmony, that was it! That was what came out of the silence – a gentle rhythm, the strain of a perfect chord, the music of the spheres, perhaps. It was enough to catch that rhythm, momentarily to be myself a part of it. In that instant I could feel no doubt of man's oneness with the universe."[44] An unexpected and rather touching demonstration of this feeling of oneness occurred at midnight on May 11. Byrd was playing a recording of Beethoven's Fifth Symphony. "The night was calm and clear. I left the door to my shack open and also my trapdoor. I stood there in the darkness to look around at some of my favorite constellations...Presently I began to have the illusion that what I was seeing was also what I was hearing, so perfectly did the music seem to blend with what was happening in the sky. As the notes swelled, the dull aurora on the horizon pulsed and quickened and draped itself into arches and fanning beams which reached across the sky until at my zenith the display attained its crescendo. The music and the night became one; and I told myself that all beauty was akin and sprang from the same substance. I recalled a gallant, unselfish act that was of the same essence as the music and the aurora."[45]

EPILOGUE

Historically, Western man's response to the extreme environments of desert and ice has much in common as well as significant differences. The desert is a less hostile environment. Human penetration of it has had a longer history. The concentric zones of home and home space are more clearly in evidence in the desert than on ice, where indeed they may be compressed to sharply defined and juxtaposed opposites – homeplace is the hut and immediately beyond is alien space, an expanse of whiteness reaching out in all directions to seemingly nowhere. Historically, also, with the exception of a few monks who by 795 A.D. might have reached as far north as Iceland in search of solitude, the deliberate attempt to penetrate the polar regions is a phenomenon of the modern period. In expressing appreciation for ice-bound wastes, the theological language so prominent among the desert hermits is naturally absent; in its place are secular equivalents such as Nansen's sense of a sublime "otherness" (the otherness of ice as distinct from the otherness of Godhead) and Byrd's feeling for cosmic oneness.

If we confine ourselves to the modern period, other differences and similarities occur. One is the justification of science, which is more prominent in polar than in desert exploration. Perhaps the difference is simply one of physical versus human science. From the eighteenth century onward, Europeans have shown an interest in human science, that is, in Egypt and the Near East for their archaeological remains and ancient history, as well as for the exotic customs of contemporary peoples. Dry lands contain vast stretches of desolation, yet in their midst are islands richly endowed with culture and history. This brings us to another important difference. Desert explorers go forth alone: one thinks of such essentially self-sufficient and self-absorbed figures as Doughty, Lawrence, and Thesiger. They have "disowned" not only a landscape but their own people and culture. For them, home is not a fount of sentiment; patriotism and the flag are not a source of inspiration. In sharp contrast, polar explorers venture forth as close-knit teams with the strong moral if not financial support of their nations. True, Byrd was "alone," but only in the strict physical sense; throughout his sojourn at Advance

154

Base he maintained regular contact by radio with his team at Little America. And we have noted the polar explorers' sentimental attachment to home. Existentially they do not feel "at home" at home, but ideologically they do: while almost constantly tempted by the frozen world they remain proud of their native place, nation, and culture.

As for the similarities in attitude toward the two extreme environments, they clearly exist and are the reasons for this comparative study. I should like to end by focusing on one such shared attitude. It is the longing to be taken out of oneself and one's habitual world into something vast, overpowering, and indifferent. If home in the narrow sense absorbs the self in its diffuse multiple sensory impressions, and if home space provides the kind of psychological distancing that makes aesthetic appreciation possible, then alien space once again offers unity but this time by overwhelming the individual. Confronted by the immensity and power of desert and ice, one cannot simply stand to the side and evaluate as though one were standing before a landscape garden and other works of art. Conflicting emotions, including fear, are aroused and simultaneously absorbed or taken over by the overmastering presence of nature. Whereas absorption into the sensory realities of home means life, the loss of self in alien space – even if it provides moments of ecstasy – means death. Explorers of desert and ice may be said to be half in love with piercing beauty and half in love with death.

Notes

1 Homer, *Odyssey* IV.
2 E. H. Bunbury, *A History of Ancient Geography among the Greeks and Romans* (2nd ed., New York: Dover, 1959) vol. 2; John Leighly, "Dry Climates: Their Nature and Distribution," *Desert Research*, Proceedings International Symposium, Research Council of Israel, special publication no. 2 (Jerusalem: 1953).
3 James Hutton, "The Theory of Earth," *Royal Society of Edinburgh*, vol. 1, part 2 (1788), p. 62.
4 Yi-Fu Tuan, *The Hydrological Cycle and the Wisdom of God* (University of Toronto Press, 1968).
5 Ralph C. Morris, "The Notion of a Great American Desert East of the Rockies," *Mississippi Valley Historical Review*, vol. 13, 1926, pp. 190–200; Martyn J. Bowden, "The Perception of the Western Interior of the United States, 1800–1870: A Problem of Historical Geosophy," *Proceedings*, Association of American Geographers, 1 (1969): 16–21.
6 Henry Nash Smith, "Rain Follows the Plow: The Notion of Increased

Rainfall for the Great Plains, 1844–1880," *Huntington Library Quarterly*, 10 (1947): 169–93.

7 J. H. L. Cumpston, *The Inland Sea and the Great River: The Story of Australian Exploration* (Sydney: Angus and Robertson, 1964).

8 Paul Carter, *The Road to Botany Bay: An Exploration of Landscape and History* (New York: Knopf, 1988), pp. 106–35.

9 John K. Wright, "The Open Polar Sea," *Geographical Review*, vol. 43 (1953): pp. 338–65.

10 R. C. Zaehner, *The Dawn and Twilight of Zoroastrianism* (New York: Putnam's, 1961), pp. 36–40.

11 See, for instance, the popular anthology *Three Hundred Poems of T'ang China* (618–906 A.D.), (Hong Kong: Yih Mei Book Company).

12 George H. Williams, *Wilderness and Paradise in Christian Thought* (New York: Harper and Brothers, 1962), pp. 11–18.

13 J. H. Simpson, *Journal of a Military Reconnaissance from Santa Fe, New Mexico, to the Navajo Country* (Philadelphia: Lippincott, 1852), p. 32.

14 W. H. Mackean, *Christian Monasticism in Egypt* (London: SPCK, 1920), pp. 135–7.

15 Robert Payne, *Jerome: The Hermit* (New York: Viking, 1951), p. 99.

16 Cassian, Conferences 9 and 19, trans. C. S. Gibson, in *Nicene and Post-Nicene Fathers* (2nd series; New York: 1984), vol. 11.

17 R. B. Blakney, *Meister Eckhart: A Modern Translation* (New York: Harper Torchbooks, 1941), pp. 200–1.

18 Norman Douglas, *Experiments* (New York: McBride and Co., 1925), pp. 19–20; *Fountains in the Sand* (London: Secker, 1925), p. 183.

19 Richard Trench, *Arabian Travellers: The European Discovery of Arabia* (Topsfield, MA: Salem House, 1986), p. 213.

20 T. E. Lawrence, *Seven Pillars of Wisdom* (New York: Doubleday, Doran and Co., 1935), p. 40.

21 G. Edward White, *The Eastern Establishment and the Western Experience: The West of Frederic Remington, Theodore Roosevelt, and Owen Wister* (New Haven: Yale University Press, 1968), pp. 80–1.

22 H. C. Allen, *Bush and Backwoods: A Comparison of the Frontier in Australia and the United States* (East Lansing: Michigan State University Press, 1959); J. M. Powell, "Images of Australia, 1788–1914," *Monash Publications in Geography* no. 3 (1972).

23 Tom Collins, *Such Is Life* (First published in 1903; Sydney: Angus and Robertson, 1962), p. 80–1.

24 Brian Elliott, *The Landscape of Australian Poetry* (Melbourne: Cheshire, 1967), p. 23.

25 Quoted in Powell, "Images," p. 10.

26 L. P. Kirwan, *A History of Polar Exploration* (Harmondsworth: Penguin, 1962); Chauncy C. Loomis, "The Arctic Sublime," in U. C. Knoepflmacher and G. B. Tennyson, eds., *Nature and the Victorian Imagination* (Berkeley: University of California Press, 1977), pp. 95–112.

27 Edward Shackleton, *Nansen the Explorer* (London: Witherby, 1959).

28 L. Nansen Hoyer, *Nansen a Family Portrait* (London: Longmans, 1957), pp. 48–9.
29 Hoyer, *Nansen*, p. 79.
30 Fridtjof Nansen, *Farthest North: Being the Record of a Voyage of Exploration of the Ship "Fram" 1893–96* (New York: Harper and Brothers, 1897), vol. 1, p. 81.
31 Nansen, *Farthest North*, vol. 2, p. 446.
32 Fridtjof Nansen, *The First Crossing of Greenland* (London: Longmans, 1892), p. 297.
33 Christopher Ralling, *Shackleton: His Antarctic Writings* (London: British Broadcasting Corporation, 1983), p. 29.
34 *Ibid.*, p. 79.
35 Nansen, *Farthest North*, vol. 2, pp. 446–7.
36 Nansen, *First Crossing*, p. 313.
37 Nansen, *Farthest North*, vol. 1, p. 1.
38 Nansen, *Farthest North*, vol. 2, p. 41.
39 *Ibid.*, p. 440.
40 Richard E. Byrd, *Alone* (First published in 1938; Los Angeles: Tarcher, n.d.), pp. 3–4.
41 Richard E. Byrd, *Discovery* (New York: Putnam's, 1935), p. 167.
42 Byrd, *Alone*, pp. 178–9.
43 *Ibid.*, pp. 25, 73–4.
44 *Ibid.*, p. 85.
45 *Ibid.*, pp. 138–9.

8

Gardens, earthworks, and environmental art

STEPHANIE ROSS

1. INTRODUCTION

Gardening was a fine art in eighteenth-century England, a full-fledged sister to painting and poetry. Landowners devoted great effort and expense to improving their estates, treatises on garden aesthetics abounded, and certain artists developed distinctive and recognizable gardening styles. Since that time, gardening has declined. Although a vast majority of Americans named gardening their favorite *hobby* in a recent Gallup survey,[1] gardening is no longer considered a fine art. Major artists do not make statements in this medium, and our sense of gardening's kinship to painting and poetry has been lost.

Though gardening has declined, high art has not retreated from the landscape. A variety of art flourishes today in sculpture gardens, artparks, and more remote locations. In his introduction to an anthology aptly titled *Art in the Land*, Alan Sonfist writes of a new group of artists "whose work makes a statement about man's relation to nature." These artists often use natural substances (earth, rocks, and plants) in their work and often construct that work outside on natural sites.[2] My concern is the relation between these recent environmental works and the eighteenth-century landscape garden.

One author in Sonfist's anthology, Michael McDonough, claims that "The true *avant garde* of architecture, the adventurous, risk-taking, experimenting, problem-seeking, redefining fringe, is not in architecture. It is in the jetties, towers, tunnels, walls, rooms, bridges, ramps, mounds, ziggurats, the buildings and landscapes, structures and constructions of environmental art."[3] In this paper, I shall challenge the genealogy McDonough has proposed. I shall argue that gardening is the true ancestor of the varied features McDonough cites, that environmental art is *gardening's avant-garde*. In tracing the

affinities between eighteenth-century gardens and present-day earthworks and environmental art, I shall also explore some more general
aesthetic issues – the threat of fraudulence, the tracing of lineage, and
the death of art.

I shall begin by describing gardens in general and documenting the
surprising symbolic powers of eighteenth-century English gardens.
Next, I shall imagine an alternative future for gardening, a fictive
scenario in which gardening persists into the twentieth century as a
high art and takes part in the ferment of modernism. Turning next to
environmental art, I shall survey some of the great variety of work
being done in this field and suggest a tentative typology. Then,
looking backwards, I shall try to establish connections between
present-day environmental art and the great gardens of the past.

2. GARDENS AND/AS ART

Gardens are so various that they defy simple definition. Consider
some possibilities. Gardens can be large or small, unbounded or
enclosed, terraced or flat, natural or geometric, with flowers or
without. They can contain blossoms, trees, lawns, and shrubs, lakes,
canals, streams, and fountains, statues, rocks, walls, and benches,
temples, follies, ruins, and grottoes. Contrast an endless expanse of
Versailles with an intimate Moorish courtyard, an English landscape
garden with a suburban perennial bed, the hanging gardens of
Babylon (actually, terraced planted ziggurats[4]) with that limiting
case, a Japanese Zen garden consisting of nothing but rocks and raked
sand.

Not only do gardens differ in features and appearance; they also
differ in purpose. We associate gardens above all with sensory
delights – colors, shapes, sounds, smells, and textures, as well as the
general kinaesthetic pleasures of moving in and through a space. But
gardens can serve other needs. Historians today trace gardens to two
distinct prototypes, (1) sacred groves and Nymphaeum dedicated to
pagan deities, and (2) utilitarian kitchen and medicinal gardens.
Thus gardens can serve spiritual or practical ends, offer places for
retreat or arenas for activity, stoke pride, yield profit, or serve the
public good.

The vast variety exhibited by gardens across time and across
cultures does not prevent us from defining the term "garden." Recall
Wittgenstein's famous discussion of the word "game" in the *Philosophical Investigations*.[5] Wittgenstein argues that the items correctly

named by a general term are united not by a core of essential properties possessed by all, but by a looser relation which he calls family resemblance. Any two items resemble one another, but no set of necessary and sufficient conditions can be found which applies to every member of the set.

Wittgenstein's notion of family resemblance applies well to gardens. For if we include amongst our examples formal gardens, landscape gardens, vegetable gardens, water gardens, Zen gardens, and more, there is no feature or set of features that they share. Nevertheless, any group of gardens has traits in common. For example, French gardens are rectilinear and architectural, like Islamic gardens, and expansive, like English landscape gardens, while the latter are naturalistic, like Chinese gardens, and flowerless, like Egyptian gardens.

Consider now gardens' status as works of art. Wittgenstein's anti-essentialist doctrine applies to the term "art" as well as to the terms "garden" and "game." A quick perusal of any aesthetics text will show that there is no agreed upon definition of art in terms of necessary and sufficient conditions.[6] Accordingly, some philosophers have formulated theories of a quite different sort. They propose that an object's status as a work of art depends not on properties manifested by that object – those that can be read off directly from it – but on nonexhibited relational properties – for example the way we treat the object in question.[7]

Two such "contextual" theories are those of George Dickie and Arthur Danto. Dickie's theory, the Institutional Theory of Art, defines art as follows: "A work of art is (1) an artifact (2) a set of the aspects of which has had conferred upon it the status of candidate for appreciation by some person or persons acting on behalf of a certain social institution (the artworld)."[8] Dickie defines the artworld in terms of a bundle of systems (i.e. the various arts: poetry, painting, dance, music, theatre, and so on) and a core personnel ("artists, producers, museum directors, museum-goers, theatre-goers, reporters for newspapers, critics for publications of all sorts, art historians, art theorists, philosophers, and [ultimately] every person who sees himself as a member...").[9] Something is art if it is sponsored and presented in the appropriate way against the background of this pervasive institution.

The strength of Dickie's theory is its ability to explain much modern art. Since the theory allows for ordinary objects to change their status and become works of art, it accommodates ready-mades like Duchamp's *Fountain* and controversial acts and events like Vito

Acconci's installation *Seedbed* (in which the artist lay under a false gallery floor and masturbated in response to viewers' walking above him).

Applied to gardens, Dickie's theory affords important insights. Not all gardens are works of art. A backyard vegetable garden or a casual perennial plot might each be designed with care and each yield pleasures and delights. But Dickie denies them the status of art because they fail condition (2). They were not consciously created to enter into the world of art. Dickie's first condition, the artifactuality requirement, also prevents all of nature from sliding over into art.

One riddle remains when Dickie's theory is applied to the natural world. What is to prevent there from being "found gardens" akin to "found art"? That is, why can't an artist declare just any piece of land to be her new work, *Garden*, in precisely the manner that Duchamp elevated snowshovels, urinals, and other quotidian things? Taking the example even further, isn't the word "garden" every bit as elastic as the word "art"? If so, our artist needn't confine herself to pieces of land but can declare, say, whatever room she happens to occupy her *Garden, Opus 1*.

If Dickie's theory were this permissive, it would indeed be at fault. But there are constraints on what can be a work of art at any given time.[10] In *Art and its Objects*, Richard Wollheim speaks of "the essential historicity of art," and Arthur Danto remarks "Not everything is possible at every time, as Heinrich Wöfflin has written, meaning that certain artworks simply could not be inserted as artworks into certain periods of history."[11] While art evolves and our conceptions of art continually change, new works (and entire new *arts*) are introduced on the coattails of existing ones. The newly established art is seen and conceptualized in terms of one that is already entrenched. For example, early American quilts could not have been considered art in 1810, yet today we encounter them in galleries and note their striking similarity to hard-edged abstract paintings.

In the case of the room-as-garden example just discussed, it is important to determine the limits of this sort of vision. Can a given item be seen in terms of literally any other? Can just anything be seen as a poem, a painting, a play, a melody, a narrative, or a garden? Nelson Goodman has claimed that any two items chosen at random will have *some* property in common.[12] He doesn't promise, however, that it will be an interesting property. And there may simply be no nonquestion-begging way to single out salient characteristics, rele-

161

vant similarities, the limits of Wittgensteinian family resemblance. I don't think Dickie intends his theory to be so permissive that, in the artworld, literally anything goes. But a defense of this claim lies beyond the scope of this essay.[13]

Whether or not Dickie's Institutional Theory is sound, the work of Arthur Danto provides additional grounds for rejecting the extreme permissive view. In *The Transfiguration of the Commonplace*, Danto offers another "contextualist" theory of art.[14] He argues that artworks are objects that *say* something, that are about the world. It follows that such works require interpretation. Their *esse* is *interpretari*.[15]

To clarify his views Danto describes various pairs of indistinguishable objects where one is a work of art but its twin is not. Two such pairs are (1) a blue necktie which Picasso has mottled green and one similarly defaced by a fingerpainting three-year-old; and (2) a 5×8 foot monochromatic red canvas by a left-leaning abstract painter and an exactly similar sample of a paint company's brightest available red. Note that we can construct garden versions of such examples. Compare (1) a wildflower garden carefully cultivated by an ecological activist and a sunny glade deep in the woods which just happens to have an exactly similar array of plants; or, (2) a vast park landscaped by Capability Brown – central lake, smooth hills, clumps of trees – and a rolling cow pasture identical in layout and grazed until smooth.

Applying Danto's doppelganger example to gardens shows that some gardens are works of art. They were created intentionally, by garden designers, and they have the capacity not only to soothe and delight but also to represent, express, arouse, amuse. In the next section, I shall describe in more detail the powers of such gardens.

3. GARDENS AS HIGH ART IN EIGHTEENTH-CENTURY ENGLAND

Gardens had special significance in eighteenth-century England. This was so for a number of reasons. First of all, eighteenth-century English gardens had political implications. The French formal garden, relentless, geometric, and expansive, had come to be associated with the reign of Louis XIV. English gardeners sought a contrasting style, a more natural and irregular layout that would celebrate English tolerance and liberty in opposition to French autocracy.[16]

Second, in eighteenth-century England, the art of gardening was considered every bit as noble as the arts of painting and poetry. For example, in 1770 Horace Walpole declared "Poetry, Painting, and

Gardening, or the science of Landscape, will forever by men of taste be deemed Three Sisters, or the Three New Graces who Dress and adorn Nature,"[17] while Thomas Whately's book *Observations on Modern Gardening*, published in the same year, opened with the claim that "Gardening, in the perfection to which it has been lately brought in England, is entitled to a place of considerable rank among the liberal arts." The traditional comparison between the arts expressed in Horace's simile 'Ut pictura poesis" (as is painting, so is poetry) was expanded to include comparisons between gardens and poems, and between gardens and paintings. These new comparisons prompted cross-fertilization among these arts and a blurring of their boundaries. Eighteenth-century gardens were expected to perform the tasks of their sister arts, to offer messages visitors could "read" and scenes they could savor.

Finally, eighteenth-century garden history is significant because gardening styles changed dramatically in the course of the century. The emblematic garden characteristic of the early 1700s was complex and allusive. It gave way to the English landscape garden which was carefully cultivated to resemble untouched nature. This stylistic shift was symptomatic of a larger change in taste – a shift from neoclassical to romantic sensibility. The fact that garden history reflected these intellectual and artistic currents shows gardening to be an ideological enterprise.

All gardens carry with them certain associations. For example, in Western culture, gardens inevitably suggest paradise, the bounty and bliss of the Garden of Eden. These Christian connotations coexist with more primitive associations – sexuality and fertility, death and regeneration, the cycle of the seasons[18] – as well as with more recent overlays ranging from the tradition of courtly love to the awareness of ecological crisis. But eighteenth-century English gardens had meaning over and above these usual associations. Many eighteenth-century writers speak of "reading" a garden, and emblematic gardens of the time did indeed function as poems, satires, treatises, and manifestos. These gardens did not, in general, contain flowers. Instead an array of sculptural and architectural features – temples, statues, grottoes, fountains, obelisks, bridges, hermitages, and more – revealed themselves as visitors strolled through the grounds. These features carried the gardens' message, but often the topography and plantings were essential as well. Let me briefly describe some examples.[19]

Probably the most renowned of all English emblematic gardens is

Lord Cobham's estate Stowe, in Buckinghamshire. An area of the garden called the Elysian Fields, designed by William Kent in the 1730s, contained three temples: a temple of Ancient Virtue, a Temple of Modern Virtue, and a Temple of British Worthies. The meaning of this ensemble becomes clear when we note the following details. The Temple of Ancient Virtue is a round classical structure based on the Temple of Vesta at Tivoli. It contains four statues (Homer, Socrates, Lycurgus, and Epaminondas) representing the greatest poet, philosopher, lawgiver, and general of the ancient world. By contrast, the Temple of Modern Virtue was built in the Gothic style and was, moreover, built as a ruin. The third and final temple was located downhill from the others across a stream. The sixteen niches in this semicircular structure housed busts of British notables: poets, philosophers, scientists, monarchs, statesmen, and warriors.

Some of the meaning of this ensemble is easy to read. Modern virtue lies in ruins alongside its ancient exemplar. The British worthies are placed downhill and so look up to their ancient predecessors. But Kent and Cobham added further layers of subtlety to give the ensemble political and religious dimensions as well. John Dixon Hunt characterizes the overall message as "anti-Stuart, anti-Catholic, pro-British."[20] Two crucial omissions underscore this message. First, Queen Anne, from whose army Lord Cobham had been dismissed, is not included among the British Worthies. And second, an inscription from Virgil's *Aeneid* is edited to remove a line in praise of the priesthood. Hunt notes the severe demands Stowe's Elysian Fields places on its viewers. They must realize the significance of different styles of architecture, recognize the quotation from Virgil and note that it is incomplete, and take into account the topography of the overall ensemble.

Another renowned eighteenth-century garden is Henry Hoare's estate Stourhead, in Wiltshire. Stourhead was created later than Stowe and differs in style, straddling the gap between early emblematic gardens like the Elysian Fields and the later landscape gardens created by Capability Brown. Stourhead is laid out as a circuit. A walk descends from the house and circles a lake, passing by carefully sited temples, bridges, grottoes, and the like. Kenneth Woodbridge has argued that the iconography of the entire ensemble is drawn from Virgil's *Aeneid*.[21] In one of Aeneas' adventures, the Cumaean sibyl leads him into the underworld to reveal the future history of Rome. Woodbridge argues that the path around the lake at Stourhead symbolizes Aeneas' journey. The descent down towards the lake and the steep climb up from the grotto represent his encounter in the underworld. Various statues and inscriptions at Stourhead support this interpretation. Overall, Woodbridge sees the garden as an extended conceit comparing Henry Hoare's life to that of Aeneas: "Henry, in his garden, celebrated the founding of Rome, just as he, like Aeneas, was establishing a family in a place."[22]

My last example is that of a ribald garden, Sir Francis Dashwood's West Wycombe Park. Sir Francis not only founded the Society of Dilettanti; he was also a member of the Hell-Fire Club. Dark rumours persist about the activities of the club, talk of orgies and bacchanals in strange monk's garb. What is clear is that West Wycombe is, in parts, an erotic garden. The central lake and canals are dammed in the form of a swan, recalling Leda and her fate. The Temple of Venus sits on a bellylike mound above the erotically shaped subterranean Venus Parlor. Forty-two erotic statues originally adorned the mound, and a brightly colored column was erected nearby. One popular source reports that the *entire* garden was laid out in the form of a nude woman: that twin mounds topped with red flowers at one end faced a triangle of dense shrubbery at the other, and that two milky fountains and a spurt of gushing water could be released from these with the turn of a switch to further underline the joke.[23]

Each of the three gardens just described is representational in the broad sense of saying something, having a subject matter, and requiring an interpretation. Each functions somewhat like a poem. The second of Walpole's two comparisons, that linking gardening and painting, is more problematic. A garden can resemble a landscape painting; a garden can copy such a painting; a painting can be of a garden. But in none of these cases does a garden function just like a representational painting, for that would require the garden to be "of" (about) some other natural scene. The very awkwardness of the phrase "garden of" shows that we don't generally attribute this sort of symbolic power to gardens. Gardeners do, however, take into account such painterly concerns as color, texture, balance, form, perspective, and light and shade in laying out grounds.

Late in the eighteenth century, the cult of the picturesque introduced one last relation between gardening and painting. Connoisseurs like Sir Uvedale Price and Richard Payne Knight came increasingly to see the world *in terms of* pictures. Viewing natural scenes, they were reminded of particular paintings. These associations heightened their viewing pleasure. In addition, Price and Knight prized just those natural features suitable for or typical of painting.

Both men developed full-blown theories of the picturesque,[24] and both advocated a picturesque style in gardening as opposed to the bland creations of Capability Brown. Some gardens which met their requirements – for example, those of Humphrey Repton – were thus ideological works which exemplified and endorsed an aesthetic theory.

4. GARDENING'S DECLINE AND AN IMAGINED REVERSAL

I have tried to indicate the range and power of eighteenth-century gardens. I have also tried to show that the era's lavish comparisons between gardening and her sister arts were not empty. If my claims are correct, then why has gardening declined? Some philosophers defend a Hegelian view according to which the death of art is an inevitable part of society's progress. Perhaps the most persuasive proponent of this view is Arthur Danto. In a recent series of papers he has refined a view according to which "art is really over with, having become transmuted into philosophy."[25]

I believe that Hegel was predicting the simultaneous death of all the arts, or at least all the arts of a given era. But I would like to speculate for a moment about the demise of individual arts.[26] Certainly today there are entire arts which are dead; consider tapestry or stained glass. Though arts decline for complex reasons, the most significant factor may well be the development of successor arts which perform the same tasks with greater power and ease. Thus oil paint offers the artist a richer palette, a more expressive surface, and a subtler range of contour, line, modeling, and shade than either tapestry or stained glass. The process of painting is also more rapid and less arduous. Although stained glass and tapestry both permit effects which cannot be achieved with paint, oil gradually became the preeminent pictorial medium.

Gardening has not been supplanted by a successor art in this manner. No new *medium* has taken over gardening's aesthetic tasks. Instead, economic and social factors have contributed to the art's decline. Gardening is labor intensive and requires vast tracts of land. The splendors of Stourhead and Stowe can't be replicated on a smaller scale, yet mass urbanization has made suitable sites scarce. Thus few today can afford to garden in the eighteenth-century style. Present-day tastes in recreation also discourage the creation of lavish gardens. The simple pleasures enjoyed by eighteenth-century aristocrats on their estates – walking, riding, hunting, conversing – are less popular in our electronic age.

Though gardening is not a high art today, I would like to speculate counterfactually for a moment and imagine a different future for the eighteenth-century English garden, one in which gardening did not decline but instead participated fully in the heady, tumultuous events as modernism altered the artworld.

There are various ways of defining modernism, postmodernism, and the *avant-garde*. I shall focus on two such definitions and ask whether gardening could have been part of the modernist enterprise. The first mark of modernism I shall consider is that proposed by Clement Greenberg in his 1939 essay "Avant-Garde and Kitsch." Greenberg claims that abstract art develops when "turning his attention away from subject matter of common experience, the poet or artist turns it in upon the medium of his own craft...These themselves become the subject matter of art and literature."[27] Arthur Danto builds a similar insight into his neo-Hegelian account of art. Suggesting that art history is best modeled by the *Bildungsroman* or novel of self-discovery, Danto sums up the progress of art as follows: "the objects approach zero as their theory approaches infinity."[28]

Might gardens participate in this progression? Can we imagine modernist, minimalist, and *avant-garde* gardens? It is certainly possible to design gardens that are spare, rectilinear, and severe, perfectly in tune with the Bauhaus aesthetic. The Brazilian gardens by Roberto Burle Marx feature masses of color and sculptural arrays of exotic plants. They are said by one writer to "owe more to cubist art than to any preceding style of landscape gardening."[29] But Greenbergian modern gardens would be both minimalist and introspective. The environment equivalent to "art about art," they would question our sense of what a garden should be. Such gardens might emphasize the process and materials of gardening, or deny such traditional garden values as beauty, variety, and originality. Imagine a garden that displays hoses, tools, and fertilizer as prominently as flowers, or one with nothing but marigolds covering varied settings and terrain that might otherwise lead us to expect roses, lilies, lilacs, lupins, violets, hollyhocks, daffodils, and more. More shocking gardens might dispense with plants altogether. Imagine a garden that is all trellises but no roses.

Stanley Cavell proposes a second mark of modernism in his paper "Music Discomposed" when he argues that questions of fraudulence and of trust are inextricably bound up with modern art.[30] As art becomes minimal, artistry becomes less apparent, and the responses "I could do that," "Anyone could do that," "A child could do that"

167

ring out. Cavell is here arguing against a certain sort of serial music, music which he calls "totally composed." He objects to such pieces because their aleatory methods prevent composers from knowing in advance how the work will sound. And this, he claims, prevents them from composing so as to satisfy themselves.

While Cavell does not, in the end, make good his charge of fraud,[31] his discussion can be extended to the art of gardening. Like serial music or minimalist paintings, gardens invite us to meditate on change and chance. All gardening incorporates some elements of chance, for plants are affected by climate, soil, pests, and disease. A gardener could introduce additional levels of randomness by buying unlabeled seeds and bulbs, by making design choices with dice or the I Ching, or by simply ceasing to prune and weed. Gardens can also pose the issues of fraudulence and trust that Cavell finds in some modern music. Consider the gardener's equivalent to John Cage's piece 4'33": well-groomed beds of soil not planted with anything at all. Alan Sonfist created a garden not unlike this. *Pool of Earth* (1975) was a fifty-foot diameter circle of fertile soil surrounded by a ring of rock in the midst of a chemical waste dump. Sonfist intended the circle to gradually reseed and rebuild the original forest. Perhaps a "found garden" would parallel even more closely Cage's views about the relative status of music and noise. Cage maintains that all sounds are worthy of attention and that music should not be specially privileged. A "found garden" which enclosed an arbitrarily selected piece of land would make a similar point about the relative status of flowers and weeds.

One garden which fits both Greenberg's and Cavell's accounts of modernism was featured in the 1985 *Home Design* magazine of the *New York Times*. This 20×20 foot garden consists of brightly colored shards of plexiglass set in a bed of gravel. A wire glass table in the center of the garden replaces the traditional garden pond, and the entire ensemble is covered with a fishnet canopy dyed bright pink. Glitter-covered trash cans cluster nearby. Martha Schwartz, the creator of this garden, confessed that it was inspired by Frank Stella's 1970s relief paintings. *The Stella Garden*, as Schwartz calls it, seems a perfect example of a modernist garden. The piece alludes wittily to the progress of twentieth-century painting. It also challenges our received views about both gardening and creativity.

I don't think the existence of *The Stella Garden* threatens my claims about the decline of gardening. For one, the work sits not in a public space or gallery setting, but in the artist's mother's back yard.

It seems thereby insulated from the factors which generate and support an *avant-garde*: urban settings, political agendas, the market power of galleries and museums. *The Stella Garden* is also isolated in another sense. It has not, to the best of my knowledge, had any significant influence on other gardens or on other works of art.

One other example of a postmodernist garden is Ian Hamilton Finlay's *Little Sparta* in southern Scotland.[32] Finlay is a sculptor and concrete poet who purchased a four-acre estate in the Scottish countryside in 1966 and has been self-consciously improving it in the manner of Shenstone and Pope. *Little Sparta* mixes traditional garden features – ponds, temples, a grotto, a sunken garden, a Roman garden, and more – with such contemporary symbols as battleships, airplanes, and a "nuclear sail." Finlay's garden is, unlike Schwartz's, open to the public and it has in fact figured in an ongoing "war" with the local tax authorities.[33] Numerous inscriptions carved in a classicizing style underscore Finlay's theme of neoclassical rearmament. The poet has taken the French Revolution with its dialectical mix of virtue and terror as the ground of both the modern era and his ongoing cultural critique.

At first glance, Finlay's garden might seem a reactionary endeavor. Like its eighteenth-century predecessors, it borrows images and inscriptions from an earlier era and uses them to voice a critical view of contemporary culture. But while Stowe and Stourhead's references to the classical world were part of the shared vocabulary of the Augustan Age, Finlay's appropriation of neoclassical style is singular and savage. Since landowners no longer improve their estates with temples, obelisks, columns, and grottos, Finlay's use of an eighteenth-century vocabulary and his juxtaposition of it with strikingly twentieth-century forms and concerns – concrete poetry, the nuclear age – mark *Little Sparta* as a highly self-conscious work. Finlay uses the neoclassical garden to make an ironic statement; he doesn't revive the garden as a viable twentieth-century art form. For this reason, *Little Sparta* is a paradigm case of a postmodern work of art.

5. EARTHWORKS AND ENVIRONMENTAL ART

I have been reinventing the history of gardening, grafting an imagined set of modernist gardens onto gardening's actual past. Together, these actual and imagined gardens – Sonfist's, Schwartz's, and Finlay's creations plus the aleatory, minimalist, Cagean, and found art possibilities I have described – show that gardening could indeed have contributed to the progress of twentieth-century art. Since this supposition is, however, contrary to fact, I would like to take another approach to demonstrating gardening's powers. Turning to some twentieth-century works, the environmental art cited by McDonough, I shall see whether a lineage can be traced backwards from this art to gardening in its prime.

The category "environmental art" is extremely diverse. Let me begin with a quick typology. I am indebted here to Mark Rosenthal's article "Some Attitudes of Earth Art: From Competition to Adoration."[34] I sort recent environmental art into seven categories. These categories are provisional, and they often overlap, but describing some of these works will help show their ties to gardens of the past. My categories are as follows:

(1) masculine gestures in the environment
    Heizer, Smithson, De Maria, Turrell
(2) ephemeral gestures in the environment
    Singer, Long
(3) environmental performance art
    Boyle, Fulton, Hutchinson, Christo
(4) architectural installations
    Holt, Aycock, Miss
(5) didactic art
    the Harrisons
(6) proto-gardens
    Sonfist, Irwin, Finlay
(7) sculpture gardens and art parks

Let me say something about each of these categories. The first contains the classic examples of what were called earthworks, works of art created by manipulating vast amounts of dirt and rock. For example, Michael Heizer's desert sculptures of the sixties include *Double Negative* (1969), in which 240,000 tons of earth were carved out of two facing cliffs,[35] and *Dissipate* (1968), in which five 12-foot-long steel-lined trenches were dug into the floor of a Nevada desert. This category includes "additive" works as well as excavations. In Robert Smithson's *Asphalt Rundown* (1969), a truckload of asphalt was poured down the side of a quarry in Rome, while the same artist's more famous work *Spiral Jetty* (1970) is a 1500-foot-long spiral of rock and earth built into Utah's Great Salt Lake. Heizer's ambitious *Complex One/City* (1972–6) is a massive illusionistic structure[36] on a remote Nevada plateau. *Complex One* seems architectural, even though it can't be entered. By contrast, Walter De Maria's *Lightning Field* (1977), a one mile square grid containing 640 18-foot steel poles, seems more an altered landscape than an essay in architecture or sculpture. James Turrell's work in progress, *Roden Crater*, can also be construed as an all-encompassing landscape or perceptual field. Turrell is subtly reshaping a volcanic crater and building rooms and chambers in which, as one writer eloquently describes, "Light from lunar, planetary, and celestial events will enter the apertures, gather, refract and self-enhance in the utter darkness, and be experienced by visitors as luminous presences, not quite space nor exactly light, but rather illusions of both."[37]

I called this first group of artworks masculine because of their scale. They are also remote and inaccessible. Traveling to see them requires braving wilderness, rattlesnakes, and the desert's climatic extremes.[38] Moreover, it is not clear from what vantage point these works *can* be seen, or are meant to be seen. For example, Elizabeth Baker states that De Maria's constructs are meant to be walked in[39] yet venturing near *The Lightning Field* during a storm would be extremely dangerous. Many of the works are documented through aerial photographs. These reveal striking affinities between these massive works and modern minimalist painting.[40] But it is unlikely that any spectator at the site could gain a similar view.

My second category of environmental art – ephemeral gestures in the environment – is typified by the early work of Michael Singer. His series *Situation Balances* (1971–3) involved rearranging fallen logs to create "networks of tenuously posed trees, buttressed by stumps."[41] Later he bundled branches and reeds and placed them in marshy areas, or wove latticelike structures of strips of wood. Richard Long's work is equally modest.[42] Carol Hall describes two of his early pieces as follows: "One work was the making of a path in a field of grass by walking back and forth for several hours, another consisted of snipping off the heads of flowers in a meadow, thus inscribing a giant X."[43] More recently, Long has been taking walks, documenting them with photographs or brief descriptions, and occasionally leaving behind geometric arrays of stones. Michael Rosenthal summarizes the work of Long and Singer: "Both view their works as ritualistic responses to the site with which they are interacting. Their largely horizontal gestures acquiesce in and complement the landscape. That these quiet gestures will be quickly erased is part of the modest ambitions of the artists when they work in nature."[44]

Some of Long's pieces – the documented walks – slide over into my third category – environmental performance art. Typical here is Mark Boyle, who beginning in 1968 asked randomly selected people to help him create an artwork. Those who agreed were blindfolded in Boyle's studio and asked to throw a dart at a map of the world. In this manner Boyle collected 1,000 randomly selected sites and has been traveling to them since 1970. At each site he takes photographs and makes castings of various surfaces. These result in shows such as *Thaw Series* (1972), in which fiberglass casts of square yards of melting snow were on display. Hamish Fulton is another artist I include in this category. Like Long, he makes walking his art form, but Fulton leaves behind no traces of his walks. He comes away only with photographs which document each walk.

Let me add works of one more sort to my Performance category. I have in mind works of art which are ephemeral, like those in category 2, but which emphasize their performance aspect by introducing artificial elements into the landscape. Paradigm cases here would include Peter Hutchinson's *Paricutin Project* (1970), in which a 300-foot-long trail of bread was laid along fault lines at the mouth of a Mexican volcano and left there for six days until mold changed the bread from white to orange. The same artist's *Threaded Calabash* (1969) involved threading five calabashes onto a twelve-foot stretch of rope and securing them underwater off the coast of Tobago until the fruit became waterlogged and sank to the ocean floor. One last piece of Hutchinson's related more closely to gardens was *Thrown Rope* (1972) in which the artist planted a row of hyacinths following the configuration of a rope he had thrown.

Christo's works have affinities with each of my first three categories. His most renowned environmental installations – *Valley Curtain* (1971–2), *Running Fence* (1976), and *Surrounded Islands* (1983) – are forceful gestures. Like Heizer's earthworks, they are massive and remote,[45] and are perhaps best viewed from the air. However, Christo's creations also have a performance aspect. Like Hutchinson's projects, they introduce artificial elements (orange curtain, white curtain, pink "skirt") into the landscape. And finally, Christo's works are short-lived. Each is assembled and dismantled within a matter of days. The site is then returned to its original condition. In this respect, Christo's works resemble those I have labeled Ephemeral Gestures.

Let me cover the remaining categories more quickly. I have grouped together Nancy Holt, Alice Aycock, and Mary Miss as three artists who create architectural installations in the landscape. Some of Holt's works are, like Heizer's and Smithson's, in remote desert sites, and many are keyed to celestial happenings. For example, her work *Sun Tunnels* (1973–6) in the Utah desert consists of four large concrete pipes oriented to mark the sunrise during summer and winter solstice. The pipes are also pierced with holes which map the constellations Draco, Perseus, Columba, and Capricorn.[46] Holt employs similar "locators" – pipes which focus and guide vision – in other works.

I have placed Helen and Newton Harrison in the separate category of didactic art. Their art is intended to draw attention to the ecological crisis confronting us, but their exhibits would fit as well in a science museum as a museum of fine art, and they are perhaps most famous for discovering how to keep rare Sri Lankan crabs happy in captivity. (The secret is to produce waves in the tank to mimic their native monsoons.)

The two artists whose work reminds me most of earlier gardens are a surprising pair, Alan Sonfist and Robert Irwin. I have placed their work in the category proto-gardens. Sonfist has created a number of *Time Landscapes*, tracts which reproduce an urban area's vanished native flora. Though didactic, like the Harrison's creations, these works truly are gardens of a sort. Thus Mark Rosenthal remarks that "Whereas Smithson pushes and manipulates earth to form his signature, Sonfist cultivates a garden."[47]

The most gardenlike of Irwin's creations is his Wellesley College installation (1980), a forty-foot-long stainless steel wall, two feet at its highest, pierced by an abstract leaflike pattern, and set in a bucolic corner of the campus. The work reflects light flickering through the trees and glistening on the nearby lake. Melinda Wortz writes that the piece alters our perception of the landscape, heightening our perception of a beautiful place. Rather than calling attention to itself as art, "the work returns us to the land."[48] I also find garden resonances in some of Irwin's indoor installations which subtly alter a gallery space, say by the addition of a narrow transparent scrim just below ceiling level along one wall. Though small, and indoors, these works envelop us in a highly charged perceptual field. This effect resembles that which some viewers attribute to De Maria's *Lightning Field*, as well as that which Turrell hopes to achieve in his *Roden Crater*.

The final category I placed in my list was that of sculpture gardens and artparks. Laumeier Park in St. Louis, Missouri, Artpark in Lewiston, New York, Parc Lullin near Geneva, Kerguehennic in

Brittany,[49] PepsiCo's world headquarters in Purchase, New York, and General Mills' headquarters in Minneapolis all resemble earlier (seventeenth- and eighteenth-century) European gardens in that all include works of art in a natural landscape. Whether these parks are functioning as gardens, or merely as museums which happen to be out of doors, depends on the relations which hold between work and site. In what follows, I shall argue that these relations are a crucial factor in understanding and interpreting these works.

6. TRACING A LINEAGE

I have described the rich variety of recent environmental art. But what might serve to connect the environmental works of today to gardens of the past? Certainly parallels abound. For example, gardening can be disruptive like the excavations of Heizer and Smithson. Gardens can contain follies like the circular constructions of Aycock and Miss. Blossoms are ephemeral like Hutchinson's loaves and calabashes, paths and benches control a visitor's perceptions like Holt's locators. Gardens create a total environment like Irwin's altered rooms. But, to repeat Goodman's caution, any two items have some properties in common. While it is intellectually satisfying to find similarities between items as disparate as eighteenth-century gardens and twentieth-century environmental art, what, if anything, follows from this exercise?

One relation which can hold between earlier and later works is that the first influenced the second. In his book *Influence in Art and Literature*, Goran Hermeren lists thirteen separate requirements which he claims characterize genuine artistic influence.[50] He distinguishes between direct and indirect influence, and between positive and negative influence. He notes that artists need not be aware of the operation of influence (p. 96), and that works of art which influenced one another need not have any "obvious and easily discovered similarities" (p. 99). Hermeren's crucial requirement is a causal one: whenever one work influences another, the artist's contact with the earlier work or with its creator is a "contributory cause" of his creation.[51]

The artistic relationship I want to characterize is looser than Hermeren's notion of influence. While I maintain that our understanding of, say, *Roden Crater*, *Lightning Field*, or *Time Landscape* is enhanced if we view these in the light of the tradition of landscape gardening, I don't claim that Turrell, De Maria, or Sonfist were necessarily thinking back to earlier gardens, nor that their works resemble such gardens in any straightforward way. For all I know, these artists never viewed or read about the eighteenth-century gardens described above. If this is so, then Hermeren's requirement of causal contact is not fulfilled, and the relation between the earlier and later works is not a simple causal one.

I propose the following principle for determining artistic legacy, for tracing a lineage from artforms of the past to those of the present. If, in understanding and interpreting later works, we see them as fulfilling some of the important functions of their predecessors, then it is proper to see the later works as descendents of those which came before. On this principle, eighteenth-century gardens and twentieth-century environmental artworks are linked if the latter works perform some of the aesthetic tasks of those gardens and do so in a way which recalls those original landscapes. It is not the case, however, that the later works *refer* to their predecessors. This stronger connection would only hold if the artist were aware of the earlier gardens and intended her audience to think back to them.

Artistic lineage is a complex concept, and the principle just proposed is extremely vague. I have not developed the notion of an aesthetic task or function used above (though I have argued that eighteenth-century gardens did much more than merely soothe or delight). When we situate works of art historically, we note both similarities and differences between them and their predecessors. Yet not all predecessors are interpretively significant. One salient similarity which links some gardens and some environmental art is that both are built landscapes in the environment. Let me try to explain the connections I see between gardens and earthworks by taking up once again the relation of work to site. In what follows, I shall borrow some distinctions from environmental artist Robert Irwin.

In his essay *Being and Circumstance*, Irwin proposes a four-fold scheme for classifying the relation between a work of art and its context.[52] Works can be (1) site dominant, (2) site adjusted, (3) site specific, or (4) site conditioned/determined. These categories form a continuum with each more context-bound than the one which preceded.

Irwin's example of site dominant art is a Henry Moore sculpture. Although a Moore *Mother and Child* might be displayed to greater effect in one setting than another, its meaning, purpose, and form are not affected by relocation. By contrast, site adjusted works make some concessions to their setting – "scale, appropriateness, place-ment, etc" (p. 26). However these works are still either made or conceived in the studio. Site specific works are those conceived with the site in mind (p. 27). Most of Richard Serra's sculpture falls within this category, and the artist might have defended his embattled piece *Tilted Arc* by arguing that since it would not be the *same* work of art if moved, it cannot be moved. Finally, site determined works are those where "the sculptural response draws all of its cues (reasons for being) from its surroundings"; the site itself "determines all facets of the 'sculptural response'" (p. 27). Here, Irwin claims, the impera-tives of the site may even override the usual marks by which we recognize an artist's oeuvre.[53]

There are problems with Irwin's categories, but they let us draw some useful distinctions among works of art. We are familiar with works of art created *in response to* a particular site. Consider Cezanne's many studies of Mt. Sainte-Victoire. Though these paint-ings testify to the artist's lifelong interest in the Provençal landscape, they aren't situated in that landscape; they hang in public and private collections throughout the world. Other works, however, are both responses *to* a site and situated *in* that site. Examples include Saarinen's *St. Louis Arch*, Serra's *Tilted Arc*, and Christo's wraps and fences. In some cases the relation between work and site becomes even more intimate: the site becomes in effect *the medium* of the work of art.

Consider Irwin's categories as applied to gardens and to environ-mental art. Surprisingly, some gardens may lack any special relation to their site. An orangerie or a botanical garden is site dominant, in Irwin's terms, if its only purpose is to produce oranges, or to display and preserve certain species of plants. The same is true of a bed of annuals planted solely to provide a striking display of color. By contrast, the eighteenth-century gardens I have been exploring do more than inhabit a site. They are responsive to that site, and they emphasize and display features which are aspects of the site itself. For example, recall that the topography of Stowe, Stourhead, and West Wycombe forms an integral part of these gardens' iconological programs.

Gardens which do not address their site, do not take it as a problem, could, it seems to me, be of botanical interest only. That is, they could only be of interest for their plantings. One might object that we could also take an interest in such added features as paths, benches, ponds, and follies, but it is hard to see how any of these could be added to a garden without taking into account prospects and viewpoints, contours and textures, the lay of the land, in short, everything that constitutes a site. Gardens which were neither site specific nor site determined would be in the land, but they would not make reference to it. It would not figure in our response to the gardens, and we would not take it into account in estimating the gardens' pleasures or success.

Of course, a garden's relation to its setting can be an adversarial one. Garden designers do not always surrender to the exigencies of a site. Consider Le Nôtre's ongoing campaign to form the gardens of Versailles from inhospitable swampland, or Brown's reputation for razing towns and rerouting rivers for the sake of his designs. In such cases, the gardener carves, shapes, alters, levels, but the resulting garden is in harmony with the conquered site. At Versailles, for instance, the relentless geometric expanse of Le Nôtre's garden reveals nothing of the underlying land but expresses perfectly his monarch's reign and aspirations. Such gardens are in fact site specific or site determined.

Many of the environmental works described in section 5 above are also site specific or site determined. The pieces I classed as ephemeral gestures (those by Long, Hutchinson, and Singer) belong in Irwin's fourth category, as do Heizer's excavations, Turrell's crater, and Irwin's gallery installation. All of Holt's locator pieces are site specific, as are Sonfist's *Time Landscapes* if we extend site to mean something like "ecological niche." All these works are in the landscape, they all manipulate that landscape, and they all make us take into account our relation to that landscape.

This then is the trait which I believe is shared by gardens, earthworks, and environmental art. It underlies their common function and grounds my claim of shared lineage. The lesser works in each of these categories (gardens, earthworks) are environmental art only in the weak sense that they are in a site; they are not responsive to it. Richer works are in a site, responsive to that site, at times about the site, and more.

Just as eighteenth-century gardens performed many of the functions of their sister arts, painting and poetry, so many pieces of environmental art have additional layers of meaning – political messages, allusions to other works of art and to theories of agency and perception. Works like Turrell's *Roden Crater*, Heizer's *Double Negative*, Singer's fragile *Situation Balances*, and Irwin's Wellesley College installation force us to rethink our place in the landscape, our roles as perceivers, enjoyers, consumers, destroyers. They raise profound metaphysical questions about permanence and change, about human will and agency. Thus these pieces are every bit as serious as the greatest of the early eighteenth-century gardens, and they make their points in much the same way. By inhabiting, addressing, and altering a site, they call into question our relations to landscape, nature, and art.

7. CONCLUSION

I began by taking issue with the claim that earthworks and environmental art are architecture's *avant-garde*. Since gardening is considered by many a branch of landscape architecture, perhaps not all that much depends on whether the works I have been discussing are *avant-garde* architecture or *avant-garde* gardens. What does matter is the connections, if any, that link seventeenth- and eighteenth-century gardens with twentieth-century earthworks and environmental art. I have argued that there are indeed important commonalities binding these arts.

My claim comes to this: these twentieth-century works are works of art, like gardens; they address the relation of work to site, like gardens; they can be ideological, like gardens; they can be beautiful, or sublime, like gardens. Overall, they force us to think deeply about nature itself, about our relation to nature, and about nature's relation to art. These deep-seated commonalities between the more ideological of the eighteenth-century gardens and these later works justify tracing a lineage linking one to the other. I have not claimed that the later works were influenced by the gardens that came before. It is not a causal chain I am tracing. Rather, I believe that many of today's environmental works fulfill the same functions as did those early gardens. They fill a space in today's artworld equivalent to that occupied by gardens two and a half centuries ago.

Notes

A version of this essay was read to the Washington University Faculty Seminar on the *avant-garde* organized by Lucian Krukowski. I thank the members of the seminar for their helpful comments. I also benefited from Tom Leddy's paper "Gardens in an Expanded Field" which I read in manuscript form.

1 "A 1986 Gallup survey conducted for the National Gardening Associ-

ation showed that for the third year in a row, gardening is the number 1 outdoor leisure activity in the United States." *New York Times*, June 4, 1987, p. 17.

2 Alan Sonfist, *Art in the Land: A Critical Anthology of Environmental Art* (New York: E. P. Dutton, 1983).

3 Michael McDonough, "Architecture's Unnoticed Avant-Garde" in A. Sonfist, ed., *Art in the Land*, p. 233.

4 Edward Hyams, *A History of Gardens and Gardening* (New York: 1971), p. 12.

5 *Philosophical Investigations*, §§66–7.

6 The history of aesthetics is filled with theories proposing competing – and incompatible – essential traits. Aristotle, Tolstoy, Croce, Langer, and Bell define art in terms of imitation, communication, intuition, expression, and significant form, respectively. Each theory brings about a sort of gerrymandering for each "redraws" the map of what is and isn't art. Since there is no one task which all works of art perform, each theory omits significant works of art from consideration.

7 A crucial paper here is Maurice Mandelbaum's "Family Resemblances and Generalizations Concerning the Arts" reprinted in *Aesthetics*, eds. George Dickie and Richard Sclafani, (New York: St. Martin's, 1977).

8 George Dickie, "What is Art? An Institutional Analysis" in *Art and Philosophy*, ed. W. E. Kennick, (New York: St. Martin's, 1979), p. 85.

9 *Ibid.*, pp. 88–9.

10 Though art remains what Morris Weitz calls an open concept.

11 Arthur Danto, *The Transfiguration of the Commonplace* (Cambridge: Harvard University Press, 1981), p. 44.

12 Nelson Goodman, "Seven Strictures on Similarity," *Problems and Projects*, (Indianapolis: Bobbs-Merrill, 1971).

13 I think theories about metaphor have some bearing on this question. Any two items *can* be juxtaposed metaphorically, but the results will often be trite, stale, misleading, or inappropriate. For example, Stanley Cavell explicates Shakespeare's metaphor "Juliet is the sun," showing the surprising and rich resonances packed into this trope. Had Romeo instead declared "Juliet is a door," the claim would have been jarring (and his love revealed as primarily sexual and opportunistic). Had he said "Juliet is a tree," we would have been completely baffled. It does not follow from this that we can state the conditions that make for good metaphors.

14 In fact, Dickie acknowledges that his own theory was inspired by the following sentence of Danto's: "To see something as art requires something the eye cannot descry – an atmosphere of artistic theory, a knowledge of history of art: an artworld." Dickie, "What is Art?", p. 81.

15 Danto, *Transfiguration*, p. 125.

16 John Dixon Hunt and Peter Willis make this point in the introduction to their anthology *The Genius of the Place: The English Landscape Garden 1620–1820* (London: Elek, 1975). Nikolaus Pevsner documents the increasing naturalness or irregularity of English gardens from the

seventeenth century on in his essay "The Genesis of the Picturesque" (*The Architectural Review*, 1944).

17 Quoted by Hunt and Willis, *Genius of the Place*, p. 11.

18 Lucy Lippard explores the connections between gardens and prehistory in her book *Overlay: Contemporary Art and the Art of Prehistory* (New York: Pantheon, 1983).

19 I discuss the iconographical programs of Stowe and Stourhead in my paper "Ut Hortus Poesis: Gardening and her Sister Arts in 18th-Century England," *British Journal of Aesthetics*, vol. 25, no. 1 (1985): 17–32.

20 John Dixon Hunt, "Emblem and Expression in the 18th-Century Landscape Garden," *Eighteenth-Century Studies*, 4 (1971): 299.

21 Kenneth Woodbridge, "Henry Hoare's Paradise," *The Art Bulletin*, 47 (1965).

22 *Ibid.*, p. 99.

23 Daniel P. Mannix, *The Hell Fire Club* (New York: Ballantine, 1959), pp. 5, 81.

24 See my paper "The Picturesque: An 18th-Century Debate." *Journal of Aesthetics and Art Criticism*, 46.2 (1987): 271–9.

25 Arthur Danto, "The End of Art," in *The Death of Art*, ed. Berel Lang, (New York: Haven, 1984), p. 8.

26 The two paragraphs which follow are drawn from my paper "Philosophy, Literature, and the Death of Art," *Philosophical Papers*, 18.1 (1989): 95–115.

27 Clement Greenberg, "Avant-Garde and Kitsch" in *Art and Culture* (Boston: Beacon Press, 1961).

28 Danto, "The End of Art," p. 31.

29 Christopher Thacker, *The History of Gardens* (Berkeley: University of California Press, 1979), p. 278.

30 "The dangers of fraud, and of trust, are essential to the experience of art." Stanley Cavell, "Music Discomposed" in *Must We Mean What We Say* (New York: Charles Scribner's and Sons, 1969), pp. 188–9. Cavell explains the situation in music a little more fully as follows: "...the possibility of fraudulence, and the experience of fraudulence, is endemic in the experience of contemporary music...its full impact, even its immediate relevance, depends upon a willingness to trust the object, knowing that the time spent with its difficulties may be betrayed," p. 188.

31 I discuss his argument in the paper, "Chance, Constraint, and Creativity: The Awfulness of Modern Music," *Journal of Aesthetic Education*, 19.3 (1985): 21–35.

32 I learned about this garden from Tom Leddy's paper "Gardens in an Expanded Field," *British Journal of Aesthetics*, 28 (1988): 327–40. *Little Sparta* is also discussed in the following works: Claude Abrioux, *Ian Hamilton Finlay: A Visual Primer* (Edinburgh: Reaktion Books, 1985); Claude Gintz, "Neoclassical Rearmament," *Art in America*, Feb. 1987 (111–17); Stephen Bann, "A Description of Stonypath," *Journal of Garden History*, 1.2 (1981): 113–44.

33 Finlay sought tax exemption for an outbuilding he converted into a

gallery. Later he remodeled it as a garden temple dedicated to Apollo ("His music; His missiles; His muses") and demanded the tax exemption appropriate to religious buildings. The Strathclyde Regional Council refused these requests, precipitating an ongoing struggle.

34 Mark Rosenthal, "Some Attitudes of Earth Art: From Competition to Adoration" in Alan Sonfist, ed., *Art in the Land*. Many writers analyze earth art in terms of gestures, but Rosenthal offers a typology of earth art very similar to mine. He proposed five categories: (1) Gestures in the Landscape (2) Enclosures in the Landscape (3) Modest Gestures in the Landscape (4) Nature for Itself (5) Idealized Landscape.

35 This account, like many of the others to follow, was drawn from Sonfist's anthology. Carol Hall's article "Environmental Artists: Sources and Directions," which describes the recent work of eighteen of the most renowned environmental artists, was especially helpful.

36 Elizabeth C. Baker describes *Complex One* in considerable detail in her article "Artworks on the Land" (in *Art and the Land*, ed. Sonfist, pp. 73–84). The work consists of a 20×110×140 foot pyramidal mound, framed by a set of cantilevered concrete piers. From a distance, *Complex One* reads as a single rectangular plane framed by bands of concrete. As the viewer approaches, this illusion fades. The mound actually inclines backwards forty-five degrees, and the concrete columns jut out in front of it.

37 From Eleanor Munro's article "Art in the Desert," *The New York Times*, Dec. 7, 1988.

38 Elizabeth Baker writes, "The experience of visiting the works is a complicated one, no small part of which is the difficulty of getting there and the exoticism of locale and lifestyle. Things can become intensely anecdotal: you learn about local economics, land purchasing in the West, enormous government land reserves, atomic test sites, snakes, trucks, and desert climates. All this, especially in the course of short visits, tends to overwhelm, so at a certain point it becomes necessary to separate the art experience from the general experience," pp. 79–80. Eleanor Munro concurs. She offers the following anecdote: "As we drove toward the town of Overton, jumping off place for the Heizer work [*Double Negative*], the temperature was pushing 120. We stopped at a gas station to ask if anyone knew the road. A well-oriented highway patrol officer with a four-wheel drive sized up our situation and growled, 'I'd rather take you up than have to go find you and bring you out.'"

Munro concludes her article with a set of warnings: "Travellers should bear in mind that sites are in semi-wilderness away from emergency facilities...Fill the gas tank and check oil at nearest station stops and never be without containers of drinkable water...Wear high-topped heavy shoes – this is rattlesnake and scorpion country – head covering and sunscreen."

39 She states that "*The Lightning Field* is slowly grasped...Perceptually it strains your attention, your sense of intervals; its boundaries are not clear once you are more than one or two units inside it. The distance between

poles is so great you strain to locate the next one – and especially the one beyond that. But psychological and supraperceptual factors seem crucial here..." p. 81. Baker wrote this after viewing a small test grid of thirty-five poles which was erected before the finished work.

40 For example, the five diagonally arrayed trenches that make up Heizer's work *Dissipate* look like a hard-edge Minimalist composition, while the five circular excavations and surrounding tire tracks that constitute *Five Conic Displacements* (1969) remind me of nothing so much as Robert Motherwell's series of *Elegies for the Spanish Republic*.

41 Kate Linkter, "Michael Singer: A Position In, and On, Nature" in *Art in the Land*, ed. Alan Sonfist, p. 185.

42 Rosenthal applies this term to Long's work in "Some Attitudes of Earth Art: From Competition to Adoration."

43 Hall, "Environmental Artists," p. 34.

44 Rosenthal, "Some Attitudes of Earth Art," pp. 66–7.

45 *Running Fence* was twenty-four and a half miles long, while *Surrounded Islands* draped thirty-five tons (6.56 million square feet) of pink polypropylene around eleven islands in Biscayne Bay.

46 Hall, "Environmental Artists," p. 29.

47 Rosenthal, "Some Attitudes of Earth Art," p. 71.

48 Melinda Wortz, "Surrendering to Presence: Robert Irwin's Aesthetic Integration," *Artforum*, Nov. 1981, p. 64.

49 These parks were written up in recent issues of *Artform* and *Art in America*.

50 Goran Hermeren, *Influence in Art and Literature* (Princeton University Press, 1975).

51 "If X influenced the creation of Y with respect to a, and if B created Y, then B's contact with X was a contributory cause of the creation of Y with respect to a," *ibid.*, p. 93.

52 Robert Irwin, *Being and Circumstance: Notes Toward a Conditional Art* (California: The Lapis Press, 1985).

53 Irwin says of site *specific* art: "...our process of recognition and understanding of the 'work of art' is still keyed (referenced) to the oeuvre of the artist. Familiarity with his or her history, lineage, art intent, style, materials, techniques, etc. are presupposed; thus, for example, a Richard Serra is always recognizable as, first and foremost, a Richard Serra," *ibid.*, p. 27.

I am not convinced that a site *determined* work would be without such stylistic markers, for even were an artistic response entirely elicited by a site, it would still be the response (action) of a particular individual and would be colored by that person's beliefs, desires, interest, habits, and so on.

9

Comparing natural and artistic beauty

DONALD W. CRAWFORD

The title of this article might trigger in the memory of some readers a famous poetic couplet:

> I think that I shall never see
> A poem as lovely as a tree.

Is such a comparison legitimate? Is it even meaningful? Just for a moment let us pursue a negative answer to this latter question by imagining that Joyce Kilmer originally wrote the poem as a student in a creative writing course, and received the following criticism from his instructor:

Although it is sometimes a good idea to begin a poem with a paradoxical thought, yours is quite confused. Your first sentence wrongly assumes that a meaningful comparison can be made between trees and poems in respect of their loveliness. But a tree is beautiful because its organic form delights the eye, while a poem's beauty lies in its expression of human thought and feeling, which is something quite different. There is no way to compare them, and the rest of your poetic effort proves the point, because all you do is slurp on about the tree, without even a nod toward great poetry. Perhaps you should try a course in the School of Business.

This is not an entirely fictitious example. Formalist genre critics such as Cleanth Brooks and Robert Penn Warren actually dismissed the validity of the poem's opening couplet, remarking that "the two kinds of loveliness, that of art and that of nature, are not comparable."[1] On the face of it, this is not a silly position, but one well worth examining.

Several important avenues of rebuttal to this criticism suggest themselves. Perhaps the most obvious rebuttal would be a defense of the classical view that artistic and natural beauty are in fact two species of the same genus, perfection of form, with artistic beauty simply imitating natural beauty. I shall begin by considering that classical conception which seems to make straightforward comparisons between the two meaningful and informative. I then shall explore other relationships between art and nature. Sometimes these allow for comparisons, although the nature of the comparison varies with the type of relationship, while other times the meaningfulness of comparisons between natural and artistic beauty is questionable. Let me make clear at the outset that I am not defending a particular way of aesthetically comparing art and nature. In fact, in many cases I am skeptical that meaningful comparisons are forthcoming. But I am also not convinced that there is a sound general argument with the conclusion that all such comparisons are pointless.

1. CLASSICAL BEAUTY: ART IMITATES NATURE

Classical beauty is based on a conception of natural beauty in which nature exhibits perfection of form in regularity and due proportion.[2] Beauty is thus something we perceive, it is not a mere affective response. Paradigms of natural beauty are living organisms and their products (flowers, seashells) as well as celestial and atmospheric phenomena (the celestial orbits, snowflakes). Natural beauty is conceived in terms of eternal laws of mathematical regularity and proportion, and it is thus linked to rationality. Natural beauty is the sensuous embodiment of seemingly intelligent design.

Nature provides the model for art: art imitates nature. Thus artistic beauty imitates the perfection – the intelligible order – visible in natural forms. Beauty arises when there is an ordered arrangement of perceptibly distinguishable parts that form a more-or-less perfect whole. In nature, beauty appears when objects or phenomena seem to be designed by intelligence; in art, beauty is found in the imitations of these perfections visible in natural forms.

If artistic beauty is thought to imitate the perfection visible in natural forms, there would seem to be no difficulty whatsoever in directly comparing natural and artistic beauty: they are two species of the same genus. We find a particular flower beautiful if it exhibits integrity or perfection as revealed in its due proportion or harmony, along with a brightness or clarity that sensuously attracts us to it and helps reveal its perfection to us. We find a painting of a flower beautiful on the same basis. On first sight that suggests a means of comparing objects with respect to their relative successful realization of a perfection of form. But there is the important question of whether due proportion is a relative notion.[3] Is *due* proportion what is normal for a *type* of thing such as a species or a natural kind? If so, there remains the possibility that any two cases of artistic and natural beauty have different kinds of integrity or perfection, formal though they both may be. For example, suppose a two-headed calf is considered ugly because it deviates from the norm; it doesn't follow that a painting which is a diptych and so deviates from the norm is not beautiful. Or even if both the two-headed calf and the diptych fail to be beautiful because they deviate from their respective norms, it doesn't follow that we can meaningfully compare them with respect to their degree of beauty.

Leaving these difficulties aside, it remains the case that the classical conditions for beauty – due proportion, harmony, integrity – all imply that a beautiful object must be made of parts, that it is a composite. This is the Aristotelian doctrine that a beautiful object must be evident to the eye and please it, so to speak, in one eyeful. Aristotle writes:

A beautiful object, whether it be a living organism or any whole composed of parts, must not only have an orderly arrangement of parts, but must also be of a certain magnitude; for beauty depends on magnitude and order. Hence a very small animal organism cannot be beautiful; for the view of it is confused, the object being seen in an almost imperceptible moment of time. Nor, again, can one of vast size be beautiful; for as the eye cannot take it all in at once, the unity and sense of the whole is lost for the spectator; as for instance if there were one a thousand miles long.[4]

Aristotle and many other writers who followed him concluded from the above principle that it is impossible for very minute and very large or vast creatures or objects to be beautiful. This raises further complications, though not necessarily insurmountable barriers, in our attempt to give a reading of the classical model which enables it to countenance meaningful comparisons between natural and artistic beauty. So what about art? Aristotle didn't flinch. By explicitly applying the principle that artistic beauty imitates nature, he concluded that the length of a story or plot is aesthetically significant: it "must be of some length, but of a length to be taken in by the memory."[5] Does that make some comparisons between art and nature informative? Do we think anything like, "That sunset would have been more beautiful if it didn't last so long! It's so difficult to distinguish the middle from the beginning and the end!"? Is an expanse of desert that seems to fade to the horizon less beautiful than one bounded by hills because it cannot be taken in all at once? I am skeptical about such comparative aesthetic judgments.

However that may be, on the classical conception natural beauty is the sensuous embodiment of perfection in a natural product – a beautiful natural thing. Natural objects are the aesthetic ideal; they provide the model for art. Thus inherent in the classical conception of beauty is its direct application to art: Art imitates nature. But if we turn to nature as dynamic and changing, do the same principles apply to dynamic art? Aristotle had no doubts but that they did. Tragedy is an imitation of nature – human nature as revealed not in individual persons but in actions of a type, and in particular in actions that are complete in themselves. For Aristotle, a plot must unfold naturally, just as a seed naturally develops into a plant which fulfills its end (realizes its final cause). Here we encounter the full power of the classical model of beauty applied to comparing art with nature. Beauty is proper proportion developing naturally to an end according to an internal principle. The experience of the beautiful is that of witnessing the process of this development or in perceiving the product at some moment of time. Natural beauty is perfection, whether found in an individual organism, a product of living things, an atmospheric phenomenon, or a natural site. The artistic analogues to these are worth noting: an individual work of art corresponds to the individual organism, a tool to a natural product like a seashell or spider web, a pyrotechnic display to an atmospheric phenomenon, and a garden to a natural site. Under this model, many comparisons might be appropriate. We recall Shakespeare's Sonnet no. eighteen, which compares a beautiful person favorably to a summer day!

2. PICTURESQUE BEAUTY

In the eighteenth century the picturesque challenged the classical conception of beauty's essential conditions of regularity and proportion. Although originally a fairly specific reaction against formalism in landscape design, from the outset the term "picturesque" also suggested ragged beggars, oxcarts in rutted dirt tracks, twisted tree trunks and limbs in moonlight, and ruins overgrown with moss and vines. These images reflect its most general early use: "a term expressive of that peculiar kind of beauty which is agreeable in a picture."[6] Although there was considerable debate in the eighteenth century as to whether the notion of "picturesque beauty" was a contradiction or a truism, the term today does not suggest an aesthetic category completely distinct from the beautiful. But picturesque beauty involves more variety and informality than was acknowledged in classical beauty.

The model of picturesque natural scenery is retained today in picture postcards. Just as in the eighteenth century, there is an emphasis on pictorial composition, not as manifest in regularity of design but instead as revealed through variety and irregularity, with emphasis on roughness of contours and texture. The aesthetic category of the picturesque related to art in two important ways. The first involved the activity of viewing picturesque scenery, adopting the perspective of the painter. The second was the creation of landscape gardens in a so-called "natural" or picturesque style, relying on "the genius of the place" rather than using geometrical plans to determine plantings, architectural sites, and garden ornaments. The picturesque garden is designed but in a way that the manipulation of nature does not immediately reveal itself. In Kant's terms, "the purposiveness in its form must seem to be as free from all constraint of arbitrary rules as if it were a product of mere nature."[7] Here the distinction between natural and artistic beauty is not in terms of an object's perceptible or exhibited qualities but instead is based on how it came to be the way it is – naturally or by art. We are back to Aristotle's original distinction.[8]

It might appear that a straightforward comparison between art and nature can be made in terms of the picturesque. Indeed, eighteenth century writers referred to the designers of picturesque landscape gardens as "improvers" of nature, adding variety, complexity, and an element of surprise to natural beauty. The very notion of "improvement" connotes that an artistic, picturesque landscape was deemed aesthetically more successful than its "unimproved" ancestor. Pope writes:

> Let not each beauty ev'ry where be spy'd,
> Where half the skill is decently to hide.
> He gain all points, who pleasingly confounds,
> Surprizes, varies, and conceals the Bounds.[9]

But a detailed analysis of the picturesque suggests a rather subtle difficulty in comparing nature and art in terms of picturesque beauty. The picturesque essentially involves a *scene*, a locality or expanse that can be seen at one time (from one perspective) by a viewer – a view. This may constitute the viewer's entire visual field or it may be only a portion of the visual field isolated or framed for perceptual attention. A *vista*, for example, is a special type of scene – a distant view seen through a framing device, such as a row of trees, an opening in a hedge, an archway. The frame accentuates the depth of field, which is an important characteristic of picturesque scenes. The scene can be purely natural, or it might contain dwellings or other evidence of human modification of nature. The degree or type of naturalness will not change the fact that a scene can only be described as what would be seen from a particular vantage point. Thus even a picturesque *natural* scene literally requires a point of view, and that means it is something over and above the natural objects and relations between them at a particular location.

We do compare picturesque scenes, both natural and artistic, with each other. The difficult question remains whether what we are doing is comparing nature with art with respect to a kind of beauty. It is true that the scenic elements in a landscape garden were placed there as a result of human design and effort, while those in an upper Alpine meadow were not. But if we compare them as *scenes* and not in terms of the objects in them, then the comparison is of a different order than when, for example, we compare the beauty of a snowflake with that of a Noam Gabo sculpture. Granted we must always look at the snowflake and sculpture from some point of view or other, but our appreciation and judgment in these latter cases is still of the objects, not of the object as seen from a particular viewing position. I am not denying that meaningful comparisons can be made. My question is whether a picturesque natural scene is accurately described simply as part of nature. If it is best described as a way in which *we see* nature, or nature as seen by us in a certain way, analogous to an artistic composition, then there is some doubt that comparisons between natural scenery and its representation or artistic creation in terms of landscapes are straightforward comparisons between nature and art.

To put the point another way, the picturesque has to be discovered or noticed *by us*. In an important sense, we compose the scene, analogous to the painter who composes the picture of the natural scene. As Santayana observed, nature in the form of landscape offers no complete compositions. The *selection* of a portion of nature as a visual field with depth and a relatively high degree of complexity that works in terms of composition, and the result is then appreciated *as nature*, seems to be the primary experience of picturesque landscapes and scenes. We frame a portion of nature, choosing what is to become our field of vision *as a composition*, in all its intricacy and complexity. It remains nature, but its beauty differs from natural beauty according to the classical conception of formal perfection in one important respect: it is literally relative to the observer. And this is relativity in a different sense than the relativist's claim that beauty is *in* the eye of the beholder. So although comparisons are meaningful, they are not straightforward comparisons between art and nature as one might assume.

3. LEVELS OF AESTHETIC SIGNIFICANCE

So far I have not introduced any complications into the concepts of artistic and natural beauty in terms of the aesthetic content of the objects being compared. In particular, I have ignored the fact that artworks are expressive and are bearers of meaning. But if one focuses on this aspect of works of art, it is easy to develop a line of criticism of the meaningfulness of comparisons between artistic and natural beauty. This would be the claim that works of art embody or express intentions, emotions and feelings, ideas and values, while nature lacks these levels of significance. On this view, artworks are intentional objects whose very existence is tied to the context of their creation and culture. To treat them as mere physical objects or events isolated from this context is not to appreciate them for what they are. To appreciate them simply as one does a waterfall, a sunset, or a butterfly is not to treat them as art. Works of art are cultural artifacts, requiring interpretation and criticism to be under-stood. If this view is correct, an inevitable conclusion follows concerning aesthetically comparing art and nature. Artworks are cultural objects, with all the significance attached thereto, and the value they have for us goes beyond an appreciation of their sen-suous surface. The aesthetic appreciation of nature, on the other hand, is restricted to this surface level. Hence there is no meaning-ful way to compare the beauty of the two, if by "artistic beauty" one is including these levels of meaning.

So might go the argument. What are we to make of it? Let's accept the premise characterizing works of art as cultural objects that would not be fully appreciated for what they are if their expressive and semantic properties were to be ignored. That leaves two possible lines of rebuttal. The first line is what I shall call the *expressive nature* view, in which it is argued that natural beauty similarly possesses expressive and semantic properties, thus allowing for meaningful comparisons between art and nature. The second line is the *Hegelian view*, which reinterprets the difference between art and nature so as to make comparisons between them both meaningful and important. I'll examine these in turn.

189

Donald W. Crawford

Expressive Nature

The *expressive nature* view takes three main forms. The first version is the position of the deist, who sees nature as God's composition and sees meaning in every leaf and flower. This argument can be found in Zen Buddhism and in American Transcendentalism, for example in Ralph Waldo Emerson's famous essay "Nature." Nature is a book to be read and, like works of art, requires interpretation and criticism to be properly understood. Children's nature stories also follow this line, finding morals in the activities of mice and beavers.

A second version attributes expression and meaning to natural beauty, although only metaphorically or analogically. A good example of this is to be found in the writings of Francis Hutcheson, who maintained that parts of nature may be seen as resembling human characteristics:

Inanimate objects have often such positions as resemble those of the human body in various circumstances: these airs or gestures of the body are indications of certain dispositions in the mind...Thus a tempest at sea is often an emblem of wrath...an aged oak cut by the plow resembles the death of a blooming hero...A fruitful fancy would find in a grove, or a wood, an emblem for every character in a commonwealth, and every turn of temper, or station in life.[10]

This is certainly a more complex response to nature than merely enjoying its pleasing forms. It seems to be the view expressed in the remainder of Joyce Kilmer's poem, which you will thank me for not quoting in full. And this view is not without its contemporary supporters.[11] There is some question whether it applies to all natural beauty, but a defender could maintain that comparisons have a point when the analogues do exist. One can meaningfully compare a particularly expressive tree with a sculpture of a human being.

A third version of the *expressive nature* view argues that natural beauty exists within a context no less significant or complex than art's cultural context, and that a proper appreciation of natural beauty must take this context into account. This is the contemporary environmentalist position, whose roots I find most clearly expressed in seventeenth-century neo-Platonism. The view is that beautiful natural objects do not exist in isolation from processes of nature. To appreciate a butterfly, one must see it as a stage in a complex life cycle, within a particular habitat, related to other organisms in the context of an evolving ecosystem, etc. The proper appreciation of a beautiful meadow sees the complex, fragile ecological balance currently existing there (the contemporary context) as well as under-standing the meadow as a stage between a lake and a wooded field (the historical context).

I find much to recommend this third view, but I think it fails to meet the argument against comparing artistic and natural beauty for two reasons. First, the environmental view essentially does away with natural beauty. The scrawniest, bleeding chicken at the lowest end of the pecking order is as rightful a candidate for appreciation as a part of the natural order as is the handsomest peacock. Anything can be appreciated from this perspective, and it is difficult to see how a place remains for judgments of relative aesthetic quality. Second, although we can concur with the environmentalist's contextualizing of nature, the fact remains that the placement of art within human culture and institutions remains an *additional* context which thwarts direct comparisons with nature. We are left only with analogies between artistic and natural beauty, without knowing how to make direct comparisons.

Hegelian Nature

There is a second major line of rebuttal to the claim that artistic and natural beauty cannot be compared because of the expressive and semantic properties attributable to the former but not to the latter. This is the Hegelian reply, which accepts the differences but argues that comparisons are perfectly in order. Hegel's position is that there is a continuum in the realization of perfection of spirit, ranging from the earth itself to the highest human forms of self-consciousness. Once we understand the principle underlying the continuum – absolute spirit – we can analyze various nodes upon it and arrive at knowledgeable comparisons. Hegel's poem would begin:

> I know that I shall never see,
> A rock as lovely as a tree.
> Nor could a tree as lovely be
> As any statue is of thee.

The Hegelian reply does not deny that natural and artistic beauty are two species of one genus, but it suggests that what is more informa-tive is that there are grades or degrees of spiritual reality or self-consciousness, the manifestation of which in perceptual forms yields beauty of different orders. Some generalizations can be made: natural beauty is as a whole deficient in comparison with art, but there are

191

varying degrees of perfection within nature as well as within art. Inanimate natural objects (crystals, for example) fall below plants, which in turn are inferior to the lower animals, and on up the hierarchy of living things the story goes. Human beings are in a privileged position, and highest of all are the activities of human beings that fully reveal self-consciousness: human art, along with religion and philosophy. Art is the sensuous or perceptible rendering of the rational. Artistic beauty is not monolithic however, and the bulk of Hegel's *Aesthetic* treats of the nature and relative value of the three types of art (symbolic, classical, romantic) and the individual arts (sculpture, architecture, music, etc.). So, for Hegel, comparison lies at the heart of understanding beauty, whether in nature or in art. Perceiving beauty in art or nature consists in coming to see the determinateness of the Ideal, and that is always relative to other possible manifestations of it.

I haven't the time nor the inclination here to take on Hegel's aesthetic system and pursue what I take to be deep philosophical problems in its articulation if not its basic conception. Let me limit myself to making three points about it. First, Hegel's aesthetics is essentially a modification of the classical theory of beauty, modified by interpreting the classical line's sensuous embodiment of perfection as the embodiment of grades of spirit and self-consciousness. It is the singularity of the principle underlying all beauty that makes comparisons possible for the Hegelian.

Second, the comparative judgments of beauty promoted by the Hegelian point of view might make sense when the items being compared are far apart on the scale of self-consciousness (a rock versus a statue). But the view seems relatively uninformative, at best, when comparing the beauty of two individuals of closely situated types – for example, a five-legged versus six-legged starfish, or a Norway spruce versus a Scotch pine. If we do think meaningful comparisons can be made here, Hegel's theory is not likely to be of much help.

Third, even comparisons between rocks and statues lose something on the Hegelian model. There is no reason to look in order to make the comparative judgment. It is arguable that for the Hegelian a rock's beauty will always be inferior to that of a statue, no matter how beautiful the former and how unsuccessful the latter. The problem with this aspect of Hegelian aesthetics is that it doesn't require perceptual discrimination and sensitivity to discern beauty. A scientific description of the characteristics of the two individual types allows one to deduce which is the more beautiful. Hegel's aesthetics seems to be a theory about art forms, not individuals.

4. INTERACTIONS BETWEEN NATURE AND ART

So far the various models we have considered for comparing artistic and natural beauty have assumed a relative separation between nature and art. The situation becomes much more complicated when, as is often the case, the two are not completely independent. In this final section I shall explore some of those complications, which in many cases seem to preclude any straightforward comparison between artistic and natural beauty.

To begin with, let us make a distinction between art which is *about* nature and art which *makes direct artistic use of* the natural environment in its realization. Nineteenth-century landscape paintings depicted the landscape, and thus related to nature in this obvious way, without modifying the part of nature they represented. The natural environment is only conceptually but not physically manipulated in traditional landscape painting. In these cases, there is a subject matter which, even if make believe, can be compared to something existing, or possibly existing, in nature. In contrast, consider how representational painting might take a different form. Suppose an artist extracts color pigment from the petals of a real flower to tint a neutral paint, which he then uses to paint a highly realistic representation of that same flower. We can compare the beauty of the representation with that of the flower itself, but to do this and nothing more would be to miss an important aspect of the work. In short, it would be a misidentification of the work for purposes of comparison. Consider another example. The Musée Rodin in Paris has some sculptures magnificently placed in the open air, but their aesthetic significance, at least as sculptures by Rodin, is not thereby changed; the sculptures do not thereby come to be about their setting. Of course an enterprising gallery director could display Rodin's *The Kiss* on a sunken platform in the middle of a lily pond, thereby incorporating the natural environment into the setting for the work. But if the natural setting itself or its interaction with the original sculpture becomes an important part of what is aesthetically appreciated, and if that goes beyond Rodin's original conception, then we may conclude that the innovation of the gallery director – using nature along with Rodin's sculpture for a presentation of his or her own works – is a new artwork, a combined- or mixed-media work.[12]

These niceties can be ignored for present purposes, but the mixture of aesthetic categories is important. Consider artworks that directly make use of the natural environment in their artistic realization, and that, when realized, are best interpreted as being at least in part about that very environment, or about our relationships to it. Here the more general concept of reference replaces resemblance or imitation as the important category in appreciating these works, and the classical model of beauty is left far behind. The question to be raised here is whether such art might be compared with natural beauty, and, if so, whether such comparisons are informative.

This distinction between art which is about nature and art which makes direct artistic use of nature also helps unravel a number of issues raised by environmental art. Some of these problems are interpretive or critical in nature, relating to the significance or aesthetic value of environmental art. Others border on the ethical, concerning the legitimacy of artistic manipulations of the environment.[13]

In previous papers, I have distinguished three different aesthetically dynamic relationships between art and nature.[14] Perhaps they can be made useful here. The first I called the *aesthetic symbiosis* of the artifactual and the natural. Here the relationship between art and nature is harmonious and the aesthetic effects range from peaceful coexistence to beneficial interaction. Outdoor sculpture and environmental constructions sometimes harmonize with their sites, drawing attention to and sometimes enhancing the aesthetic qualities of the natural setting. The same is sometimes true of architectural constructions, such as a castle or a monastery perched on a dramatic elevation, a farmstead nestled in a verdant valley, or a domestic dwelling adapted to a natural site. In such cases the aesthetic qualities of the building may be enhanced by the natural setting while at the same time the aesthetic qualities of the natural setting are highlighted or gain in stature. The comparison of artistic and natural beauty is not at issue here in any straightforward way; instead, whatever the conceptions may be of the two, they are merely being brought together.

The second dynamic relationship between the artifactual and the natural I termed *dialectical*. In general, in a dialectical relationship the two elements of the relationship are conflicting forces whose interaction brings into being some third object – the product of their interaction. The emergent third object may become a new object of aesthetic appreciation, one which results from the synthesis of opposing forces, artifactual and natural. In some cases the synthesis need not negate or dissolve either the natural or the artifactual; each may retain its identity, and the aesthetic significance of each is dependent upon the interaction between the two – hence the term "dialectical." I found this relationship exemplified by Robert Smithson's *Spiral Jetty*, by Christo's *Valley Curtain, Running Fence*, and *Surrounded Islands*, and by some ruins *in situ*. Since in such cases the aesthetic object is essentially a product of the natural and the artistic, any direct comparison between artistic and natural beauty seems inapplicable.

A third dynamic relationship is also possible. The symbiotic relationship is harmonious coexistence; the dialectical relationship is synthesis through conflicting interaction. There remains the possibility of an interaction between art and nature which results in destruction of one by the other – the domination of nature by art or of art by nature. I called this relation *parasitic*, and the examples I cited were endless rows of tract homes eradicating the natural landscape. The artistic domination of nature to the point of nature's subordination or eradication is possible even if highly controversial. In this context I presented two fictitious examples from contemporary environmental sculpture. In the first an artist dynamites a small, isolated hill, leveling it, destroying all natural vegetation; he fully documents the event and displays the documentation in a gallery. In the second example, the artist pours various types of oil on the surface of a lake to create striking color patterns that change over time; in effect he uses the lake surface as his canvas. Under our current climate which values our respect for nature, these examples invite a comparison between artistic and natural beauty, but the comparison is not obviously an aesthetic one, unless one characterizes the aesthetic in broader parameters than in the past. There may be good reason to do that, that is, to argue that a formalist analysis of those works is inadequate. This raises the question whether, in the absence of any other higher order principles, comparisons to either artistic or natural beauty are in order unless one has a higher order principle in terms of which the comparisons are being made.

We need to recognize, however, that in many cases of contemporary environmental sculpture the work succeeds only because the natural setting or an aspect of nature functions as a part of the work. In such cases, nature is used to refer to that very relationship (whether harmonious, dialectical, or parasitic). These complex relationships between art and nature preclude direct comparisons with natural or artistic beauty, at least on traditional models of aesthetic evaluation.

5. CONCLUSION

In this essay I have explored the implications of diverse models of the relationship between art and nature with respect to the issue of comparing artistic and natural beauty. The conclusions I have reached might not be as categorical as one would like. But there are some general conclusions with important implications for aesthetic theory. First, if one adheres to a single primary aesthetic principle that can be exemplified to varying degrees, then one can make comparisons between artistic and natural beauty. For example, the classical organic unity principle and its modern formalist relatives allow for such comparisons, as does the Hegelian principle of manifestation of Spirit. Second, the view that art and nature are appreciated aesthetically for quite different reasons does not necessarily rule out meaningful comparisons between the two. One can opt for the *expressive nature* position, such as the environmentalist's, which allows for metaphorical comparisons between natural and artistic beauty. The other alternative seems to be a reversion to the apples-and-oranges school, in which case there is no choice but to give bad marks to poets like Joyce Kilmer.

Notes

1 Cleanth Brooks and Robert Penn Warren, *Understanding Poetry*, 3rd. edition. (New York; Holt, Reinhart, and Winston, 1960), p. 289. This criticism is noted by Michael Hancher in a stimulating article, "Poems versus Trees: The Aesthetics of Monroe Beardsley," *The Journal of Aesthetics and Art Criticism*, 31.2 (winter 1972): 181. Hancher goes on to show how the aesthetics of Monroe Beardsley deprecates the aesthetic value of nature. Beardsley's view is that objects have aesthetic value insofar as they have the instrumental capacity to effect an aesthetic experience, and an aesthetic experience is characterized by certain qualities – especially unity, complexity, and intensity – which are supposed to be correlative to the presence of those same qualities in the aesthetic object (*ibid.*, p. 184). Beardsley then argues that works of art have the special function of providing aesthetic experiences: they do it best, and most dependably, and they alone do it in the highest magnitude

(M. C. Beardsley, *Aesthetics: Problems in the Philosophy of Criticism* (New York: Harcourt Brace and World Inc., 1958), p. 530).

Hancher argues, correctly I think, that Beardsley's general criteria do not in themselves factor art over nature. Rather it is Beardsley's specific interpretation of the third criterion – intensity – to mean the intensity of human regional or expressive qualities, that seems to lead to his conclusion that nature falls short of art in its capacity to provide aesthetic experiences.

2 "For beauty includes three conditions, *integrity* or *perfection*, since those things which are impaired are by the very fact ugly; due *proportion* or *harmony*; and lastly, *brightness* or *clarity*, whence things are called beautiful which have a bright color." *Summa Theologica*, question 39, article 8, in *Basic Writings of Saint Thomas Aquinas*, trans. Lawrence Shapcote, (New York: Random House, 1945), vol. 2, p. 443.

3 There is also the issue of whether "due proportion" can be read in a sufficiently value-neutral way so that it can function as a criterion of beauty. I have discussed this briefly in "Art into Nature: Decoration, Incursion, or Revelation?" in *The Reasons of Art*, Peter J. McCormick, ed., (University of Ottawa Press, 1985), pp. 234–6.

4 Aristotle, *Poetics*, 7, 1450b–1451a; trans. S. H. Butcher, in *Aristotle, On the Art of Poetry* (Indianapolis: Bobbs-Merrill, Inc., Liberal Arts Press, 1956), pp. 11–12.

5 *Ibid.*, 1451a5; p. 12.

6 William Gilpin, *An Essay on Prints* (1768), p. 2.

7 Immanuel Kant, *Critique of Judgement*, section 45.

8 Aristotle, *Physics*, book II.

9 Alexander Pope, "Epistle to Richard Boyle, Earl of Burlington" (1731), lines 53–6; included as Epistle IV in *Moral Essays: In Four Epistles to Several Persons* (1734). See also Humphrey Repton's "Red Books".

10 Francis Hutcheson, *An Inquiry into the Original of Our Ideas of Beauty and Virtue* (1725), 4.1.

11 Mark Sagoff, "On Preserving the Natural Environment," *Yale Law Journal*, 84 (1974): 205–67.

12 This example raises questions concerning the interpretive activity of gallery directors through their choice of display conditions. There is, of course, a continuum here, running from more-or-less neutral presentation (which cannot be specified absolutely but is relative to a given work and perhaps even the viewer), to a modest interpretation, to a more manifest critical statement (for example, by juxtaposition), all the way to the use of an existing work to make a new one. Nelson Goodman has argued that the primary function of museums is to implement works of art, to make them work, as distinct from the execution of the work, which he characterizes as the whole process of making it. He concludes that "implementation is the process of bringing about the aesthetic functioning that provides the basis for the notion of a work of art." Nelson Goodman, "Implementation of the Arts." *The Journal of Aesthetics and Art Criticism*, 40.2 (spring 1982): 28.

13 "Art into Nature: Decoration, Incursion, or Revelation?" in P. J. McCormick, ed., *The Reasons of Art* (University of Ottawa Press, 1985), pp. 232–42.
14 In the article cited in the previous note as well as in "Nature and Art: Some Dialectical Relationships," *Journal of Aesthetics and Art Criticism,* 42.1 (autumn 1983): 49–58.

10

Appreciating art and appreciating nature

ALLEN CARLSON

I. THE CONCEPT OF APPRECIATION

The concept of appreciation is common to both art appreciation and nature appreciation. However, it is usually not examined in the relevant theoretical work. Writings on appreciating art by art critics and art historians seldom touch on it. Nature literature may exemplify it but typically does not discuss it. Investigations of aesthetic appreciation by aestheticians dwell on the nature of the aesthetic and have little to say about appreciation. That the concept is not discussed is a pity, for it is central both to philosophical aesthetics and to our day to day dealings with such matters. Not only are the notions of art appreciation and nature appreciation in common usage, but we move with ease from the appreciation of landscapes to that of landscape paintings, from appreciating Van Gogh's *The Starry Night* to appreciating the starry heavens above. Yet the nature of appreciation is far from clear and what is involved in each of these two central cases – appreciating art and appreciating nature – remains obscure.

Thus, some clarification of appreciation is useful. To achieve it, since our topic is the appreciation of both art and nature, it is appropriate to consider a philosophical tradition which in its infancy thought nature at least as significant as art as an object of aesthetic appreciation. The tradition ties appreciation to notions such as disinterestedness. Although this position like most others in philosophical aesthetics is more concerned with the aesthetic than with appreciation, it yet provides insight into the nature of appreciation. Equally important, it points the way to a flaw in much philosophical thinking about appreciation – a flaw which apparently stems from its myopic focus on the aesthetic. Both the insight and the flaw can be clarified, adequately for present purposes, by considering the recent version of the position presented by Jerome Stolnitz and the attack on it by George Dickie.[1] Stolnitz's elaboration of "the aesthetic attitude" illustrates the insight; Dickie's elaboration of "the myth of the aesthetic attitude" brings out the flaw.

Stolnitz's version of the disinterestedness position focuses on a special attitude, the aesthetic attitude, defined as "disinterested and sympathetic attention to and contemplation of any object of awareness whatever, for its own sake alone."[2] True to the tradition, Stolnitz does not directly discuss aesthetic *appreciation*. However, it is to be treated, it may be assumed, as related notions such as "aesthetic experience" which are "defined by reference to" the aesthetic attitude.[3] Thus, aesthetic appreciation would be defined as the total appreciation engaged in while this attitude is being taken. Consequently, insights into the nature of appreciation are provided in Stolnitz's remarks about taking the aesthetic attitude.

The most fundamental of these insights about aesthetic appreciation concerns what may be termed its scope. Although at points in its history the disinterestedness tradition apparently judged certain kinds of objects to be closed to disinterested attention and therefore essentially nonaesthetic, the tradition by and large emphasizes a broad scope for appreciation. This is cited by Stolnitz as one of two major reasons for preferring this line of approach to others. In Stolnitz's version of the position the scope is in fact "limitless" in that the "aesthetic attitude can be adopted toward 'any object of awareness whatever.'"[4] The recognition of such a scope for aesthetic appreciation is particularly important for understanding nature appreciation, for nature, noted for diversity, comes in all shapes and sizes and all types and kinds, many seemingly not tailor-made for appreciation as are paradigmatic works of art.

A second significant dimension of appreciation can be clarified by noting how it differs from some other notions utilized in the tradition and in fact contained in Stolnitz's definition – notions such as contemplation and awareness. Here Stolnitz's appeal to the concept of an attitude is helpful, although often it is simply misleading. As Stolnitz emphasizes, attitudes are directive, they organize, orientate, and guide. This directive nature "prepares us to *respond*" and the responsiveness of appreciation separates it from passive states such as contemplation or awareness.[5] Indeed, Stolnitz thinks it "safe" to use the word "contemplation" only after stressing that taking the aesthetic attitude is an "alert and vigorous" business in which we focus "discriminating attention" upon the object, "'key up' our capacities of imagination and emotion to respond to it," and engage in a range of emotional, cognitive, and physical "activity."[6] In this way appreciation is severed from what Stolnitz describes as the "blank, cow-like stare" often associated with contemplation, with disinterestedness, and with the aesthetic itself.[7] Rather it is aligned with the slogan Stolnitz adopts from a psychologist: "Appreciation...is awareness, alertness, animation."[8]

The active nature of appreciation helps to illuminate the flaw that mars the tradition's treatment of it, a flaw central to Dickie's attack. The problem develops because, unlike either a blank, cow-like stare which needs no guidance or serene contemplation which needs only a little, active appreciation requires considerable guidance. Stolnitz relies on attitudes here which, since they organize, orientate, and guide, provide by means of the aesthetic attitude a *general aesthetic criterion* for the guidance of appreciation. Dickie attacks this as the first way the disinterestedness tradition "misleads aesthetic theory": the way it sets "the limits of aesthetic relevance."[9] This may be called the issue of aesthetic relevance, the issue of how to guide appreciation or, more precisely, how to determine what is relevant to the appreciation of particular objects. It is not only the issue upon which the disinterestedness treatment of appreciation stumbles, it is a key issue in any such treatment.

The tradition's problems with aesthetic relevance stem from a tension among its essential elements. The tension is present throughout the tradition but is especially evident in Stolnitz's definition which requires attention to be both disinterested and sympathetic. Disinterestedness pulls toward the general criterion of aesthetic relevance, sympathy in the other direction. The tension is illuminated by the responsive nature of appreciation. By contrast, the blank cow-like stare can be both disinterested and sympathetic. What does it matter? It does not respond. But since appreciation is responsive, to sympathetically respond it must, as Stolnitz says, "accept the object 'on its own terms,'" "follow the lead of the object and respond in concert with it" – only in this way can we "relish its individual quality."[10] On the other hand, disinterestedness requires an experience which "at its best, seems to isolate both us and the object from the flow of experience," one in which the object "is divorced from its interrelations with other things."[11] The question is which "other things," in particular which, as Stolnitz puts it, "thoughts or images or bits of knowledge which are not present within the object itself" are relevant to its appreciation?[12] The tradition's answer – the general criterion of aesthetic relevance – is that it depends on whether any such thought, image, or bit of knowledge is "aesthetic" which in turn "depends on whether it is compatible with the attitude of 'disinterested attention.'"[13] The upshot is that much that might enhance the appreciation of an object – help us to "relish its individual quality" – is condemned as nonaesthetic and therefore as irrelevant to aesthetic appreciation.

Thus, the elaborations of disinterestedness and sympathy place these two concepts at odds. To make the conflict perfectly clear only requires the right kinds of objects. In responsive appreciation we must "follow the lead of the object" yet isolate and divorce it and ourselves from "its interrelations with other things," unless such things are compatible with "disinterested attention." But what if an object does not lead in that direction, what if it resists being isolated and divorced from its interrelations? Indeed, although some works of art may be "aesthetic" in the sense that they readily yield to being – in fact are explicitly created to be – so isolated and divorced, many other works and most nonart, and nature in particular, are precisely not "aesthetic" in this limiting sense. Thus, to respond to such objects as if they were is not to follow their lead, not to be sympathetic to them, not to appreciate them. Does this mean that these "nonaesthetic" objects which cling to their interrelations with other things are therefore closed to "disinterested attention"? This cannot be, for, as noted, at least at this late date in the tradition, the aesthetic attitude is limitless, it can be taken toward "any object of awareness whatever." It becomes clear that something must go.

As is typical in such cases, however, the reaction is an over-reaction. It is clear that something must go and what has gone is most of the disinterestedness tradition along with its insight concerning appreciation. The isolation of the appreciator and the object and the divorcing of the latter from its interrelations, all seemingly required by disinterestedness, are taken, with some justification, to after all reduce appreciation to the notorious cow-like stare. With this *reductio* in mind, critics lose sight of the rich, expansive, and responsive notion of appreciation contained in the tradition. Indeed, some reactions are more extreme. Dickie, for example, overreacting to his own critique, seemingly rejects the very concept of the aesthetic: "there is no reason to think that there is a special kind of aesthetic consciousness, attention, or perception. Similarly, I do not think there is any reason to think that there is a special kind of aesthetic appreciation."[14] This may be to throw out the baby with the bath water, but it has a point: The problem with the disinterestedness tradition, as with philosophical aesthetics in general, is that too much attention is paid to the concept of the aesthetic and too little to that of appreciation. The attempt to accommodate the former warps disinterestedness and therefore appreciation itself into a restrictive and isolating state, caricaturizable as the cow-like stare. A shift of emphasis to the latter yields a different picture.

Interesting enough, such a shift of emphasis, together with its happy consequences, is evident within the disinterestedness tradition itself. For example, once Stolnitz moves from philosophical analysis of the aesthetic attitude to consideration of art appreciation, the story changes dramatically. Instead of the strict application of the general criterion of aesthetic relevance, we find concerning, for instance, the issue of relevant knowledge: "We need not, however, condemn all 'knowledge about' as aesthetically irrelevant...'Knowledge about' is relevant under three conditions: when it does not weaken or destroy aesthetic attention to the object, when it pertains to the meaning and expressiveness of the object, and when it enhances the quality and significance of one's immediate aesthetic response to the object."[15] Note that only the first condition accommodates the aesthetic; the latter two aim at enhancing the appreciation of the object. With the emphasis thus shifted to appreciation, sympathy outweighs disinterestedness, and we truly "follow the lead of the object." Moreover, it is now not the blind leading the blind, for the aestheticizing cow-like stare gives way to appreciation not only responsive to the object but informed by knowledge about it.

The shift of emphasis to appreciation is followed up by Paul Ziff. Ziff's treatment is informative in that it retains the insights of the disinterestedness position without embracing its flaws.[16] The essence of his account is the notion of an "act of aspection," the way of attending to an object which in part constitutes its appreciation.[17] Ziff argues that different acts of aspection are appropriate in the appreciation of, for example, works of art of different kinds, styles, and schools. Thus, knowledge of a work's history and nature dictates the proper acts of aspection: Appreciation is a set of activities not only responsive to the object but incorporating knowledge of it as an essential component. Ziff further argues not simply that "anything that can be viewed is a fit object for aesthetic attention," but that "anything viewed makes demands."[18] That objects of appreciation make demands means that following the lead of the object rules out

the possibility of anything like a general criterion of aesthetic relevance. Since objects of appreciation obviously differ a great deal, so
does what is relevant to and involved in their appreciation: "As the
character of the objects attended to vary, the character of the actions,
the conditions, and the requisite qualities, skills, and capacities of the
person may also have to vary, if attention to the objects is to be
aesthetically worthwhile."[19] Thus, the appreciation of each of, to use
Ziff's examples, Leonardo's *Ginevra de' Benci, Mona Lisa,* the *Barry
McKenzie* comic strip, an alligator basking in the sun, or a pile of
dried dung requires engaging in different acts of aspection, using
different capacities and skills, and knowing different things. The
general criterion of aesthetic relevance is replaced by object given
indications of appreciative relevance.

Stolnitz's and Ziff's remarks on appreciation demonstrate that
although philosophical aesthetics has relatively little to say about the
concept, it is yet possible to derive from its investigation of the
aesthetic some useful observations. Ironically it is precisely in
drawing back from the tradition's obsession with the aesthetic that
the concept of appreciation is brought into focus. The obsession with
the aesthetic inhibits a proper understanding of appreciation by
pulling in the direction of a passive state of limited scope, restricted
by a general criterion of aesthetic relevance, and comparable to a
blank, cow-like stare. By contrast, the concept of appreciation which
can be coaxed from philosophical aesthetics, seemingly almost
against its will, reveals appreciation as engaged mental and physical
activity applicable to any object whatever, exceedingly responsive to
that object, and guided almost exclusively by its nature.

We may conclude this discussion of appreciation by asking, in light
of the object-orientated nature of appreciation, what remains of the
idea that the tradition attempts to capture with concepts such as
disinterestedness? What becomes of the isolating attention intended
to divorce both the object and the appreciator from all that is
irrelevant to the object's appreciation? In fact there is in the object-
orientated notion a significant residue of this idea. It is that to follow
the lead of the object and be guided by it is to be "object-ively"
guided. This sense of objective is the most basic: It concerns the
object and its properties and is opposed to subjective in the sense of
concerning the subject and its properties. Appreciating objectively in
this sense is appreciating the object as and for what it is and as and for
having the properties it has. It is in opposition to appreciating
subjectively in which the subject – the appreciator – and its prop-

erties are in some way imposed on the object, or, more generally, something other than the object is imposed on it.

Thus, the insight of the disinterestedness part of the tradition is that insofar as appreciation is disinterested it is objective. And when it fails to be, it is in a corresponding sense subjective and involves viewing the object as something it is not or as having properties it does not have. Thus, appreciation is isolating only in the sense that both object and appreciator must be divorced from that which is not true of the object. In short, it is the false that is incompatible with disinterested attention and therefore irrelevant to aesthetic appreciation. The insight contained in the passive, blank, cow-like stare is that it limits itself to the dull, objective truth. Moreover, in that disinterestedness constitutes part of the analysis of the aesthetic, aesthetic appreciation is therefore no more *or less* than appreciation in this sense objective. To appreciate something aesthetically is to appreciate it as and for, to use the phrase Butler coined in another context, "what it is, and not another thing." No wonder everything is open to aesthetic appreciation.

The notion of object-orientated aesthetic appreciation which thus emerges from philosophical aesthetics is precisely the kind of concept required for a fruitful investigation of appreciating art and appreciating nature. Given the "limitless" scope which it grants appreciation, such a notion is especially useful in understanding the appreciation of diverse kinds of things, such as works of art and natural objects. Moreover, the concept of object-orientated appreciation facilitates the constructive comparison of different kinds of appreciation, of art appreciation and nature appreciation, without the assimilation of one to the other. Without a concept of appreciation which allows, indeed requires, appreciative activity to respond directly to and to vary according to the nature of different kinds of objects, there is a danger of all appreciation being assimilated to one model – typically that of the appreciation of the most conventional kind of art. However, although it must not be taken as the model for all other forms of appreciation, the appreciation of conventional and therefore paradigmatic works of art is yet the proper starting point for any investigation of different kinds of appreciation.

II. APPRECIATING ART: DESIGN APPRECIATION

What is involved in the appreciation of paradigmatic works of art or, more precisely, what is paradigmatic art appreciation? Given the object-orientated nature of appreciation, there must be diverse kinds of art appreciation, each requiring engaging in different physical and mental acts of aspection, using different capacities and skills, and knowing different things. Indeed, they may have little in common, not even the utilization of any one sense modality. Nonetheless, the question is what is central to all these many diverse kinds of appreciation – what in general is significant in art appreciation? Seemingly the only possible answer is the appreciation of design: Paradigmatic art appreciation must be at least appreciation of a thing as something designed and therefore as something which is the creation of a designer. To put it another way, appreciation of art *qua* art must be appreciation *qua* creation of an artist.

That art appreciation is artist or designer centered seems an obvious point, but it is not always fully appreciated in philosophical aesthetics. To some extent the prominence of the disinterestedness tradition is responsible. As noted, when developed in certain ways, the notion of disinterestedness requires that the object of appreciation be isolated and divorced from its interrelationships with other things, its appreciation being strictly constrained by the general criterion of aesthetic relevance. The result is a purified aesthetic object, divorced from its own history, even from the fact that it is the product of a designer. Moreover, in recent philosophy of art criticism this perverse offspring of disinterestedness gives comfort to and joins with anti-intentionalism in an attempt to ban almost any knowledge of the artist from the appreciation of his creations.[20] Thus, the disinterestedness tradition, with a little assistance, completely obscures the designer-centered nature of paradigmatic art appreciation.

This line of thought, however, stems from the same mishandling of disinterestedness that obscures the object-orientated nature of appreciation. Consider the fact that even if a work is explicitly designed by its creator to be an isolated, pure aesthetic object, narrowly "aesthetic" in the sense required by the general criterion of aesthetic relevance, it is nonetheless still *designed by its creator* to be that way. Thus, appreciation which to any extent follows the lead of the object, although it may appropriately ignore many other facts about such an object, simply cannot ignore the central fact that the object is designed to be the way it is – that its being designed is the essence of its being "what it is, and not another thing." Consequently, in that appreciation is objective in the sense noted in section I, the fact that paradigmatic art appreciation is designer centered likewise cannot be ignored. The failure to appreciate this is one of the major ways philosophical aesthetics is misled by its disregard for the concept of appreciation and its obsession with the aesthetic.

Whatever the state of affairs in philosophical aesthetics, the point that art appreciation must focus on the artist is seemingly taken for granted by art critics and art historians. A glance at the treatment of the point in some classic discussions of the history of art is revealing. For example, E. H. Gombrich opens *The Story of Art* with the uncompromising claim that: "There really is no such thing as Art. There are only artists."[21] He elaborates by stressing that "what we call 'works of art' are not the results of some mysterious activity, but objects made by human beings for human beings" – objects designed such that "every one of their features is the result of a decision by the artist."[22] Indeed, Gombrich characterizes the artist as the ultimate designer, one who "must always be 'fussy' or rather fastidious to the extreme," obsessed with, as he puts it, "whether he has got it 'right'."[23] Gombrich discusses what he calls "that modest little word 'right'" at great lengths so that we may "begin to understand what artists are really after."[24]

The theme that art appreciation is designer centered is similarly evident in the introductory chapter of H. W. Janson's classic textbook, *History of Art*, aptly titled "The Artist and His Public." In discussing originality in artistic creation, Janson notes that appreciation of the ancient bronze, *Thorn Puller*, is destroyed by the knowledge that the piece is not the creation of a designing intellect, but rather an *ad hoc* combination of preexisting parts. He claims that with this knowledge "we no longer see it as a single, harmonious unit but as a somewhat incongruous combination."[25] When we cannot appreciate the bronze as a designed whole, as the creation of a designer, its appreciation as a work of art is not possible. Observations of the kind exemplified by Gombrich and Janson support the view that at the center of appropriate appreciation of conventional works of art is the idea that the object of appreciation is a designed object, an object created such that all its significant qualities are, as Gombrich stresses, results of decisions by a designer. This kind of appreciation, the essence of paradigmatic art appreciation, may be called design appreciation.

What are the significant features of design appreciation? The object must be appreciated as a designed object – but what does this entail? Designed objects involve three key entities: the initial design, the object embodying this design, and the individual who embodies the design in the object. With the first, the design, the central issue is what is being done or what the undertaking is or, as it is sometimes put in artistic discussions, what problem is being solved or, as it is put, rather unfortunately, in some literature in aesthetics, what the artist's intentions are. With the second, the object, what is important are its given properties, its strengths, weaknesses, limits and potentials, what can and can not be done with it, what is a use, and what an abuse, of it. With the third, the individual, what is most central are his abilities and skills, his talents, as a designer, both at the individual and the human level, and the ways these talents are used to embody the design in the object.

Design appreciation involves awareness and understanding of the three entities and their central properties. Especially important is awareness and understanding of the interplay among them and of the ways they function, severally and jointly, to achieve this interplay, for the interplay embodies the design and thereby determines the nature of the object of appreciation. In this sense design appreciation is object orientated: Knowledge of the nature of the object dictates relevant acts of aspection and guides the appreciative response. A part of this response involves making judgments about the interplay, ones which assess the designed object in terms of the talents of the designer and the undertaking set by the initial design – judgments such as whether the object is a success or failure, good or bad, or, as it is often put, whether it "works" or, as Gombrich puts it, whether it is "right." Such judgments, together with the mental and physical acts of aspection required for making them, are at the core of design appreciation – and thus essential to paradigmatic art appreciation.

III. APPRECIATING ART: ORDER APPRECIATION

Design appreciation is essential to paradigmatic art appreciation, but, as noted, the latter must not be unthinkingly taken as the model for all other forms of appreciation. Consideration of some unconventional works of art and their nonparadigmatic yet appropriate appreciation is more helpful in understanding the appreciation of nonart and that of nature in particular. As an initial case in point, consider what is called action painting; a specific example is Jackson Pollock's *One* (#31). Its creation is described by art historian Werner Haftmann: "The canvas is placed on the ground. Casting off all intellectual control, the painter moves over it with complete spontaneity; the liquid paint dripping from his brush or from a tin with holes in it weaves the trace of his gestures into a dense filigree."[26] Haftmann adds that a "work so produced is a direct record of the psyche" and that the process of production came to be regarded by Pollock as "pure action, an intricate trance-like choreography" the trace of which "registers the artist's inner life."[27]

What should be said about action painting concerning design, object, and artist? First, there does not seem to be an initial design which becomes embodied in the object. Haftmann says that such art is composed of and "by motor energies."[28] However, even if an embodied design is lacking, the "motor energies" yet form a pattern, which is a function of the interplay between the other two entities. Thus, Janson says of Pollock's works: "The actual shapes visible... are largely determined by the internal dynamics of his material and his process: the viscosity of the paint, the speed and direction of its impact upon the canvas, its interaction with other layers of pigment."[29] In this way the object and its properties achieve a greater significance than they have in more conventional art: They are no longer constrained by an attempt to make them embody a particular given design; rather they in part strongly determine a resultant pattern.

The role of the artist is more perplexing. Haftmann characterizes him as moving with "complete spontaneity" and as "casting off all intellectual control." Pollock remarked in 1947: "When I am in my painting, I'm not aware of what I'm doing."[30] However, Pollock also noted in 1951, perhaps in response to the criticism that he, to quote Janson, "is not sufficiently in control of his medium," that: "When I am painting I have a general notion as to what I am about. I *can* control the flow of paint: there is no accident."[31] Janson's cowboy analogy is illuminating: "Pollock does not simply 'let go' and leave the rest to chance, He is himself the ultimate source of energy for these forces, and he 'rides' them as a cowboy might ride a wild horse, in a frenzy of psychophysical action."[32] Such an artist is not happily described as a designer, creating objects such that, as Gombrich puts it, "every one of their features is the result of a decision." Rather the artist has only "a general notion" of what he is about and provides "the ultimate source of energy" for the creation of the object, but not much more. The role of the artist therefore becomes similar to that of the object and its given properties: The artist is not the embodier of a design but rather only one force among others, which working together determine a pattern.

However, although in one sense the artist is assimilated to his materials, he also acquires another feature. Even if an individual is an artist, not every set of drippings, spatterings, and dribblings he initiates "weaves the trace of his gestures into a dense filigree." Not every pattern is an appreciable pattern. Pollock's *One*, in the Museum of Modern Art, is subtitled #31 and as Janson says, following up his cowboy metaphor, Pollock "does not always stay in the saddle."[33] What happens when he falls out? Where are the paintings *One* (#s 1–30)? It seems not every pattern is *selected* as an object of appreciation. Perhaps those selected are only those which seem to reveal "motor energies" or demonstrate "internal dynamics" of materials and process or actually "weave the trace" of the artist's gestures and "directly record" his "psyche." In short, appreciable patterns are those which reveal, or at least can be seen as revealing, an *order*, those which are or can be seen as the marks of the forces which have ordered the drips, spatters, and dribbles into whatever pattern they form. Thus, although the artist loses his role as designer, he acquires the role of selecting ordered and hence appreciable patterns.

Two additional cases, less conventional than action painting and rather more what is called anti-art, further develop the themes introduced by Pollock's work. The first involves Dada experiments with "automatic" writing and drawing and "chance" poetry and collage, especially as developed by Tristan Tzara and Hans Arp. Haftmann reports: "Tzara would draw slips of paper with words inscribed on them from a hat, and present the resulting combination of words as a poem; Arp allowed cut-outs of free or geometric shapes to arrange themselves in a random order, then pasted them on a surface, and presented the result as a picture."[34] He further notes: "In the course of such experiments, Arp also used automatic drawing, i.e., irrational, spontaneously traced forms rising from the un-conscious."[35]

The key elements introduced in these experiments are spontaneity, randomness, and chance. Moreover, unlike Pollock who somewhat unconvincingly claims that "there is no accident," these artists embrace random chance as a significant part of the process. Janson claims: "The only law respected by the Dadaists was that of chance."[36] Thus, and this is especially clear concerning "automatic" works, the artist is completely reduced to a force not unlike his materials – a force played upon by chance. The focus is not on *recording* the artist's "psychophysical action" but on the spon-taneous working out of the unconscious, the irrational. The artist's role is retained only insofar as there is after-the-fact alteration or, as with Pollock, selection of certain results rather than others. For example, Janson reports that Arp sometimes "cautiously adjusted" a "'natural' configuration."[37] Moreover, some selection must play a part in the overall process; not every one of Arp's experiments achieved the status of *Collage with Squares Arranged According to the Laws of Chance*, a work in the Museum of Modern Art.

The element of selection comes completely into its own only in another kind of anti-art. Although evident in the Dadaist movement, it is most perfectly exemplified in those works of Marcel Duchamp called found art. When Duchamp selected a urinal, a bottle rack, or a typewriter cover for display as a found object, selection itself became the heart of the process. Moreover, it is the fact of selection which is significant, rather than exactly what is selected, for in many instances one object does as well as another. In some surrealist experiments with found objects chance is in fact the means of selection. For example, Salvador Dali suggests: "Each of the experimenters is given an alarm-watch which will go off at a time he must not know. Having this watch in his pocket, he carries on as usual and at the very instant the alarm goes off he must note where he is and what most strikingly impinges on his senses."[38] The fact of selection is all that counts; the object selected is left totally to chance.

Dadaist and surrealist art, more so than Pollock's, brings out the fact that all these works have little to do with traditional artistic and aesthetic concerns. For example, Dali claims the point of surrealist experiments is to realize "to what extent objective perception depends upon imaginative representation."[39] Haftmann reports that in general such techniques are "methods for opening the way to the store of images preserved in the unconscious. Their purpose is never to produce 'art'; all of them are conceived merely as instruments for exploring man's potentialities."[40] In a similar way, Duchamp's pieces, Dada experiments, and even Pollock's paintings seem to have no artistic or aesthetic basis. The urinal was not selected, in spite of what George Dickie suggests, because of "its gleaming white surface."[41] Duchamp says: "A point that I want very much to establish is that the choice of these Readymades was never dictated by aesthetic delectation. The choice was based on a reaction of *visual indifference* with a total absence of good or bad taste."[42] Likewise, the Dada experiments, as those of surrealism, aim not at artistic or aesthetic qualities but at "new psychological discoveries" – "a release of the forces of the subconscious."[43] And Pollock's paintings, as noted, are a means of producing "a direct record of the psyche."[44]

Allen Carlson

The lack of regard for artistic and aesthetic concerns displayed by these works has ramifications for their appreciation. The works are not designed nor even selected to either solve conventional artistic problems or exemplify traditionally important aesthetic qualities such as grace or delicacy. Yet the forces of creation or selection operate such that these objects have appreciable patterns – patterns ordered by and revelatory of these forces. But the creation or selection, and hence the ordering, is typically accomplished by reference to some general ideas or beliefs having little to do with aesthetics or with art in a traditional sense. Instead the ideas or beliefs characteristically concern the way these works can reveal the nature and the order of things such as the subconscious, the unconscious, the human mind, the human condition. Thus, anything like a general criterion of *aesthetic* relevance is completely irrelevant and even paradigmatic design-focused art appreciation seems quite out of place. Such appreciation is appropriate for artistically designed aesthetic objects and gets little purchase on unconventional works of art and anti-art. Some other form of appreciation is required.

The form of appreciation required may be called, in contrast to design appreciation, order appreciation, for to the extent that these works have anything comparable to a design, it is only an ordered pattern. The exact nature of such appreciation can be elaborated by further pursuing the comparison with design appreciation and the entities involved: the initial design, the object embodying the design, and the individual who embodies the design. As noted, the first is absent; there is no given design embodied in an object. However, for designed objects the initial design indicates what is being done, what the undertaking is. Thus, if this task is to be accomplished for an object with only an ordered pattern, it must be by some other means. In fact at least something similar is accomplished by the ideas and beliefs which play a role in the creation or selection of the object. Although they are typically nonartistic and nonaesthetic, they yet indicate if not what is being done, then at least what is going on in an ordered object. Thus, they help make the ordered pattern visible and intelligible somewhat as the initial design does for the designed object. Consequently, awareness and understanding of them and their interplay with the other entities is significant in order appreciation, as is the comparable knowledge of the initial design in design appreciation.

The remaining two entities, although not absent, are greatly altered. The object embodying the design no longer embodies a

212

design and the individual who embodies the design is no longer a designer. The object is a thing shaped and molded by a combination of forces: initially, its own given properties, its strengths, weaknesses, limits and potentialities, but also the forces of random chance and of the artist acting upon it – and acting with control only barely more significant than exercised by the object or by chance. Thus, as the third entity is only one force among many, he is in large part assimilated to the other forces – a part of the process and the materials rather than a master of them. But the third entity also has another role: He selects from what these forces, including his own, produce, and in selecting relies on some general ideas and beliefs in light of which the object's pattern seems visible and intelligible – can be perceived and understood as ordered by the forces which produce it. To put it another way, he selects by means of a general account, a story, or a theory that helps to make the object appreciable.

The additional role for the third entity is a significant factor in order appreciation. The new role is a traditional spectator role and therefore as the artist's original role is assimilated to processes and materials, the new role is similarly assimilated to the appreciator. This is not surprising for works such as the Dada and surrealist pieces are called experiments in part because any appreciator can conduct them; they are experiments *in appreciation*. In summary, then, in order appreciation an individual *qua appreciator* selects objects of appreciation from things around him and, as noted, does so by reference to a general nonaesthetic and nonartistic account which, by revealing the order imposed by the various forces, random and otherwise, which produce the selected objects, makes them appreciable. As in design appreciation, in order appreciation awareness and understanding of the entities involved – the order, the forces which produce it, the story which illuminates it – and the interplay among them is essential, but the focus is switched from a designed object created by an artist to an ordered object selected by an appreciator.

IV. APPRECIATING NATURE: DESIGN APPRECIATION

Frequently the appreciation of nature is assimilated to the appreciation of art. Such an assimilation is both a theoretical mistake and an appreciative pity. On the theoretical level, it typically involves misunderstanding not only appreciation but also one or both of art and nature. On the appreciative level, it can result in either failing to appreciate nature at all or appreciating it in an inappropriate manner

– relying on the wrong information, engaging in the wrong acts of aspection, and having the wrong response. As Ronald Hepburn points out in a classic discussion of appreciating nature: If our "aesthetic education" instills in us "the attitudes, the tactics of approach, the expectations proper to the appreciation of art works only," we "either pay very little aesthetic heed to natural objects or else heed them in the wrong way." We "look – and of course look in vain – for what can be found and enjoyed only in art."[45]

The theoretical mistake of assimilating nature appreciation and art appreciation, as some other mistakes noted, can be traced in part to the disinterestedness tradition. However, at times in its history, especially in its beginnings, the tradition assimilated the appreciation of art to that of nature rather than the other way around. Nonetheless, whichever way it goes the assimilation is a mistake. When generated by disinterestedness, the mistake has the same roots as that of ignoring the designed nature of art noted in section II. When the notion of disinterestedness is treated such that the object of appreciation is isolated and divorced from its interrelationships, and its appreciation is constrained by the general criterion of aesthetic relevance, the stage is set for the assimilation. According to this construal of disinterestedness, both works of art and natural objects are in appreciation more or less severed from their natures and their histories. Thus, both kinds of objects may be appreciated in the same way: as pure aesthetic objects. The result is one form of appreciation – *aesthetic* appreciation – which appropriately applies to any and all kinds of things. Art appreciation and nature appreciation collapse into one.

As argued in section I, however, this construal of disinterestedness is a mishandling of the concept. With it, not only do all forms of appreciation collapse into one, also, as noted, all seemingly collapse into the blank, cow-like stare. Thus, the key to avoiding this path to the assimilation of art and nature appreciation is the same as that to avoiding the stare: the key is the object-orientated nature of appreciation. This understanding of appreciation, as it facilitates the recognition of the designer-centered nature of paradigmatic art appreciation, also both closes down this route to the assimilation and points toward the proper understanding of nature appreciation. However, the coast is not yet clear. Even with object-orientated appreciation and without mishandling disinterestedness, there are yet means to assimilate art and nature appreciation. Indeed, the temptation to assimilate them is seemingly so strong that one suspects that the desire for assimilation is in fact the cause and mistakes such as mishandling disinterestedness only an effect.

A second path to the assimilation of art appreciation and nature appreciation involves a tradition even more venerable than that of disinterestedness. This route recognizes the object-orientated nature of appreciation and follows the lead of the object. It also recognizes paradigmatic art appreciation as design focused. Thus, it takes design appreciation as basic and assimilates all other appreciation, including nature appreciation, to it. All that is required to accomplish the assimilation is construing nature as the creation of a designer. And if nature is to be so construed, most cultural traditions have ample resources to support the construal. In the West many forms of theism seem adequate for the purpose and can thereby play a role in the assimilation of nature appreciation to art appreciation. Nelson Potter nicely puts the point: "The theist sees the world as throughout the product of God's design and plan...For such a theist it may seem that there is *no difference* between art-appreciation and nature-appreciation, since both are the products of intentional design."[46] He notes that on this view any account of the appreciation of art "would be directly applicable to Nature, where *God* is the artist."[47]

This means of assimilating art appreciation and nature appreciation also has difficulties. Potter, for example, claims it construes "God in a naive and excessively anthropomorphic fashion" and consequently fails "to realize that God is so different from man that even as we regard Nature as the product of God's handiwork, we are aware that the model of a human artist and his intentions and his artwork is inadequate to understand our appreciation of beauty in nature."[48] He therefore opts to "bid farewell to those theists who think that conceiving of God as a divine Philip Johnson is an adequate model for the appreciation of beauty in nature."[49] Potter's conclusion is probably correct. It seemingly follows not only from Potter's concerns, but also from any more general lack of confidence in the theist world view. In any case it is a conclusion that has wide acceptance.

However, accepting the conclusion that nature is not usefully conceptualized as the creation of a designer leaves us with a problem concerning its appreciation – a problem which in the West has become increasingly acute since the end of the nineteenth century. In an insightful discussion of Ruskin's agonizing confrontation with it, Peter Fuller succinctly summarizes the issue: "Once the illusion that the world was the handiwork of God had been jettisoned, then the whole base of aesthetics needed to be re-examined."⁵⁰ Thus, the role of theism in the attempt to assimilate nature appreciation to art appreciation, together with what is perhaps the ultimate failure of this attempt, brings into sharp focus what may well be the central theoretical problem concerning the appreciation of nature: the problem of how to understand such appreciation given that paradigmatic art appreciation is analyzed as design appreciation but nature is not construed as the creation of a designer.

This problem about nature appreciation is perplexing enough that it leads to radical solutions. For example, in what he calls the "Human Chauvinistic Aesthetic," Don Mannison reaches the startling conclusion that "Nature cannot be the object of aesthetic appreciation" by arguing that "only *human* artifacts can be objects of aesthetic judgement," for "'artistry' is an essential component of an aesthetic judgement" – "The conceptual structure of an aesthetic judgement...includes a reference to a creator; i.e. an artist."⁵¹ A similar conclusion is drawn by Robert Elliot, who argues that "an apparently integral part of aesthetic evaluation depends on viewing the aesthetic object as an intentional object, as an artifact, as something that is shaped by the purposes and designs of its author" and that this is not possible with nature for "Nature is not a work of art."⁵² As Elliot brings out, a concern of the Human Chauvinistic Aesthetic is that nature does not seem open to evaluative aesthetic judgments such as whether it is good or bad, a success or failure. This concern is legitimate, but drawing from it the conclusion that nature cannot be an object of aesthetic appreciation is without doubt an overreaction, not unlike Dickie's abandoning of the concept of the aesthetic. But even were it not, the conclusion would still be unacceptable. It offends against the truism noted in section I that aesthetic appreciation is applicable to any object of awareness whatever. Moreover, it is not established by the arguments offered in its defense.⁵³

What is important here, however, is seeing how the conclusion that nature cannot be an object of aesthetic appreciation stems in part from not recognizing the object-orientated nature of appreciation. As noted in section I, this concept, by ridding itself of anything like the general criterion of aesthetic relevance, allows for, indeed requires, different kinds of aesthetic appreciation as a function of the object of appreciation. Thus, all appreciation need not and should not be assimilated to the model of paradigmatic, design-centered art appreciation. In short, the position that nature appreciation cannot be aesthetic stems from a failure to recognize that there are alternatives to design appreciation. This fact is significant. If the position is a possible solution to the problem of how to understand nature appreciation when paradigmatic art appreciation is design focused and nature is not designed, then recognizing that there are alternatives to design appreciation makes evident a more plausible solution. The solution lies not in denying that the appreciation of nature can be aesthetic but rather in considering the alternatives to design appreciation. Thus, although in itself wrongheaded, the attempt to abandon the aesthetic appreciation of nature points towards a fruitful line of thought.

That nature appreciation is to be understood in light of alternatives to design appreciation is also suggested, ironically enough, by one aspect of the theist view. That view assimilates nature appreciation to art appreciation only by *construing* nature such that it fits the model of design appreciation. In this way the theist view brings out the fact that with object-orientated appreciation the way we construe the object of appreciation – the general account or the story we accept about it – determines the nature of its appreciation. With paradigmatic works of art this fact is obscured, for there is little dispute and therefore no alternative stories about them: No one doubts that they are creations of designers and typically there is considerable agreement about the details of their histories. However, when there is less clarity and agreement, as with nature, then alternative stories abound and form part of the basis for appreciation. Thus, with nature the story accepted about it, the ideas and beliefs we have about it, are pivotal factors in its appreciation. In this way nature is similar to those works of art and anti-art for which the appropriate appreciation is, as noted in section III, order appreciation. Moreover, order appreciation is an alternative to design appreciation such as is required to solve the problem of how to understand the appreciation of nature without forcing it into the model of design appreciation.

V. APPRECIATING NATURE: ORDER APPRECIATION

The idea of order appreciation as a model for the appreciation of nature is worth exploration. It is suggested by more than just that the appreciation of nature, like that of the works of art and anti-art for which order appreciation is appropriate, is shaped by the stories we tell about it. It is also suggested by other similarities and relationships between such works of art and anti-art and the objects of nature. There is, for instance, the fact that the works called found objects need not be limited to urinals, bottle racks, or typewriter covers, but can be themselves natural objects, as Haftmann points out, "a root, a mussel, a stone."[54] Likewise, consider the fact that a work such as Dali's surrealist experiment is not made less significant if the "alarm-watch" goes off when the "experimenter" is, for example, in a forest rather than in his bathroom. If order appreciation is the form of appreciation relevant to such works, it is seemingly as relevant in the forest as it is in the bathroom.

Especially revealing of the relevance of order appreciation to the appreciation of nature are the claims of the artists who initiated these works of art and anti-art. For example, it is said such art "urges man to identify himself with nature" and is itself comparable to the objects of nature.[55] Arp, for instance, claims that: "These paintings, sculptures, objects should remain anonymous and form a part of nature's great workshop as leaves do, and clouds, animals, and men. Yes, man must once again become a part of nature."[56] Of automatic poetry, in particular, he says: "Automatic poetry comes straight out of the poet's bowels or out of any other of his organs that has accumulated reserves...He crows, swears, moans, stammers, yodels, according to his mood...Neither the Postillon of Longjumiau, nor the Alexandrian, nor grammar, nor aesthetics, nor Buddha, nor the Sixth Commandment are able to constrict him."[57] Nor, it might be added, can the appreciation of such poetry be constricted by the general criterion of aesthetic relevance. Thus, Arp concludes: "His poems are like nature; they stink, laugh, and rhyme like nature. Foolishness, or at least what men call foolishness, is as precious to him as a sublime piece of rhetoric. For in nature a broken twig is equal in beauty and importance to the clouds and the stars."[58]

On the assumption that order appreciation provides the correct model for the appreciation of nature, such appreciation has the following general *form*: An individual *qua* appreciator selects objects of appreciation from the things around him and focuses on the order imposed on these objects by the various forces, random and otherwise, which produce them. Moreover, the objects are selected in part by reference to a general nonaesthetic and nonartistic story which helps make them appreciable by making this order visible and intelligible. Awareness and understanding of the key entities – the order, the forces which produce it, and the account which illuminates it – and of the interplay among them dictate relevant acts of aspection and guide the appreciative response. If this indicates the form of nature appreciation as modeled on order appreciation, it is yet only part of understanding such appreciation. As the Human Chauvinistic Aesthetic reminds us in denying that nature appreciation is aesthetic: "Nature is not a work of art." Consequently, even though modeled on order appreciation, nature appreciation differs in certain substantive ways from the appreciation of those works of art and anti-art for which order appreciation is also appropriate. Following the lead of the object, as demanded by the object-orientated nature of appreciation, helps bring out these differences.

As noted, the theist view that nature appreciation, like paradigmatic art appreciation, is design focused ironically suggests the alternative view that nature appreciation involves order appreciation. This is because the theist view brings out clearly the role played in nature appreciation by our story of it. In this way it also makes clear that with order appreciation to follow the lead of an object is to follow the lead of our story about it. And even if we, like Potter, reject the theist view of nature as designed, we are yet left with a variety of stories the lead of which we could follow. In one sense any of these stories can do the job required by order appreciation. Relevant stories derive from various religious and folk traditions, explaining nature if not as designed by yet as involving in some way the actions of, for example, one all-powerful god, many lesser gods, entities such as spirits, demons, fairies, or heroes, or whatever. However, in part because such accounts lose much of their appeal without the element of design and in part because of the appeal of an alternative story, these stories, with the possible exception of that of the all-powerful god, do not play a crucial role in our aesthetic appreciation of nature. What plays this role, and has increasingly done so in the West since the seventeenth century, is the alternative account given by natural science.[59]

In view of the object-orientated nature of appreciation it is not surprising that the story provided by natural science functions in the aesthetic appreciation of nature. On the one hand, that science, natural or otherwise, is relevant to nature appreciation gathers plausibility in that, as noted in section I, object-orientated appreciation is objective: It focuses on an object as what it is and as having the properties it has. Science is the paradigm of that which reveals objects for what they are and with the properties they have. Thus, it not only presents itself as the source of objective truth, it brands alternative accounts as subjective falsehood and therefore, in accord with objective appreciation, as irrelevant to aesthetic appreciation. In this way the significance of science in the aesthetic appreciation of nature is in part a legacy of the notion of disinterestedness. On the other hand, that the science relevant to nature appreciation is natural science follows rather obviously from object-orientated appreciation. This is one important difference between the order appreciation of nature and that of works of art and anti-art. For the latter the relevant stories, as noted in section III, are typically metaphysical, mystical, or psychological. However, it is no surprise that humanistic stories and the human sciences are relevant to the appreciation of artifacts while the natural sciences are relevant to the appreciation of nature. What else should following the lead of the object indicate?

The *content* of nature appreciation can now be added to its form. Its form, as noted, centers on the entities significant to order appreciation: order, the forces which produce it, and the account which illuminates it. Its content is as follows: First, the relevant order is that typically called the natural order. Second, since there is no artist, not even one assimilated to processes and materials, the relevant forces are the forces of nature: the geological, biological, and meteorological forces which produce the natural order by shaping not only the planet but everything that inhabits it. Although these forces differ from many that shape works of art, awareness and understanding of them is vital in nature appreciation, as is knowledge of, for example, Pollock's role in appreciating his action painting or the role of chance in appreciating a Dada experiment. Third, the relevant account which makes the natural order visible and intelligible is, as noted, the story given by natural science – astronomy, physics, chemistry, biology, genetics, meteorology, geology as well as the particular explanatory theories within these sciences. Awareness and understanding of evolutionary theory, for example, is relevant to appreciating the natural order as revealed in flora and fauna; without such knowledge the biosphere may strike us as chaotic.[60]

The remaining significant factor in order appreciation is the role of *selection* by an individual *qua* appreciator. And indeed in nature appreciation the appreciator must select particular objects of appreciation from, as Arp says, "nature's great workshop." However, here again there is a significant difference from the appreciation of works of art and anti-art. Although selection plays a key role in the order appreciation of these artistic endeavors, it has a somewhat less significant role in nature appreciation. Unlike the situation concerning such works, all of nature necessarily reveals the natural order. Although it may be easier to perceive and understand in some cases than in others, it is yet present in every case and can be appreciated once our awareness and understanding of the forces which produce it and the story which illuminates it are adequately developed. In this sense all nature is equally appreciable and therefore selection among all that the natural world offers is not of much ultimate importance. As Arp observes, "in nature a broken twig is equal in beauty and importance to the clouds and the stars."

If all nature "is equal in beauty and importance," this is a significant difference not simply between nature appreciation and the order appreciation of some works of art and anti-art but between nature appreciation and art appreciation in general. However, it is in part explained by design appreciation's inappropriateness for nature. An important aspect of design appreciation is judging the object in terms of the talents of the designer and the undertaking set by the initial design – assessing, as noted in section II, whether it is good or bad, a success or failure, or, as Gombrich puts it, whether it is "right." The fact of a designer and an initial design makes design appreciation appropriate for conventional works of art and such judgments a key aspect of their appreciation. Likewise, the absence of these entities makes design appreciation not appropriate for nature and these kinds of judgments not an aspect of its appreciation. Natural objects are not such that their appreciation involves judging whether they are "right" in Gombrich's sense; in this sense they are all more or less equally right. Thus, to the extent that they are appreciable at all, all are more or less equally appreciable – equal in beauty and importance. As noted, that judgments of this kind do not apply to nature is part of the argument for the Human Chauvinistic Aesthetic. It is now clear that what follows from this is almost the opposite of the conclusion that nature cannot be an object of aesthetic appreciation.

The appropriateness of order appreciation to nature, as the inappropriateness of design appreciation, is also useful in explaining why natural objects, unlike works of art, are more or less equally appreciable. In order appreciation instead of judging a work a success or failure in light of a design and designer, there is only appreciating an object as ordered in light of a story. Although such stories may differ, each, indeed this is much of the point of constructing them, illuminates nature as ordered – either by making its order visible and intelligible or by imposing an order on it. Thus, although such stories are in one sense nonaesthetic, in another sense they are exceedingly aesthetic. They illuminate nature as ordered and in doing so give it meaning, significance, and beauty – qualities those giving the stories find aesthetically appealing. Thus, unlike design appreciation which focuses on aesthetic qualities which result from embodying an initial design in an object, order appreciation focuses on aesthetic qualities which result from applying an after-the-fact story to a preexistent object. Moreover, the aesthetic qualities resulting from ordering nature one way or another figure in the general attractiveness of one story as opposed to another. Thus, over the long run, stories develop so as to provide as much and as universal aesthetic appeal as possible. In this way the stories that play a role in the order appreciation of nature work toward making natural objects all seem equally aesthetically appealing.[61]

One final contrast between appreciating art and appreciating nature can be brought out by reference to differences between design and order appreciation. What lies behind a designed object is a designer and therefore in design appreciation part of our appreciative response is directed towards another intellect not unlike our own. He and his design are something towards which we can feel the empathy and the closeness typical of our relationships with other humans. Yet there is distance for it is an *other* towards which our feelings are directed. By contrast, all that lies behind an ordered object is a story, the account which illuminates the order. Thus, in order appreciation part of our appreciative response is directed towards whatever is in our story. And be that an all-powerful god, a folklore of demons and fairies, or a world of natural forces, it is something by its nature distinct from and beyond humankind, something essentially alien. Our appreciative response is to a mystery we will seemingly never fully comprehend. Yet it is *our* story – our god, our folklore, our science – in light of which we respond and therefore there is, after all, a closeness. Perhaps not the closeness typical of our relationships with other humans, but maybe something more like that typical of our relationships with our pets – or at least our pet theories.

Given these differences between design and order appreciation, appreciating art and appreciating nature should exemplify different kinds of ambivalences: On the one hand, in appreciating art we are aware that the work is a human creation, an artifact, and therefore open to our appreciation and to our understanding, our judgment, our mastery. However, we must also be aware that even if we master it completely, it is yet not our own, but someone else's creation that we master. On the other hand, in appreciating nature we are aware that the object is alien, a mystery, and therefore ultimately beyond our appreciation and beyond our understanding, our judgment, our mastery. However, we may also be aware that insofar as we achieve some mastery of it, it is by means of our own beliefs, our own story, our own creation that we do so. Thus, perhaps nature is easiest to appreciate when our account of it is simplistic anthropomorphic folklore: a story of almost human gods or godlike human heroes not unlike that of so-called primitive peoples who are said to feel exceptionally close to nature. With such folklore nature should be very approachable, for it is illuminated not only by our own story but in terms of beings much like ourselves. Likewise, perhaps works of art are easiest to appreciate when they are our own works. For most of us, however, to appreciate art is to confront the quintessentially human by way of *the other*, while to appreciate nature is to confront either an almighty god or blind natural forces by way of ourselves. In neither confrontation is appreciation necessarily easy, yet in each can be found aesthetic experiences of great richness and power. However, it is no surprise if typically only the confrontations with nature are marked by overwhelming wonder and awe.

Notes

1 Stolnitz's version of the position is in Jerome Stolnitz, *Aesthetics and Philosophy of Art Criticism: A Critical Introduction* (Boston: Houghton Mifflin, 1960). Dickie's initial and best-known version of his attack is George Dickie, "The Myth of the Aesthetic Attitude," *American Philosophical Quarterly* 1 (1964): 56–65.
2 Stolnitz, *Aesthetics*, p. 35.
3 *Ibid.*, p. 42.
4 *Ibid.*, p. 39.
5 *Ibid.*, p. 33. Stolnitz's italics.
6 *Ibid.*, pp. 37–8.
7 *Ibid.*, p. 37.
8 *Ibid.* Stolnitz is quoting Kate Hevner, "The Aesthetic Experience: A Psychological Description," *Psychological Review* 44 (1937): 249.
9 Dickie, "Myth of the Aesthetic Attitude," p. 61.
10 Stolnitz, *Aesthetics*, p. 36.
11 *Ibid.*, p. 52.
12 *Ibid.*, p. 53. Stolnitz puts what he calls the problem of aesthetic relevance as follows: "Is it ever 'relevant' to the aesthetic experience to have thoughts or images or bits of knowledge which are not present within the object itself? If these are ever relevant, under what conditions are they so?" This way of putting it emphasizes one aspect, perhaps the most important, of what I call the issue of aesthetic relevance.
13 *Ibid.*, p. 54.
14 George Dickie, *Art and the Aesthetic: An Institutional Analysis* (Ithaca,

NY: Cornell University Press, 1974), p. 40. In a similar fashion in "The Myth of the Aesthetic Attitude" Dickie states that "an underlying aim of this essay is to suggest the vacuousness of the term 'aesthetic'," Dickie, "Myth of the Aesthetic Attitude," p. 64.

15 Stolnitz, *Aesthetics*, p. 58. Stolnitz's brief discussion on pages 57–60 of the relevance of knowledge to appreciation is excellent. It should be read by anyone who wishes to properly teach "art appreciation."

16 I have elsewhere discussed in detail how Ziff's account of aesthetic appreciation seemingly avoids the major difficulties of both the disinterestedness tradition and alternative "conceptual" approaches. See "Critical Notice of Ziff, *Antiaesthetics: An Appreciation of the Cow with the Subtile Nose*," *Canadian Journal of Philosophy* 17 (1987): 919–34.

17 Paul Ziff, "Reasons in Art Criticism," in Paul Ziff, *Philosophical Turnings: Essays in Conceptual Appreciation* (Ithaca, NY: Cornell University Press, 1966), p. 71.

18 Paul Ziff, "Anything Viewed" in Paul Ziff, *Antiaesthetics: An Appreciation of the Cow with the Subtile Nose* (Dordrecht: Reidel, 1984), p. 136.

19 *Ibid.*, p. 135. I have taken the liberty of adding commas to this quote. It is worth noting that the object-orientated nature of appreciation suggested by Ziff also becomes more explicit in Stolnitz in his later writings. In his insightful 1978 Presidential Address to The American Society for Aesthetics he characterizes disinterestedness as involving "scrupulous regard for the qualitative individuality of the object" and, as Ziff, speaks of the object itself as making "demands" – "demands that must be met if the thing is to be savored for what it uniquely is." See Jerome Stolnitz, "The Artistic and the Aesthetic 'in Interesting Times'," *Journal of Aesthetics and Art Criticism* 37 (1979): 401–13.

20 In the classic anti-intentionalist piece, for example, Wimsatt's and Beardsley's forbidden "external evidence" is more than simply artist's intentions; it is also knowledge, "revelations" as they say, about the artist. See W. K. Wimsatt Jr., and Monroe C. Beardsley, "The Intentional Fallacy," *Sewanee Review* 54 (1946): 468–88.

21 E. H. Gombrich, *The Story of Art* (London: Phaidon, 1950), p. 5.

22 *Ibid.*, pp. 12–13.

23 *Ibid.*, p. 14.

24 *Ibid.*

25 H. W. Janson, *History of Art: A Survey of the Major Visual Arts from the Dawn of History to the Present Day* (Englewood Cliffs: Prentice-Hall, 1969), p. 13.

26 Werner Haftmann, *Painting in the Twentieth Century: An Analysis of the Artists and their Work* (New York: Praeger, 1965), p. 348.

27 *Ibid.*

28 *Ibid.*, p. 349.

29 Janson, *History of Art*, p. 540.

30 Jackson Pollock, "Three Statements, 1944–1951" in Herschel B. Chipp, ed., *Theories of Modern Art: A Sourcebook by Artists and Critics* (Berkeley: University of California Press, 1968), p. 548.

31 Janson, *History of Art*, p. 540; Pollock, "Three Statements," p. 548.
32 Janson, *History of Art*, p. 540.
33 *Ibid.*
34 Haftmann, *Painting in the Twentieth Century*, p. 183.
35 *Ibid.*
36 Janson, *History of Art*, p. 534.
37 *Ibid.*
38 Salvador Dali, "The Object Revealed in Surrealist Experiment" in Chipp, *Theories of Modern Art*, p. 423.
39 *Ibid.*
40 Haftmann, *Painting in the Twentieth Century*, p. 190.
41 George Dickie, "A Response to Cohen: The Actuality of Art" in George Dickie and R. J. Sclafani, eds., *Aesthetics: A Critical Anthology* (New York: St. Martin's, 1977), p. 199.
42 Marcel Duchamp, quoted in Anne d'Harnoncourt and Kynaston McShine, eds., *Marcel Duchamp* (New York: Museum of Modern Art, 1973), p. 89. The quote is given in Timothy Binkley, "Piece: Contra Aesthetics," *Journal of Aesthetics and Art Criticism* 35 (1977): 275. Binkley's piece is very useful concerning what he calls "Art Outside Aesthetics."
43 Haftmann, *Painting in the Twentieth Century*, pp. 182–3.
44 *Ibid.*, p. 348.
45 R. W. Hepburn, "Aesthetic Appreciation of Nature" in H. Osborne, ed., *Aesthetics and the Modern World* (London: Thames and Hudson, 1968), p. 53. I discuss the unfortunate consequences of appreciating nature in terms of some particular artistic models in "Appreciation and the Natural Environment," *Journal of Aesthetics and Art Criticism* 37 (1979): 267–75, reprinted in Patricia H. Werhane, ed., *Philosophical Issues in Art* (Englewood Cliffs: Prentice-Hall, 1984), pp. 519–31. In that article I distinguish three models of appreciation which I call the object, the landscape, and the environmental models. The former two fit with the appreciation of certain traditional art objects, but do not do justice to the aesthetic appreciation of nature. By contrast the environmental model is especially appropriate for the aesthetic appreciation of the natural world. These distinctions bring out important differences between appreciating art and appreciating nature which, although they complement and support the contrasts elaborated in this article, need not and cannot be reiterated here. Their importance and relevance to the issues addressed here should be evident even though throughout this article for convenience I simply speak of appreciating art objects and natural objects, rather than art objects and natural environments.
46 Nelson Potter, "Aesthetic Value in Nature and In the Arts" in Hugh Curtler, ed., *What is Art?* (New York: Haven, 1983), p. 142. Potter's italics.
47 *Ibid.*, p. 143. Potter's italics.
48 *Ibid.*, pp. 143–4.
49 *Ibid.*, p. 144.

50 Peter Fuller, "The Geography of Mother Nature" in D. Cosgrove and S. Daniels, eds., *The Iconography of Landscape: Essays on the Symbolic Representation, Design and Use of Past Environments* (Cambridge University Press, 1988), p. 25.
51 Don Mannison, "A Prolegomenon to a Human Chauvinistic Aesthetic" in Don Mannison, Michael McRobbie, and Richard Routley, eds., *Environmental Philosophy* (Canberra: Australian National University, 1980), pp. 216, 212–13. Mannison's italics.
52 Robert Elliot, "Faking Nature," *Inquiry* 25 (1982): 90.
53 I do not consider these arguments here as I discuss Elliot's presentation of them in detail in "Nature and Positive Aesthetics," *Environmental Ethics* 6 (1984): 5–34. Moreover, the unacceptability of the conclusion is perhaps more evident in light of the way it requires the abandonment of the concept of the aesthetic, than from the weaknesses in the arguments for it. In this way the Human Chauvinistic Aesthetic has something in common with the "Aesthetics of Engagement" proposed by Arnold Berleant. In response to some of the problems traditional aesthetics pose for the aesthetic appreciation of nature, Berleant develops a view of the relevant experiences of both nature and art which abandons so much of the tradition that it brings into question the degree to which such experiences are in any sense aesthetic or even, for that matter, appreciative of their objects. See, for example, Berleant's "The Aesthetics of Art and Nature" in this volume. On this view the aesthetic appreciation of art and that of nature are assimilated to one another not simply at the expense of the aesthetic appreciation of nature but seemingly at the expense of the aesthetic appreciation of anything whatsoever. However, Berleant's view, as those of both Dickie and the Human Chauvinistic Aesthetic, is an unnecessary overreaction. The problems which motivate it can be handled by recognizing the object-oriented nature of appreciation, as I suggest here, and by bringing it together with an environmental model of appreciation such as I develop in "Appreciation and the Natural Environment." Taking this tack avoids the absurdity to which theories of the engagement or involvement type lend themselves: that the relevant experiences of nature, art, or whatever are neither very aesthetic nor especially appreciative of their objects, but rather more like what Goodman characterized as the "Tingle-Immersion" variety. See N. Goodman, *Languages of Art* (New York: Bobbs-Merrill, 1968), p. 112. For example, it is ironic that in rightly attempting to avoid the tradition's major pitfall, the blank, cow-like stare, Berleant comes full circle and ends up promoting a kind of "sensory immersion" experience of both nature and art – an experience which can be equally unknowing, equally blank. But it is not surprising. As should be evident from the traditional attempts to assimilate appreciating art and appreciating nature, such attempts to assimilate the experiences of radically different kinds of things frequently do so, at least in part, by downplaying the substantive content of the experiences. A somewhat related position, Noël Carroll's "being moved by nature" view is also to a certain extent an "immersion

view" which does not emphasize much of the substantive cognitive content of our appreciative experiences of nature. See his "On Being Moved by Nature: Between Religion and Natural History" in this volume. However, Carroll does not present his view as an alternative account of our appreciation of nature, but only as a "co-existing model" designed to elaborate a certain dimension of that appreciation. As such, the "being moved by nature" view makes a valuable contribution to furthering our understanding of our aesthetic appreciation of the natural world.

54 Haftmann, *Painting in the Twentieth Century*, p. 191.
55 Hans Arp, "Abstract Art, Concrete Art" in Chipp, *Theories of Modern Art*, p. 391.
56 *Ibid.*, p. 390.
57 *Ibid.*, p. 391.
58 *Ibid.*
59 I defend a quasi-historical account of the growth of the role of science in the aesthetic appreciation of nature in "Nature and Positive Aesthetics," specifically pp. 20–4. A classic discussion of the topic is Marjorie Hope Nicolson, *Mountain Gloom and Mountain Glory* (Ithaca, NY: Cornell University Press, 1959).
60 I argue for the importance of scientific knowledge to the aesthetic appreciation of nature in other articles; see, for example, "Nature and Positive Aesthetics," "Nature, Aesthetic Judgment, and Objectivity," *Journal of Aesthetics and Art Criticism* 40 (1981): 15–27, reprinted in C. Cloutier and C. Seerveld, eds., *Opuscula Aesthetica Nostra: Aesthetics and the Arts in Canada* (Edmonton: Academic Printing and Publishing, 1984), pp. 87–99, and "Saito on the Correct Aesthetic Appreciation of Nature," *Journal of Aesthetic Education* 20 (1986): 85–93.
61 I develop the line of thought of this paragraph more fully in "Nature and Positive Aesthetics," specifically pp. 24–34 and in "Critical Notice of Rolston, *Philosophy Gone Wild*," *Environmental Ethics* 8 (1986): 163–77.

11

The aesthetics of art and nature

ARNOLD BERLEANT

The title of this essay masks a deliberate ambiguity, one that is, in fact, its central issue. Few would deny the possibility of obtaining aesthetic satisfaction from both works of art and from nature, customarily in the case of the first and under certain conditions in the other. But what sort of satisfaction is this, and is it the same kind in nature as in art?

The usual course, perhaps the most intuitively obvious, is to recognize that aesthetic value exists in both domains but for historical and philosophical reasons to find, like Diffey and Carlson, that the kind of appreciation each encourages is essentially different.[1] Another possibility is to join Ross in associating contemporary environmental art with seventeenth- and eighteenth-century gardens, then regarded as a high art, demonstrating a unity of art and nature in both, and implying that they share a common aesthetic.[2] A third possibility, the converse of this, is to take environmental appreciation as the standard and to reinterpret the artistic aesthetic by the natural. The question hidden in my title, then, is whether there is one aesthetic or two, an aesthetic that encompasses both art and nature or one aesthetic that is distinctively artistic and another that identifies the appreciation of natural beauty.

This is more than a question in the grammar of number, and it is, in my judgment, more than a minor issue in aesthetics. Rather, it provokes some of its central concerns: the nature of art, the identifying features of aesthetic appreciation, and the larger connections of such experience with matters once regarded as philosophically central but now largely consigned to the margins, matters Diffey calls noumenal and transcendent and Tuan identifies in the aesthetic response to extreme environments.[3] It may indeed be that environment is no peripheral matter, either aesthetically or philosophically,

228

and that ultimately it engages the very heart of philosophy. It is, in fact, the intent of this essay to suggest this, to move towards a naturalizing of aesthetics, as it were, and its identification as a critical dimension of the value that binds together the many domains of the human world.

A part of this project, the one that will occupy me here, is to consider whether aesthetics harbors two dissimilar types of phenomena, one concerning art and another nature, or whether both actually involve a single all-embracing kind of experience which requires a comprehensive theory to accommodate it. It would be coy to plead uncertainty at this point in the discussion, for it is indeed my purpose to make a case for a general theory without, at the same time, denying the diversity of individual experience and divergent cultural factors in our encounters with art and nature. A universal aesthetic must acknowledge these differences, and its ability to do so is the test of its success. For it is precisely the failure of traditional aesthetics to accommodate the enlargement of the objects, activities, and occasions that have characterized much of the art of the past hundred years that is the cause of our present dilemma concerning nature and art.

ONE AESTHETICS OR TWO?

Professor Carlson turns to Stolnitz's characterization of the modern traditional view that aesthetic appreciation requires a special attitude, and it is a useful statement of what that attitude entails.[4] The watchword is, of course, "disinterested," for Kant's legacy in making it central in appreciation has shaped the course of aesthetics over the past two centuries.[5] It is precisely by setting aside interest, "either of sense or of reason," that we become capable of receiving aesthetic satisfaction. Assuming a disinterested attitude frees us from the distractions of practical purposes and permits us to dwell freely on an object or a representation of it, which we then can regard as beautiful.

This definition of the boundaries of the aesthetic carries important implications. To aid in achieving disinterestedness it is important to circumscribe art objects by clear borders, and the classical arts exhibit many features which seem designed to accomplish this: the frame of a painting, the pedestal for sculpture, the proscenium arch in theatre, the stage for dance, music, and other performing arts. To some extent these were deliberate developments. Shaftesbury, who preceded Kant and actually provided much of the originality of conception to which Kant later gave philosophical order and structure, had argued that art must be enclosed within borders instead of spreading across walls, ceilings, and staircases, so that it may be grasped in a single view. It became important to isolate the object of beauty, singling it out for its special aesthetic qualities, which succeeding generations of aestheticians have attempted to identify. This view led, too, to a focus on the internal attributes of the art object, such as its self-sufficiency, completeness, and unity. These traits came to identify the character and object of aesthetic appreciation and they set the direction of aesthetic inquiry that has dominated discussion to the present.[6]

By circumscribing the domain of aesthetics, this formulation recognized a distinct aesthetic sensibility and encouraged a body of scholarship that came to constitute the new discipline of aesthetics. However, it also had some awkward consequences. How, for example, does one deal with architecture? If we put enough distance between ourselves and a building, we may possibly comprehend it in a single view. But surely there is more to a building than a distant visual object. A building is meant to be entered, to be moved through, to house activities of some sort. The only recourse of traditional aesthetics, then, is to place these various roles in separate domains, as Vitruvius divided architecture into firmness, utility, and beauty.[7] Indeed, that has been the regular ploy of aesthetics when forced to defend the integrity of beauty against the incursions of utility: separate the various aspects of the object to keep art from being sullied by any association with practical activities or ends.

Compromise, then, permitted architecture to retain its place among the fine arts. But it was an uneasy compromise, for in practice it is impossible to maintain for long any real division between beauty and utility. Not only can form and function be related, but the perception of space, surface, sound, and pattern can profoundly affect a building's practical success, influencing the movement, the efficiency, the very mood and attitude of its users. Nor can the performing arts retain their purity as contemplative objects by separating them physically from their surroundings. For despite the tactic of placing musical and dance performances in their separate space above the plane occupied by the audience, these arts possess the uncanny ability to insinuate themselves into our bodies, stirring up somatic and affective responses, and engaging us in ways that are difficult to reconcile with the contemplative ideal. It is even harder to distance oneself from literature, for here the art employs our very consciousness to lead us into its enchanted realm. In fact, it seems that we have a theory of the arts that is actually modeled on only one kind, the visual arts of painting and sculpture, and which has been extended to the others at the price of plausibility. And even in the visual arts its appropriateness can be questioned.[8]

Some serious problems encumber traditional aesthetics, then, in the domain of the fine arts. But what happens when this conception of art becomes the model for appreciating nature? Here even greater difficulties appear. Shaftesbury had wanted to deal with beauty in nature as contemplative and not as active, of practical use, owned, or involved with desires.[9] And indeed there are devices that seem to turn environment into a contemplative object – the scenic outlook over a panoramic landscape, an allée viewed from a terrace, a French formal garden.

Yet does aesthetic appreciation cease when we enter a path to move into the landscape or walk down the allée? Most gardens, even the French, draw us into intimate views, encouraging us to make a reciprocal contribution through our movement and change of location and vantage. Moreover, the distancing that is so important a part of traditional appreciation is difficult to achieve when one is surrounded by the "object." As with earth art, we are on the same plane, in the same space as the blossom or tree we are regarding. In fact, what the Japanese garden accomplishes by requiring our active cooperation in walking and positioning ourselves simply extends factors present in all environmental experience.[10] In order to safeguard aesthetic contemplation one may be forced, ironically, to abandon nature entirely in favor of its representation in art. It is easier to contemplate a landscape painting rather than a landscape design, for painting frames the scene, offering it as an object for disinterested regard. There are no annoying insects to distract one, no wind to ruffle one's hair, no precarious footing or dizzying drops. One can adopt a disinterested stance without danger and fear of disruption.

The inadequacies of traditional aesthetics for the appreciation of nature rest on still different grounds. Some commentators associate the enjoyment of art with the appreciation of the skill and originality that went into creating the art object. For them, art appreciation centers on our admiration of the creativity embodied in the design of a work. Since this is not present in nature, one must have recourse to something different in an aesthetics of nature. Carlson takes this tack, and is led to conclude that a separate aesthetic is needed, one that bases our appreciative response on the awareness, selection, and understanding of the order by which natural forces have produced the objects we admire. The appreciation of order in nature, then, replaces the appreciation of design in art. Each provides the basis of a separate aesthetic, one for art and another for nature, and traditional aesthetics remains intact.

This solution to the different sorts of appreciation in art and nature remains indebted to the traditional aesthetics of Shaftesbury and Kant. For its central premise is that appreciation is directed toward an aesthetic object – a designed object in art, an ordered object in nature. And indeed this dual aesthetic is a reasonable consequence of that premise: Such dissimilar objects seem to require different accounts of their creation and meaning.

It is more than coincidental that both the traditional theory and the dualistic compromise rest on the premise of objectification. Yet does this premise follow from the appreciative experience of art and nature or is their perception rather dictated by the theory? A world of objects is easier to circumscribe and control, but is this the world of lived experience?[11] If we regard the painting of a landscape from a disinterested distance, we get a contemplative object, but what of the appreciation of an actual landscape? Here the problems with objectification are more troublesome. It is, as we have seen, far more difficult to objectify environment than art.

But does the objectification premise in fact survive in either case? For it is not nature alone which troubles conventional aesthetics. In fact, its applicability to painting lasted barely a century, although whether it ever really suitably accounted for aesthetic fulfillment is itself debatable.[12] Yet since the impressionists' dissolution of represented objects into atmosphere and of art objects into perceptual experiences, the visual arts have increasingly followed the nonconfining pattern of the other arts. The picture frame has come to function not so much as an enclosure than as a facilitator for focusing our gaze into the painting, and this internal focusing eludes the kind of objectification that the traditional aesthetic intended to facilitate.

Such developments in painting make reference to the beholder, and the viewer's participation is required to complete the work. What the multiple planes of cubism do in fragmenting static objects, the intense energy of the futurist does in dissolving dynamic ones: both transform objects into experiences. As optical art forces an interplay between eye and painting, photorealism confronts the viewer with its giant images. And sculpture, which would seem to preserve the separateness of the object by removing it to a higher spatial plane, even sculpture has followed the same course, not just by emphasizing the dynamic forces of the work, as with Bourdelle, but by stressing the powers that emanate from the piece to energize the surrounding space and, like the *Laocoön*, entrap the viewer. Yet this merely emphasizes the charmed space, the magical effusion of all good sculpture. More recent work has, of course, tended to dispense with the pedestal entirely and lead the viewer into physical interplay, as with Calder's stabiles and Di Suvero's ride 'em pieces. And as Ross points out, earthworks and environmental art extended far beyond the restrictive conventions of the traditional model by the use they may make of natural substances and by the bond they may project to their site. These works involve the viewer as well, not only through the forceful message they may embody about our relation to nature, but by the direct physical participation that appreciation often requires. We are beginning to discover that the history of the modern arts is more a history of perception than a history of objects, and that perception, moreover, is not just a visual act but a somatic engagement in the aesthetic field. Such a development the traditional object-orientated theory is hard put to account for.

If conventional aesthetics impedes our encounter with the arts, it obstructs even more the appreciation of nature. For much, perhaps most of our appreciative experience of nature exceeds the limits of a contemplative object and refuses to be constrained within discrete boundaries. If we are going to need a separate aesthetic for nature, why be burdened with a model so alien to experience? From the difficulties in distancing nature and in assimilating natural objects to the appreciative requirement of design, what seems to be needed is an account appropriate to the distinctive qualities and demands of environment. What form might this take?

AN AESTHETICS OF NATURE

There is an irony in the persistent division between the *Naturwissenschaften* and the *Geisteswissenschaften*, that sharp distinction between the natural and the cultural sciences which gives intellectual status to the separation between nature and art: The hard sciences deal with nature, the soft ones with culture. For the distinction is belied when art, as one of the domains of culture, does no better than emulate the scientific model by adopting its conventions of objectification, distancing, and disinterested (i.e. contemplative) regard. Yet not only is this inadequate for explaining the arts, as we have just seen. The division between nature and culture is misleading in yet another respect: it misrepresents nature.

For nature cannot be disposed of as easily as the classic account would have it. Nature, in the sense of the earth apart from human intervention, has mostly disappeared. We live in a world profoundly affected by human action, not just in the nearly complete destruction of the planet's primeval wilderness or in the distribution of flora and fauna far from their original habitats, but in the alteration of the shape and character of the earth's surface, its climate, its very atmosphere.

It is true that, unlike cultural artifacts, nature seems obdurate: it may bend but it will not disappear. Yet it bends in strange ways. We are beginning to realize that the natural world is no independent sphere but is itself a cultural artifact. Not only is nature affected pervasively by human action; our very conception of nature has emerged historically, differing widely from one cultural tradition to another. What we mean by nature, our beliefs about wilderness, the recognition of landscape, our very sense of environment have all made an historical appearance and have been understood differently at different times and places.[13] No wonder that an aesthetics that aspires like the sciences to universality has difficulty accommodating nature.

There are good reasons, then, for the fact that until recently philosophers have not devoted much attention to the aesthetics of nature. Yet it was the very philosopher who attempted to formalize the structure of a universal aesthetics, Immanuel Kant, who took an important step here. His idea of the sublime captures one aspect of the aesthetic experience of nature – the capacity of the natural world to act on so monumental a scale as to exceed our powers of framing and control, and to produce in their place a sense of overwhelming magnitude and awe. This is the same condition about which Tuan writes so compellingly in considering the extreme environments of desert and ice. These environments deserve the appellation "sublime" because an overpowering nature here bursts beyond the bounds that permit disinterested contemplation and assimilates the human presence.

Perhaps the sublime offers a clue for identifying a distinctive aesthetics of nature that is unrelated to the traditional theory of the arts.[14] For we need no longer pursue the hopeless effort to assimilate environmental appreciation to artistic satisfaction by objectifying and contemplating an object or scene of nature with a sense of disengagement, or by replacing the design of art with the order of nature. Why not reserve the disinterested contemplation of a discrete object for art, and develop a different aesthetic for natural appreciation, one that acknowledges the experience of continuity, assimilation, and engagement that nature encourages? The sublime may provide the very direction we need.

Throughout the development of the notion of the sublime there persists the sense of boundless magnitude and power. In the first century A.D. Longinus identified it in literature as "the echo of greatness of spirit."[15] Burke, in the mid-eighteenth century, associated the sublime in literature with the emotion of terror and its power over the imagination.[16] But it was Kant who discovered its applicability to nature, where the boundaries of form and purposiveness, through which the beautiful inheres in art, in some instances no longer impose restraint and control. While natural beauty is like art in the purposive order of its forms, this, Kant claimed, does not apply to the sublime. The sublime, in fact, is not in nature but in our mind, and it is only through the idea of reason, through the subjective construction of judgments, that we can establish the cognitive order of purposiveness. In what Kant called the mathematically sublime, where the magnitude of natural things surpasses our aesthetic imagination, and in the dynamically sublime, in which the might of nature overwhelms us and produces fear, the aesthetic satisfaction we feel comes from our ability to grasp them, the first by our capacity to comprehend great size intellectually, the second by our contemplation of nature's power from a secure position, thus turning the initial pain into pleasure.[17] For Kant, then, both the fact of the sublime and its peculiar satisfaction are to be found in the mind from aesthetic experience and its cognitive comprehension. Once again the convenient Cartesianism of the western tradition comes to the rescue, saving us from the terror of overwhelming magnitude and might by the purposive order of thought.

That ploy is, however, no longer available; that is why nature will not stay within its prescribed limits but breaks out to engulf us. We can no longer, in ignorance of history and of experience, spin great webs of learning out of very little substance, as Bacon once described the scholastic process, and contain the natural world within the constructions of the mind.[18] The safety sought in seeing ourselves separate from nature we now know to be specious. What, then, if we start by recognizing that connectedness? Here the sublime may serve not as an exceptional case but as a clear model for the aesthetic experience of nature. For it is through the very sense of magnitude and might which Kant identified that we may grasp the true proportions of the nature—human relation, where awe mixed with humility is the guiding sentiment. This is clearly a factor in the appeal Tuan recognizes that solitude has for desert hermit and arctic explorer alike: the intensity that goes with great simplicity and physical austerity, and the sense of harmony with nature that may accompany it.

Yet one need not immerse oneself in an extreme environment to achieve that qualitative sense of unity. The boundlessness of the natural world does not just surround us; it assimilates us. Not only are we unable to sense absolute limits in nature; we cannot distance the natural world from ourselves in order to measure and judge it with complete objectivity. Nature exceeds the human mind, not just because of the limits of our present knowledge, not only because of the essentially anthropomorphic character of that knowledge so that we can never go beyond the character and boundaries of our cognitive process, but by the recognition that the cognitive relation with things is not the exclusive relation or even the highest one we can achieve. The proper response to this sense of nature is awe, not just from its magnitude and power, but from the mystery that is, as in a work of art, part of the essential poetry of the natural world. What is boundless is, then, the ultimately ungraspable breadth of nature. And terror is the appropriate response to a natural process that exceeds our power and confronts us with overwhelming force, the ultimate consequence of a scientific technology where humans have become the inescapable victims of their own actions.

Is aesthetic pleasure possible under these circumstances? Clearly not, if we think it necessary to exercise ultimate control by objectifying and contemplating nature. But if the sublime becomes our model and we accept the unity of the natural world, then we must identify the qualitative character of our experience which becomes central on those occasions when aesthetic appreciation dominates. They are times of sensory acuteness, of a perceptual unity of nature and human, of a congruity of awareness, understanding, and involvement mixed with awe and humility, in which the focus is on the immediacy and directness of the occasion of experience. Perceiving environment from within, as it were, looking not *at* it but *in* it, nature becomes something quite different; it is transformed into a realm in which we live as participants, not observers.[19] The consequences are not de-aestheticizing, as the eighteenth century would have it, but intensely and inescapably aesthetic.

236

Nor need we look for occasions of a natural aesthetic only in the bold and dramatic places where Kant finds them: the ultimate immeasurableness of the universe, great gray cloud masses accompanied by crashes and flashes of thunder and lightning, a powerful hurricane, the moving mass of a mighty waterfall, the sight of the boundlessness or the overwhelming tumult of the ocean, the all-embracing vault of the starry heavens.[20] These are powerful occasions, to be sure, and Kant locates their sublimity sensitively, not in the intellectual comprehension of their processes and extent, but in the perceptual grasp of their force and range. One cannot distance oneself from such events; in fact, part of the aesthetic power of such occasions lies in our vulnerability. Survival and safety clearly supersede the aesthetic dimension when actual danger threatens, but our personal involvement adds to the perceptual intensity of such situations. The lookout platform of a cathedral steeple or a skyscraper, a boardwalk beyond which storm waves are crashing on the shore, a hilltop during a lightning storm mix a touch of fear with the qualitative intensity of aesthetic perception, adding spice to the savor.

But there are gentler occasions on which we engage the natural world: canoeing a serpentine river when the quiet evening water reflects the trees and rocks along the banks so vividly as to allure the paddler into the center of a six-dimensional world; camping beneath pines black against the night sky; walking through the tall grass of a hidden meadow whose tree-defined edges become the boundaries of the earth. The aesthetic mark of all such times is not disinterested contemplation but total engagement, a sensory immersion in the natural world that reaches the still uncommon experience of unity. Joined with acute perceptual consciousness and enhanced by the felt understanding of assimilated knowledge, such occasions can become clear peaks in a cloudy world, high points in a life dulled by habit and defensive disregard.

Moreover, it is not the sublime alone that encourages an aesthetics of engagement; natural beauty can do so as well, once we are liberated from the formalistic requirements of discreteness and order. For unlike its representations, nature does not come framed, and we can take as much aesthetic delight in profusion and continuity as we have been taught to find in symmetry and regularity. The attraction of a spreading patch of bunchberry or a stand of wild columbine on the forest floor does not lie in its stimulus to the free play of imagination alone, as Kant would have it, but on color, shape, poignant simplicity, delicacy and, as much as anything, its gratuitousness and

237

profusion.[21] Formal order is but one source of aesthetic satisfaction, not the *sine qua non* of beauty. Part of the appreciation of natural beauty lies in the fascination with intricate detail, subtle tone, endless variety, and the imaginative delight in what we would call in a human artifact marvelous invention, all as part of an environmental setting with which we, as appreciative participants, are continuous. Forgoing the requirements of objectification and order, we can discover beauty in a rippling brook and a fire on the hearth, to cite Kant's examples, as much as in a Van Ruisdael or a Hobbema painting of them.

AN AESTHETICS FOR NATURE AND ART

Engagement, then, is the direction in which an aesthetics of nature can lead us. Yet adopting a participatory aesthetics not only transforms our appreciation of nature but the nature of our appreciation more generally. There is another alternative to the strategies of assimilating natural beauty to the arts or constructing separate accounts for each: The aesthetics of nature can serve as the model for appreciating art.

For continuity and perceptual immersion occur in our experience of art as much as in nature. Ross points in environmental art to the connection of the object with its site. In fact, by functioning in important ways like seventeenth- and eighteenth-century English gardens, the appreciation of many earthworks and environmental art works rests on their ties with the perceiver through the meanings and associations they evoke, as well as in the sensory bonds with site and viewer that they exert. Sculpture, in fact, provides a significant test case of the adaptability of art to aesthetic engagement. While it appears to lend itself perfectly to traditional aesthetics, sculpture directly contradicts those conventions when it takes the form of earthworks and environments. Here art and nature are joined through the ties these works have with their site and with their perceivers. Moreover, neither site nor perceiver has sharp boundaries; each combines with the other into a single total experience.

Similarly, both art and nature may exhibit some degree of order. Associating design with art mistakenly generalizes from a common but not universal formal order, since design is but a genetic explanation of the order that may be found in art. Moreover, one is not even obliged to take the essentially Kantian tack of finding order in nature to qualify it for aesthetic appreciation. While there is formal structure in a quartz crystal and a starfish as there is in the symmetry of the Taj Mahal and Notre Dame Cathedral, art, like nature, has its share of deliberate disarray. We can find as much disorder in the opening movements of Bach's great organ Toccatas in C major and D minor and in Debussy's through-composed songs as in the irregular curve of a beach or the scattering of daisies in a field.

What draws together natural beauty and the arts are some commonalities in our relation and response: Both can be experienced perceptually; both can be appreciated aesthetically; and more particularly still, both can function reciprocally with the appreciator, enticing the participant to join in a unified perceptual situation. Such appreciation requires a radically different aesthetic from eighteenth-century disinterestedness. I call this an aesthetics of engagement, and it is one that environmental appreciation especially encourages.[22]

Applying this model to art appreciation leads, then, to restructuring the usual approach to art. It also suggests ways of resolving certain problems that result from adopting separate forms of appreciation for nature and for art. Diffey raises some interesting issues here, one of which has to do with appreciating the beauty of the beloved. This may be seen as an aspect of natural beauty that attaches to the human person, and it usually harbors an element of sexual desire, sometimes diffuse, sometimes specific.[23] Appreciation here is hardly disinterested, and the tradition in aesthetics has always had difficulty accommodating itself to this sense of beauty since, as Plato observed in the *Hippias Major*, sexual desire is not confined to the distance receptors of sight and hearing. Need we then, like Plato, be obliged to drop any claim to beauty here? Obviously yes, if we are committed to aesthetics of disinterested contemplation; no, if we accept an aesthetics of engagement. For the beauty of the sexually beloved does not lie in possession, itself never an intrinsic value. Nor does it lie in arousal, which is self-directed, or in idealization, which rests on objectification. To appreciate such beauty for its own sake rests on recognizing its inherent value, a value that dwells in the sensuous and other perceptual qualities of the situation and not on disinterestedness, and this is possible on an occasion of engagement.[24] Like most human values, sexuality need not be either entirely biological or sublimated into something ideal. Appreciating the beauty of the beloved in sexual desire is fulfilled in the quality of an entire human situation as it is enhanced by mutual contribution and mutual appreciation. This is precisely what an engaged aesthetic

239

honors, and it accords with the sense of beauty we discover in sensual love.

Again, can nature reveal the transcendent as art is capable of doing? As with sexual beauty one can easily be seduced away from the aesthetic character of the situation, in the one case by indulging in a fixation on gratification, in the other by abandoning oneself entirely to some surpassing state. To reach the supersensible through communion with nature as with art is to forgo the aesthetic in experience entirely in favor of mystical transcendence. Whatever the attractions that may have, it turns art or nature merely into a vehicle for achieving the state. And this loses the awareness of the intrinsic character of that experience where art or nature must be irrevocably present, which is an uncontested condition of the aesthetic.

But there is something here which nature shares with art, and which poets like Wordsworth recognize truly. Perhaps, as Diffey notices, there is an easy transition to the sublime, though I suspect that both terms, "beauty" and "sublime," require radical redefinition once one no longer associates the first with objects and the second with transcendence. Perhaps the truth approached by transcendence lies in the quality of unity with nature which aesthetic engagement encourages. The perceived sense of continuity of our human being with the dynamic forms and processes of the natural world is a central factor in the aesthetic appreciation of nature, and it accounts for a touch of the sublime in the feeling of awe which accompanies that occasion. Transcendence no longer, we still retain the quality of numinousness in the sense of immanence we sometimes obtain in nature and art. And this is the fulfillment of aesthetic engagement.

What we grasp in the wilder states of nature we appreciate too in its more cultivated forms. Those environments where art and nature are deliberately fused, gardens, are one way a natural aesthetic is employed to evoke the sense of continuity with nature. Here cultural forms and traditions mediate that unity, as they mediate every mode of experience, for there is a world of difference between a Japanese garden and a French garden, a telling indication of the different worlds those cultures create. While this union of art and nature was deliberately cultivated during the seventeenth and eighteenth centuries, the impulse to fuse them persists, and not only in modern environmental sculpture. The same union of art and nature occurs in modern architecture that is sensitive to its site, in urban planning that responds to geomorphological and geographical considerations, in site specific sculpture, in the design of urban parks, in viewer-activated art. A single aesthetic applies to nature and to art because, in the final analysis, they are both cultural constructs, and so we are not talking about two things but about one.

An aesthetics of engagement thus encompasses both art and nature, and it does what we hope any good account will do – solve more problems than it creates. Moreover, aesthetic engagement offers more than a theoretical advantage; it opens regions of experience that have been closed to aesthetic appreciation by theories that have subsisted by exclusion. By extending appreciation to nature in all its cultural manifestations, the entire sensible world is included within the purview of aesthetics. This hardly makes the world any the more beautiful; if anything it confronts us with the failures of taste which have so far marked most industrial and commercial activities in this century. But if environment, which is nature as we live it, can have aesthetic value, so then can actions be condemned which ignore or deny that value. A universal aesthetic is therefore an aesthetic of the universe, and it offers us a goal to work for as well as a standard by which to judge our success.

Notes

1 T. J. Diffey, "Natural Beauty without Metaphysics"; Allen Carlson, "Appreciating Art and Appreciating Nature"; both in this volume.
2 Stephanie Ross, "Gardens, Earthworks, and Environmental Art," in the present volume.
3 Diffey, "Natural Beauty," Yi-Fu Tuan, "Desert and Ice: Ambivalent Aesthetics," in the present volume.
4 Jerome Stolnitz, Aesthetics and Philosophy of Art Criticism: A Critical Introduction (Boston: Houghton Mifflin, 1960), ch. 1., quoted in Carlson, "Appreciating Art." I term this the modern traditional view, since it is associated with the rise of modern aesthetics in the eighteenth century. There is a much older tradition which is, I believe, closer to the position I develop here. Both are critically elaborated in my book, Art and Engagement (Philadelphia: Temple University Press, 1991).
5 Immanuel Kant, Critique of Judgement (1790), section 5. See also sections 43 and 45.
6 Anthony Ashley Cooper, Third Earl of Shaftesbury, "A Notion of the Historical Draught of Tablature of the Judgment of Hercules" (1712); and Characteristics of Men, Manners, Opinions, Times (1711) (New York: 1900), vol. 1, p. 94; vol. 2, pp. 136–7, 130–1. I have explored the historical development of traditional aesthetics at some length in "The Historicity of Aesthetics I," The British Journal of Aesthetics 26.2 (spring 1986): 101–11; and "The Historicity of Aesthetics II," 26.3 (summer 1986): 195–203.

7 "*Firmitas, Utilitas, Venustas.*" Marcus Vitruvius Pollio, *De Architectura Libri Decem* (1st century B.C.), bk. 1, ch. 2.

8 See Berleant, *Art and Engagement*, ch. 3.

9 Anthony Ashley Cooper, Third Earl of Shaftesbury, *Characteristics*, part III, section II. Cited in A. Hofstadter and R. Kuhns, eds., *Philosophies of Art and Beauty* (New York: Modern Library, 1964), pp. 246–7.

10 I argue against the objectification premise in "Art without Object," in *Creation and Interpretation*, eds., Stern, Rodman, and Cobitz (New York: Haven, 1985), pp. 63–72.

11 This question implicates the large phenomenological literature on the lifeworld, raising issues that can only be broached here. One, of surpassing importance, is whether the lifeworld is itself a historico-cultural construct, and whether the arts of the past hundred years are fulfilling a function the arts have often had of serving as the vanguard of cultural change, a change from a lifeworld of discrete objects to one of essential connections and continuities.

12 The thesis of *Art and Engagement* is that the traditional theory never really gave a satisfactory account of the actual workings of the arts and that it owes its influence to its compatibility with the classic philosophic tradition rather than to its theoretical success in explaining the arts. See especially chs. 1 and 2.

13 The meanings we assign and the understanding we have of nature, wilderness, forest, and landscape have changed dramatically over time. See, for example, Keith Thomas, *Man and the Natural World* (London: Allen Lane, 1983); Marvin W. Mikesell, "Landscape," in P.W. English and R.C. Mayfield, eds., *Man, Space, and Environment* (New York: Oxford, 1972), pp. 9–15; David Lowenthal, "Is Wilderness 'Paradise Enow?': Images of Nature in America," *Columbia University Forum* (1964), pp. 34–40; Yi-Fu Tuan, *Topophilia, A Study of Environmental Perception, Attitudes, and Values*, (Englewood Cliffs, NJ: Prentice-Hall, 1974).

14 References here to traditional aesthetics are not meant to overlook the variety of different theories that have been proposed in the past. My claim is that they do nonetheless possess certain generic features, whether they rely for their identity on imitation, emotion, expression, symbol, or language. See Berleant, *Art and Engagement*, ch. 1. In *The Theory of the Arts* (Princeton University Press, 1982), Francis Sparshott relates the various theories differently, deriving all later developments from what he calls "the classic line." See also Arnold Berleant, *The Aesthetic Field* (Springfield, IL: C. C. Thomas, 1970), ch. 1, "Surrogate Theories of Art."

15 Longinus, *On the Sublime*.

16 Edmund Burke, *Philosophical Enquiry into the Origin of our Ideas of the Sublime and Beautiful* (1757).

17 Immanuel Kant, *Critique of Judgement*, trans. J. H. Bernard (New York: Hafner, 1951), sections 23–30.

18 Francis Bacon, *The Advancement of Learning*, First Book (1605), in Francis Bacon, *Essays, Advancement of Learning, New Atlantis, and*

Other Pieces, ed. R. F. Jones (Garden City, New York: Doubleday, Doran, 1937), p. 202.

19 I can only mention this here, not make a case for it. That is undertaken in Berleant, *Art and Engagement*, chs. 3 and 4.

20 Kant, *Critique*, sections 26, 28, 29.

21 *Ibid.*, section 22.

22 This is no developed case for extending the model of environmental appreciation to the arts. That is something I have undertaken elsewhere. But it serves at least to indicate its possibility and direction. See my essay, "The Environment as an Aesthetic Paradigm," *Dialectics and Humanism*, 15.1–2 (1988): 95–106.

23 "Natural" beauty here, as elsewhere, is a misnomer. Like all forms of nature, human beauty is very much a human, cultural construct, not just by techniques of physical enhancement, but in the selection of desirable body types, physiognomies, personalities, behavior patterns, and the like.

24 See Arnold Berleant, "The Sensuous and the Sensual in Aesthetics," *The Journal of Aesthetics and Art Criticism*, 23.2 (winter 1964): 185–92; reprinted in *Philosophical Essays on Curriculum*, (Philadelphia: Lippincott, 1969), eds. R. S. Guttchen and B. Bandmann, pp. 306–17.

12

On being moved by nature: between religion and natural history

NOËL CARROLL

I. INTRODUCTION

For the last two and a half decades – perhaps spurred onwards by R. W. Hepburn's seminal, wonderfully sensitive and astute essay "Contemporary Aesthetics and the Neglect of Natural Beauty"[1] – philosophical interest in the aesthetic appreciation of nature has been gaining momentum. One of the most coherent, powerfully argued, thorough, and philosophically compelling theories to emerge from this evolving arena of debate has been developed over a series of articles by Allen Carlson.[2] The sophistication of Carlson's approach – especially in terms of his careful style of argumentation – has raised the level of philosophical discussion concerning the aesthetic appreciation of nature immensely and it has taught us all what is at stake, logically and epistemologically, in advancing a theory of nature appreciation. Carlson has not only presented a bold theory of the aesthetic appreciation of nature; he has also refined a methodological framework and a set of constraints that every researcher in the field must address.

Stated summarily, Carlson's view of the appreciation of nature is that it is a matter of scientific understanding; that is, the correct or appropriate form that the appreciation of nature – properly so called – should take is a species of natural history; appreciating nature is a matter of understanding nature under the suitable scientific categories. In appreciating an expanse of modern farm land, for example, we appreciate it by coming to understand the way in which the shaping of such a landscape is a function of the purposes of large-scale agriculture.[3] Likewise, the appreciation of flora and fauna is said to require an understanding of evolutionary theory.[4]

Carlson calls his framework for nature appreciation the natural environmental model.[5] He believes that the strength of this model is that it regards nature as (a) an environment (rather than, say, a view) and (b) as natural. Moreover, the significance of (b) is that it implies that the appreciation of nature should be in terms of the qualities nature has (and these, in turn, are the qualities natural science identifies). Carlson writes "for significant appreciation of nature, something like the knowledge and experience of the naturalist is essential."[6]

My major worry about Carlson's stance is that it excludes certain very common appreciative responses to nature – responses of a less intellective, more visceral sort, which we might refer to as "being moved by nature." For example, we may find ourselves standing under a thundering waterfall and be excited by its grandeur; or standing barefooted amidst a silent arbor, softly carpeted with layers of decaying leaves, a sense of repose and homeyness may be aroused in us. Such responses to nature are quite frequent and even sought out by those of us who are not naturalists. They are a matter of being emotionally moved by nature. This, of course, does not imply that they are noncognitive, since emotional arousal has a cognitive dimension.[7] However, it is far from clear that all the emotions appropriately aroused in us by nature are rooted in cognitions of the sort derived from natural history.

Appreciating nature for many of us, I submit, often involves being moved or emotionally aroused by nature. We may appreciate nature by opening ourselves to its stimulus, and to being put in a certain emotional state by attending to its aspects. Experiencing nature, in this mode, just is a manner of appreciating it. That is not to say that this is the only way in which we can appreciate nature. The approach of the naturalist that Carlson advocates is another way. Nor do I wish to deny that naturalists can be moved by nature or even to deny that something like our nonscientific arousal by nature might be augmented, in some cases, by the kind of knowledge naturalists possess. It is only to claim that sometimes we can be moved by nature – *sans* guidance by scientific categories – and that such experiences have a genuine claim to be counted among the ways in which nature may be (legitimately) appreciated.

Carlson's approach to the appreciation of nature is reformist. His point is that a number of the best-known frameworks for appreciating nature – which one finds in the literature – are wrongheaded *and* that the model of appreciation informed by naturalism which he endorses is the least problematic and most reasonable picture of what nature appreciation should involve. In contrast, I wish to argue that there is at least one frequently indulged way of appreciating nature which Carlson has not examined adequately and that it need not be abjured on the basis of the kinds of arguments and considerations Carlson has adduced. It is hard to read Carlson's conclusions without surmising that he believes that he has identified *the* appropriate model of nature appreciation. Instead, I believe that there is one form of nature appreciation – call it being emotionally moved by nature – that (a) is a longstanding practice, (b) remains untouched by Carlson's arguments, and (c) need not be abandoned in the face of Carlson's natural environmental model.

In defending this alternative mode of nature appreciation, I am not offering it in place of Carlson's environmental model. Being moved by nature in certain ways is one way of appreciating nature; Carlson's environmental model is another. I'm for coexistence. I am specifically *not* arguing that, given certain traditional conceptions of the *aesthetic*, being moved by nature has better claims to the title of *aesthetic* appreciation whereas the environmental model, insofar as it involves the subsumption of particulars under scientific categories and laws, is not an *aesthetic* mode of appreciation at all. Such an objection to Carlson's environmental model might be raised, but it will not be raised by me. I am willing to accept that the natural environmental model provides *an* aesthetic mode of appreciating nature for the reasons Carlson gives.

Though I wish to resist Carlson's environmental model of nature appreciation as an exclusive, comprehensive one, and, thereby, wish to defend a space for the traditional practice of being moved by nature, I also wish to block any reductionist account – of the kind suggested by T. J. Diffey[8] – that regards our being moved by nature as a residue of religious feeling. Diffey says, "In a secular society it is not surprising that there will be a hostility towards any religious veneration of natural beauty and at the same time nature will become a refuge for displaced religious emotions."[9] But I want to stress that the emotions aroused by nature that concern me can be fully secular and have no call to be demystified as displaced religious sentiment. That is, being moved by nature is a mode of nature appreciation that is available between science and religion.

In what follows I will try to show that the kinds of considerations that Carlson raises do not preclude being moved by nature as a respectable form of nature appreciation. In order to do this, I will review Carlson's major arguments – which I call, respectively:

246

science by elimination, the claims of objectivist epistemology and the order argument. In the course of disputing these arguments, I will also attempt to introduce a positive characterization of what being moved by nature involves in a way that deflects the suspicion that it should be reduced to displaced religious feeling.

II. SCIENCE BY ELIMINATION

Following Paul Ziff, Carlson points out that in the appreciation of works of art, we know what to appreciate – in that we can distinguish an artwork from what it is not – and we know which of its aspects to appreciate – since in knowing the type of art it is, we know how it is to be appreciated.[10] We have this knowledge, as Vico would have agreed, because artworks are our creations. That is, since we have made them to be objects of aesthetic attention, we understand what is involved in appreciating them.[11]

However we explain this feature of artistic appreciation, it seems clear that classifying the kind and style of an artwork is crucial to appreciating it. But with nature – something which in large measure it is often the case that we have not made – the question arises as to how we can appreciate it. By what principles will we isolate the appreciable from what is not, and how will we select the appropriate aspects of the nature so circumscribed to appreciate? In order to answer this question, Carlson explores alternative models for appreciating nature: the object paradigm, the landscape or scenery model, and the environmental paradigm.[12]

The object paradigm of nature appreciation treats an expanse in nature as analogous to an artwork such as a nonrepresentational sculpture; as in the case of such a sculpture, we appreciate its sensuous properties, its salient patterns and perhaps even its expressive qualities.[13] That is, the object model guides our attention to certain aspects of nature – such as patterned configurations – which are deemed relevant for appreciation. This is clearly a possible way of attending to nature, but Carlson wants to know whether it is an aesthetically appropriate way.[14]

Carlson thinks not; for there are systematically daunting disanalogies between natural expanses and works of fine art. For example, a natural object is said to be an indeterminate form. Where it stops is putatively ambiguous.[15] But with artworks, there are frames or framelike devices (like the ropes and spaces around sculptures) that tell you where the focus of artistic attention ends. Moreover, the

247

formal qualities of such artworks are generally contingent on such framings.[16]

Of course, we can impose frames on nature. We can take a rock from its natural abode and put it on a mantlepiece. Or, we can discipline our glance in such a way as to frame a natural expanse so that we appreciate the visual patterns that emerge from our own exercise in perceptual composition. But in doing this, we work against the organic unity in the natural expanse, sacrificing many of those real aesthetic features that are not made salient by our exercises in visual framing, *especially* the physical forces that make the environment what it is.[17] And in this sense, the object paradigm is too exclusive; it offends through aesthetic omission.

Thus, Carlson confronts the object paradigm with a dilemma. Under its aegis, either we frame – literally or figuratively – a part of nature, thereby removing it from its organic environment (and distracting our attention from its interplay with many real and fascinating ecological forces) OR we leave it where it is, unframed, indeterminate, and bereft of the fixed visual patterns and qualities (that emerge from acts of framing). In the first case, the object model is insensitive; in the second, it is, putatively, inoperable.

A second paradigm for nature appreciation is the landscape or scenery model. This also looks to fine art as a precedent; it invites us to contemplate a landscape as if it were a landscape painting. Perhaps this approach gained appeal historically in the guidebooks of the eighteenth century which recommended this or that natural prospect as affording a view reminiscent of this or that painter (such as Salvator Rosa).[18] In appreciating a landscape as a piece of scenery painting, we attend to features it might share with a landscape painting, such as its coloration and design.

But this, like the object model, also impedes comprehensive attention to the actual landscape. It directs our attention to the visual; but the full appreciation of nature comprises smells, textures and temperatures. And landscape painting typically sets us at a distance from nature. Yet often we appreciate nature for our being amidst it.[19] Paintings are two-dimensional, but nature has three dimensions; it offers a participatory space, not simply a space that we apprehend from outside.

Likewise, the picture frame excludes us whereas characteristically we are included as a self in a setting in the natural expanses we appreciate.[20] Thus, as with the object model of nature appreciation, the problem with the scenery model is that it is too restrictive to accommodate all the aspects of nature that might serve as genuine objects of aesthetic attention.

Lastly, Carlson offers us the natural environment model of appreciation. The key to this model is that it regards nature as nature. It overcomes the limitations of the object model by taking *as essential* the organic relation of natural expanses and items to their larger environmental contexts. The interplay of natural forces like winds are as significant as the sensuous shapes of the rock formations that are subject to them. On this view, appreciating nature involves attending to the organic interaction of natural forces. *Pace* the scenery model, the totality of natural forces, not just those that are salient to vision, are comprehended. Whereas the scenery paradigm *proposes* nature as a static array, the natural environment approach acknowledges the dynamism of nature.

Undoubtedly the inclusiveness of the natural environment model sounds promising. But the question still remains concerning which natural categories and relations are relevant to attending to nature as nature. It is Carlson's view that natural science provides us with the kind of knowledge that guides us to the appropriate *foci of* aesthetic significance and to the pertinent relations within their boundaries.

In order to aesthetically appreciate art, we must have knowledge of the artistic traditions that yield the relevant classificatory schemes for artists and audiences; in order to aesthetically appreciate nature, we need comparable knowledge of different environments and of their relevant systems and elements.[21] This knowledge comes from science and natural history, including that which is embodied in common sense. Where else could it come from? What else could understanding nature as nature amount to? The knowledge we derive from art criticism and art history for the purposes of art appreciation come from ecology and natural history with respect to nature appreciation.

Carlson writes: "What I am suggesting is that the question of *what* to aesthetically appreciate in the natural environment is to be answered in a way analogous to the similar question about art. The difference is that in the case of the natural environment the relevant knowledge is the commonsense/scientific knowledge which we have discovered about the environment in question."[22]

The structure of Carlson's argument is motivated by the pressure to discover some guidance with respect to nature appreciation that is analogous to the guidance that the fixing of artistic categories does with works of art. Three possibilities are explored: the object paradigm, the scenery paradigm and the natural environment paradigm. The first two are rejected because they fail to comprehensively track all the qualities and relations we would expect a suitable framework for the appreciation of nature to track. On the other hand, the natural environment model is advanced not only because it does not occlude the kind of attentiveness that the alternative models block, but also because it has the advantage of supplying us with classificatory frameworks which play the role that things like genres do with respect to art, while at the same time these categories are natural (derived from natural history).

Stated formally, Carlson's argument is basically a disjunctive syllogism:

(1) All aesthetic appreciation requires a way of fixing the appropriate *loci* of appreciative acts.

(2) Since nature appreciation is aesthetic appreciation, then nature appreciation must have a means of fixing the appropriate *loci* of appreciative acts.

(3) With nature appreciation, the ways of fixing the appropriate *loci* of appreciative acts are the object model, the scenic model and the natural environment model.

(4) Neither the object model nor the scenic model suit nature appreciation.

(5) Therefore, the natural environment model (using science as its source of knowledge) is the means for fixing the *loci* of appreciative acts with respect to nature appreciation.

Of course, the most obvious line of attack to take with arguments of this sort is to ask whether it has captured the relevant field of alternatives. I want to suggest that Carlson's argument has not. Specifically, I maintain that he has not countenanced our being moved by nature as a mode of appreciating nature and that he has not explored the possibility that the *loci* of such appreciation can be fixed in the process of our being emotionally aroused by nature.

Earlier I conjured up a scene where standing near a towering cascade, our ears reverberating with the roar of falling water, we are overwhelmed and excited by its grandeur. People quite standardly seek out such experiences. They are, pretheoretically, a form of appreciating nature. Moreover, when caught up in such experiences our attention is fixed on certain aspects of the natural expanse rather than others – the palpable force of the cascade, its height, the volume of water, the way it alters the surrounding atmosphere, etc.

This does not require any special scientific knowledge. Perhaps it only requires being human, equipped with the senses we have, being small and able to intuit the immense force, relative to creatures like us, of the roaring tons of water. Nor need the common sense of our culture come into play. Conceivably humans from other planets bereft of waterfalls could share our sense of grandeur. This is not to say that all emotional responses to nature are culture-free, but only that the pertinent dimensions of some such arousals may be.

That is, we may be aroused emotionally by nature, and our arousal may be a function of our human nature in response to a natural expanse. I may savor a winding footpath because it raises a tolerable sense of mystery in me. Unlike the scenery model of nature appreci- ation, what we might call the arousal model does not necessarily put us at a distance from the object of our appreciation; it may be the manner in which we are amidst nature that has moved us to the state in which we find ourselves. Nor does the arousal model of nature restrict our response to only the visual aspects of nature. The cascade moves us through its sound, and weight, and temperature, and force. The sense of mystery awakened by the winding path is linked to the process of moving through it.

Perhaps the arousal model seems to raise the problem of framing, mentioned earlier, in a new way. Just as the object model and the scenery model appeared to impose a frame on an otherwise indeter- minate nature, similarly the arousal model may appear to involve us in imposing emotional gestalts upon indeterminate natural expanses. Nevertheless, there are features of nature, especially in relation to human organisms, which, though they are admittedly "selected," are difficult to think of as "impositions."

Certain natural expanses have natural frames or what I prefer to call natural closure: caves, copses, grottoes, clearings, arbors, valleys, etc. And other natural expanses, though lacking frames, have features that are naturally salient for human organisms – i.e., they have features such as moving water, bright illumination, etc. that draw our attention instinctually toward them. And where our emotional arousal is predicated on either natural closure or natural salience, it makes little sense to say that our emotional responses, focused on said features, are impositions.

An emotional response to nature will involve some sort of selective attention to the natural expanse. If I am overwhelmed by the grandeur of a waterfall, then certain things and not others are in the forefront of my attention. Presumably since I am struck emotionally by the grandness of the waterfall, the features that are relevant to my

251

response have to do with those that satisfy interests in scale, notably large scale. But my arousal does not come from nowhere. The human perceptual system is already keyed to noticing salient scale differentials and the fact that I batten on striking examples of the large scale is hardly an imposition from the human point of view.

Suppose, then, that I am exhilarated by the grandeur of the waterfall. That I am exhilarated by grandeur is not an inappropriate response, since the object of my emotional arousal is grand – i.e., meets the criteria of scale appropriate to grandeur, where grandeur, in turn, is one of the appropriate sources of exhilaration. In this case, our perceptual make-up initially focuses our attention on certain features of the natural expanse, which attention generates a state of emotional arousal, which state, in turn, issues in reinforcing feedback that consolidates the initial selective gestalt of the emotional arousement experience. The arousal model of nature appreciation has an account of how we isolate certain aspects of nature and why these are appropriate aspects to focus upon; that is, they are *emotionally* appropriate.

Perhaps Carlson's response to this is that emotional responses to nature of the sort that I envision are not responses to nature as nature. This route seems inadvisable since Carlson, like Sparshott, wants us to think of the appreciator of nature as a self in a setting which I understand as, in part, a warning not to divorce human nature from nature.[23] Admittedly, not all of our emotional arousals in the face of nature should be ascribed to our common human nature, rather than to what is sectarian in our cultures, but there is no reason to preclude the possibility that some of our emotional arousals to nature are bred in the bone.

Conceding that we are only talking about *some* of our appreciative responses to nature here may seem to open another line of criticism. Implicit in Carlson's manner of argument seems to be the presupposition that what he is about is identifying the one and only form of nature appreciation. His candidate, of course, is the environmental model which relies heavily on natural science.

I have already argued that this model is not the only respectable alternative. But another point also bears emphasis here, namely, why presume that there is only one model for appreciating nature and one source of knowledge – such as natural history – relevant to fixing our appreciative categories? Why are we supposing that there is just one model, applying to all cases, for the appropriate appreciation of nature?

On being moved by nature

That the appreciation of nature sometimes may involve emotional arousal, divorced from scientific or commonsense ecological knowledge, does not disallow that at other times appreciation is generated by the natural environment model. Certainly a similar situation obtains in artistic appreciation. Sometimes we may be emotionally aroused – indeed, appropriately emotionally moved – without knowing the genre or style of the artwork that induces this state. Think of children amused by capers of *Commedia dell'arte* but who know nothing of its tradition or its place among other artistic genres, styles and categories. Yet the existence of this sort of appreciative response in no way compromises the fact that there is another kind of appreciation – that of the informed connoisseur – which involves situating the features of the artwork with respect to its relevant artistic categories.

I want to say that the same is true of nature appreciation. Appreciation may sometimes follow the arousal model or the natural environment model. Sometimes the two models may overlap – for our emotions may be aroused on the basis of our ecological knowledge. But, equally, there will be clear cases where they do not. Moreover, I see no reason to assume that these are the only models for the appropriate response to nature. In some cases – given the natural closure and salience of arrays in nature – the object model may not be out of place for, given our limited perceptual capacities, structured as they are, nature may not strike us as formally indeterminate.

My basic objection to Carlson is that emotional arousal in response to nature can be an appropriate form of nature appreciation and that the cognitive component of our emotional response does the job of fixing the aspects of nature that are relevant to appreciation. Here, I have been assuming that emotional arousal, though cognitive, need not rely on categories derived from science. But Carlson sometimes describes his preferred source of knowledge as issuing from common sense/science. So perhaps the way out of my objection is to say that with my cases of being moved by nature, the operative cognitions are rooted in commonsense knowledge of nature.

A lot depends here on what is included in commonsense knowledge of nature. I take it that for Carlson this is a matter of knowing in some degree how nature works; it involves, for example, some prescientific, perhaps folk, understanding of things like ecological systems. That I know, in my waterfall example, that the stuff that is falling down is water is not commonsense knowledge of nature in the way that Carlson seems to intend with phrases like common sense/science. For the knowledge in my case need not involve any systemic knowledge of nature's working of either a folk or scientific origin. And if this is so, then we can say that we are emotionally moved by nature where the operative cognitions that play a constitutive role in our response do not rely on the kind of commonsense systemic knowledge of natural processes that Carlson believes is requisite for the aesthetic appreciation of nature. And, perhaps even more clearly, we can be moved by nature where our cognitions do not mobilize the far more formal and recondite systemic knowledge found in natural history and science.

III. THE CLAIMS OF OBJECTIVIST EPISTEMOLOGY

One reason, as we have just seen, that prompts Carlson to endorse natural history as the appropriate guide to nature appreciation is that it appears to provide us with our only satisfactory alternative. I have disputed this. But Carlson has other compelling motives for the type of nature appreciation he advocates. One of these is epistemological. It has already been suggested; now is the time to bring it centerstage.

Echoing Hume's "Of the Standard of Taste," Carlson's impressive "Nature, Aesthetic Judgment and Objectivity" begins with the conviction that certain of the aesthetic judgments that we issue with respect to nature – such as "The Grand Tetons are majestic" – are or can be appropriate, correct or true. That is, certain aesthetic judgments of nature are objective. Were someone to assert that "The Grand Tetons are paltry," without further explanation, our response would converge on the consensus that the latter assertion is false.

However, though the conviction that aesthetic judgments of nature can be objective is firm, it is nevertheless difficult to square with the best available models we possess for elucidating the way in which aesthetic judgments of art are objective. Indeed, given our best models of the way that aesthetic judgments of art are objective, we may feel forced to conclude that aesthetic judgments of nature are relativistic or subjective, despite our initial conviction that aesthetic judgments of nature can be objective.

So the question becomes a matter of explaining how our aesthetic judgments of nature can be objective. This is a problem because, as just mentioned, reigning accounts of how aesthetic judgments of art are objective have been taken to imply that aesthetic judgments of nature cannot be objective.

In order to get a handle on this problem, we need, of course, to understand the relevant theory of art appreciation which ostensibly renders nature appreciation subjective or relative. The particular theory that Carlson has in mind is Kendall Walton's notion of categories of art. This theory is an example of a broader class of theories – that would include institutional theories of art – which can be usefully thought of as cultural theories. Roughly speaking, cultural theories of art supply the wherewithal to ground aesthetic judgments of art objectively by basing such judgments on the cultural practice and forms – such as artistic genres, styles and movements – in which and through which artworks are created and disseminated.

On Walton's account, for example, an aesthetic judgment concerning an artwork can be assessed as true or false. The truth value of such judgments is a function of two factors, specifically: the non-aesthetic perceptual properties of the artwork (e.g., dots of paint), and the status of said properties when the artwork is situated in its correct artistic category (e.g., pointillism). Psychologically speaking, all aesthetic judgments of art, whether they are subjective or objective, require that we locate the perceived, nonaesthetic properties of the artwork in some category. For example, if an uninformed viewer finds the image in a cubist painting woefully confused, it is likely that that viewer regards the work in terms of the (albeit wrong) category of a realistic, perspectival representation.

However, logically speaking, if an aesthetic judgment is true (or appropriate), then that is a function of the perceived, nonaesthetic properties of the artwork being comprehended within the context of the correct category of art. In terms of the preceding example, it is a matter of viewing the painting in question under the category of cubism. Consequently, the objectivity of aesthetic judgments of art depends upon identifying the correct category for the artwork in question.

A number of circumstances can count in determining the category of art that is relevant to the aesthetic judgment of an artwork. But some of the most conclusive depend on features relating to the origin of the work: such as which category (genre, style, movement) the artist intended for the artwork, as well as cultural factors, such as whether the category in question is a recognized or well-entrenched one. These are not the only considerations that we use in fixing the relevant category of an artwork; but they are, nevertheless, fairly decisive ones.

However, if these sorts of considerations are crucial in fixing the relevant categories of artworks, it should be clear that they are of little moment when it comes to nature. For nature is not produced by creators whose intentions can be used to isolate the *correct* categories for appreciating a given natural expanse nor is nature produced with regard for recognized cultural categories. But if we cannot ascertain the correct category upon which to ground our aesthetic judgments of nature, then those judgments cannot be either true or false. Moreover, since the way in which we fix the category of a natural object or expanse appears to be fairly open, our aesthetic judgments of nature appear to gravitate towards subjectivity. That is, they do not seem as though they can be objective judgments, despite our starting intuition that some of them are.

The structure of Carlson's argument revolves around a paradox. We start with the conviction that some aesthetic judgments of nature can be objective, but then the attempt to explain this by the lights of our best model of aesthetic objectivity with respect to the arts, indicates that no aesthetic judgment of nature can be objective (because there are no *correct* categories for nature). Carlson wants to dissolve this paradox by removing the worry that there are no objective, aesthetic judgments of nature. He does this by arguing that we do have the means for identifying the relevant, *correct* categories that are operative in genuine aesthetic judgments of nature. These are the ones *discovered* by natural history and science.

For example, we know that the relevant category for aesthetically appreciating whales is that of the mammal rather than that of fish as a result of scientific research. Moreover, these scientific categories function formally or logically in the same way in nature appreciation that art historical categories function in art appreciation. Thus, the logical form, though not the content, of nature appreciation corresponds to that of art appreciation. *And* insofar as the latter can be objective in virtue of its form, the former can be as well.

Another way to characterize Carlson's argument is to regard it as a transcendental argument. It begins by assuming as given that nature appreciation can be objective and then goes on to ask how this is possible – especially since there does not seem to be anything like correct categories of art to ground objectivity when it comes to nature appreciation. But, then, the possibility of the objectivity of nature appreciation is explained by maintaining that the categories discovered by natural history and science are available to play the role in securing the objectivity of aesthetic judgments of nature in a way that is analogous to the service performed by art historical categories for art.

Thus, for epistemological reasons, we are driven to the view of nature appreciation as a species of natural history. Effectively, it is advanced as the only way to support our initial intuitions that some aesthetic judgments of nature can be objective. Moreover, any competing picture of nature appreciation, if it is to be taken seriously, must have comparable means to those of the natural environment model for solving the problem of the objectivity of nature appreciation.

Of course, I do not wish to advance the "being moved by nature" view as competing with the natural environment approach. Rather, I prefer to think of it as a coexisting model. But even as a coexisting model, it must be able to solve the problem of objectivity. However, the solution to the problem is quite straightforward when it comes to being emotionally moved by nature.

For, being emotionally moved by nature is just a subclass of being emotionally moved. And on the view of the emotions that I, among many others, hold, an emotion can be assessed as either appropriate or inappropriate. In order to be afraid, I must be afraid of *something*, say an oncoming tank. My emotion – fear in this case – is directed; it takes a particular object. Moreover, if my fear in a given case is appropriate, then the particular object of my emotional state must meet certain criteria, or what are called "formal objects" in various philosophical idioms.

For example, the formal object of fear is the dangerous. Or, to put the point in less stilted language: if my fear of the tank (the particular object of my emotion) is appropriate, then it must satisfy the criterion that I believe the tank to be dangerous to me. If, for instance, I say that I am afraid of chicken soup, but also that I do not believe that chicken soup is dangerous, then my fear of chicken soup is inappropriate. C. D. Broad writes: "It is appropriate to cognize what one takes to be a threatening object with some degree of fear. It is inappropriate to cognize what one takes to be a fellow man in undeserved pain or distress with satisfaction or with amusement."[24]

Of course, if emotions can be assessed with respect to appropriateness and inappropriateness, then they are open to cognitive appraisal. Ronald deSousa says, for example, that "appropriateness is the truth of the emotions."[25] We can assess the appropriateness of the emotion of fear for an emoter in terms of whether or not she believes that the particular object of her emotion is dangerous. We can, furthermore, assess whether the appropriateness of her fear ought to be shared by others by asking whether the beliefs, thoughts or patterns of attention that underpin her emotions are the sorts of beliefs, thoughts or patterns of attention that it is reasonable for others to share. Thus we can determine whether her fear of the tank is objective in virtue of whether her beliefs about the dangerousness of the tank, in the case at hand, is a reasonable belief for the rest of us to hold.

Turning from tanks to nature, we may be emotionally moved by a natural expanse – excited, for instance, by the grandeur of a towering waterfall. All things being equal, being excited by the grandeur of something that one believes to be of a large scale is an appropriate emotional response. Moreover, if the belief in the large scale of the cascade is one that is true for others as well, then the emotional response of being excited by the grandeur of the waterfall is an objective one. It is not subjective, distorted, or wayward. If someone denies being moved by the waterfall, but agrees that the waterfall is large scale and says nothing else, we are apt to suspect that his response, as well as any judgments issued on the basis of that response, are inappropriate. If he does not agree that the waterfall is of a large scale, and does not say why, we will suspect him either of not understanding how to use the notion of large scale, or of irrationality. If he disagrees that the waterfall is of a large scale because the galaxy is much much larger, then we will try to convince him that he has the wrong comparison class – urging, perhaps, that he should gauge the scale of the waterfall in relation to human scale.

In introducing the notion of the "wrong comparison class," it may seem that I have opened the door to Carlson's arguments. But I do not think that I have. For it is not clear that in order to establish the relevant comparison class for an emotional response to nature one must resort to scientific categories. For example, we may be excited by the grandeur of a blue whale. I may be moved by its size, its force, the amount of water it displaces, etc., but I may think that it is a fish. Nevertheless, my being moved by the grandeur of the blue whale is not inappropriate. Indeed, we may be moved by the skeleton of a *Tyrannosaurus rex* without knowing whether it is the skeleton of a reptile, a bird, or a mammal. We can be moved by such encounters, without knowing the natural history of the thing encountered, on the basis of its scale, along with other things, relative to ourselves.

Such arousals may or may not be appropriate for us and for others. Moreover, judgments based on such emotional responses – like "that whale excites grandeur" or "The Grand Tetons are majestic" – can be objective. Insofar as being moved by nature is a customary form of appreciating nature, then it can account for the objectivity of some of our aesthetic judgments of nature. Thus, it satisfies the epistemological challenge whose solution Carlson appears to believe favors only his natural environment model for the aesthetic appreciation of nature. Or, to put it another way, being moved by nature remains a way of appreciating nature that may coexist with the natural environment model.

At one point, Carlson concedes that we can simply enjoy nature – "we can, of course, approach nature as we sometimes approach art, that is, we can simply *enjoy* its forms and colors or *enjoy* perceiving it however we may happen to."[26] But this is not a very deep level of appreciation for Carlson, for, on his view, depth would appear to require objectivity. Perhaps what Carlson would say about my defense of being moved by nature is that being emotionally aroused by nature falls into the category of *merely* enjoying nature and, as an instance of that category, it isn't really very deep.

Undoubtedly, being moved by nature may be a way of enjoying nature. However, insofar as being moved by nature is a matter of being moved by appropriate objects, it is not dismissable as enjoying nature in whatever way we please. Furthermore, if the test of whether our appreciation of nature is deep is whether the corresponding judgments are susceptible to objective, cognitive appraisal, I think I have shown that some cases can pass this test. Is there any reason to think that being moved by nature must be any less deep a response than attending to nature with the eyes of the naturalist?

I would be very suspicious of an affirmative answer to this question. Of course, part of the problem is that what makes an appreciative response to nature shallow or deep is obscure. Obviously, a naturalist's appreciation of nature could be deep in the sense that it might go on and on as the naturalist learns more and more about nature, whereas a case of emotional arousal with respect to nature might be more consummatory. Is the former case deeper than the latter? Are the two cases even commensurable? Clearly, time alone cannot be a measure of depth. But how exactly are we to compare appreciative stances with respect to depth?

Maybe there is no way. But if the depth of a response is figured in terms of our intensity of involvement and its "thorough-goingness,"[27] then there is no reason to suppose that being moved by nature constitutes a shallower form of appreciation than does appreciating nature scientifically. The Kantian apprehension of sublimity[28] – and its corresponding aesthetic judgment – though it may last for a delimited duration, need not be any less deep than a protracted teleological judgment.

Again, it is not my intention to dispute the kind of appreciation that Carlson defends under the title of the natural environment model. It is only to defend the legitimacy of an already well-entrenched mode of nature appreciation that I call being moved by nature. This mode of nature appreciation can pay the epistemological bill that Carlson presupposes any adequate model of nature appreciation should accommodate. It need not be reducible to scientific appreciation, nor must it be regarded as any less deep than appreciation informed by natural history.

Of course, it may seem odd that we can appreciate nature objectively this way when it seems that a comparable form of appreciation is not available to art. But the oddity here vanishes when we realize that to a certain extent we are able to appreciate art and render objective aesthetic judgments of artworks without reference to precise art historical categories. One may find a fanfare in a piece of music stirring and objectively assert that it is stirring without any knowledge of music history and its categories. Being emotionally aroused by nature in at least certain cases need be no different.

Carlson may be disposed to question whether being emotionally moved by nature is really a matter of responding to nature as nature. Perhaps he takes it to be something like a conceptual truth that, given the culture we inhabit, attending to nature as nature can only involve attending to it scientifically. However, if I am taken with the grace of a group of deer vaulting a stream, I see no reason to suppose that I am not responding to nature as nature. Moreover, any attempt to regiment the notion of responding to nature as nature so that it only strictly applies to scientific understanding appears to me to beg the question.

IV. ORDER APPRECIATION

The most recent argument that Carlson has advanced in favor of the natural environmental model of nature appreciation is what might be called the order argument.[29] In certain respects, it is reminiscent of his earlier arguments, but it does add certain new considerations that are worth our attention. Like his previous arguments, Carlson's order argument proceeds by carefully comparing the form of nature appreciation with that of art appreciation.

One paradigmatic form of art appreciation is design appreciation.

Design appreciation presupposes that the artwork has a creator who embodies the design in an object or a performance, and that the design embodied in the artwork indicates how we are to take it. However, this model of appreciation is clearly inappropriate for nature appreciation since nature lacks a designer.

Nevertheless, there is another sort of art appreciation which has been devised in order to negotiate much of the *avant-garde* art of the twentieth century. Carlson calls this type of appreciation order appreciation. When, for example, we are confronted by something like Duchamp's *Fountain*, the design of the object does not tell us how to take it or appreciate it. Instead, we rely on certain stories about how the object came to be selected by Duchamp in order to make a point. These stories inform us of the ideas and beliefs that lead an *avant-garde* artist to produce or to select (in the case of a found object) the artwork.

These stories direct us in the appropriate manner of appreciating the object; they guide us in our selection of the relevant features of the work for the purposes of appreciation. They do the work with unconventional, experimental art that design does with more traditional art. For example, our knowledge, given a certain art historical narrative, of Surrealism's commitment to revealing the unconscious, alerts us to the importance of incongruous, dreamlike juxtapositions in paintings by Dali.

For Carlson, design appreciation is obviously ill-suited to nature appreciation. On the other hand, something like order appreciation appears to fit the case of nature appreciation. We can appreciate nature in terms of the forces that bring natural configurations about, and we can be guided to the relevant features of nature by stories. But where do these stories come from? At an earlier stage in our culture, they may have come from mythology. But at this late date, they come from the sciences, including astronomy, physics, chemistry, biology, genetics, meteorology, geology and so on. These sciences, and the natural histories they afford, guide our attention to the relevant forces that account for the features of nature worthy of attention.

Basically, Carlson's most recent argument is that art appreciation affords two possible models for nature appreciation: design appreciation and order appreciation. Design appreciation, however, is clearly inadmissable. That leaves us with order appreciation. However, the source of the guiding stories pertinent to the order appreciation of nature differ from those that shape order appreciation with respect to art. The source of the latter is art history while the source of the former is natural history.

But once again Carlson's argument is open to the charge that he has not canvased all of the actual alternatives. One's appreciation of art need not fall into either the category of design appreciation or order appreciation. We can sometimes appreciate art appropriately by being moved by it. Moreover, this is true of the *avant-garde* art that Carlson suggests requires order appreciation as well as of more traditional art.

For example, Man Ray's *The Gift* is an ordinary iron with pointed nails affixed to its smooth bottom. Even if one does not know that it is a specimen of Dada, and even if one lacks the art-historical story that tells one the ideology of Dada, reflecting on *The Gift* one may readily surmise that the object is at odds with itself – you cannot press trousers with it – in a way that is brutally sardonic and that arouses dark amusement. Similarly, one can detect the insult in Duchamp's *Fountain* without knowing the intricate dialectics of art history, just as one may find certain Surrealist paintings haunting without knowing the metaphysical, psychological and political aims of the Surrealist movement.

As it is sometimes with art, so is it with nature. In both cases, we may be emotionally moved by what we encounter without any really detailed background in art history or natural history. With respect to both art and nature, emotional arousal can be a mode of appreciation, and it is possible, in a large number of cases, to determine whether the emotional arousal is appropriate or inappropriate without reference to any particularly specific stories of either the art-historical or the natural-history varieties.

A parade or a sunset may move us, and this level of response, though traditionally well-known, need not be reduced to either design appreciation or order appreciation, nor must it be guided by art history or by natural history. Insofar as Carlson's approach to both art and nature appears wedded to certain types of "professional" knowledge as requisite for appreciation, he seems to be unduly hasty in closing off certain common forms of aesthetic appreciation. This is not said in order to reject the sort of informed appreciation Carlson advocates, but only to suggest that certain more naive forms of emotive, appreciative responses may be legitimate as well.[30]

I have argued that one form of nature appreciation is a matter of being aroused emotionally by the appropriate natural objects. This talk of the emotions, however, may seem suspicious to some. Does it really seem reasonable to be emotionally moved by nature? If we feel a sense of security when we scan a natural expanse, doesn't that sound just too mystical? Perhaps, our feeling, as Diffey has suggested, is some form of displaced religious sentiment. Maybe being moved by nature is some sort of delusional state worthy of psychoanalysis or demystification.

Of course, many emotional responses to nature – such as being frightened by a tiger – are anything but mystical. But it may seem that others – particularly those that are traditionally exemplary of aesthetic appreciation, like finding a landscape to be serene – are more unfathomable and perhaps shaped by repressed religious associations. However, I think that there is reliable evidence that many of our emotional responses to nature have a straightforwardly secular basis.

For example, in his classic *The Experience of Landscape*,[31] and in subsequent articles,[32] Jay Appleton has defended the view that our responses to landscape are connected to certain broadly evolutionary interests that we take in landscapes. Appleton singles out two significant variables in our attention to landscape – what he calls prospect (a landscape opportunity for keeping open the channels of perception) and refuge (a landscape opportunity for achieving concealment).

That is, given that we are the kind of animal we are, we take a survival interest in certain features of landscapes: open vistas give us a sense of security insofar as we can see there is no threat approaching, while enclosed spaces reassure us that there are places in which to hide. We need not be as theoretically restrictive as Appleton is and maintain that these are the major foci of our attention to landscape. But we can agree that features of landscape like prospect and refuge may cause our humanly emotional responses to natural expanses in terms of the way they address our deep-seated, perhaps tacit, interests in the environment as a potential theatre of survival.

Thus, when we find a natural environment serene, part of the cause of that sense of serenity might be its openness – the fact that nothing can approach us unexpectedly across its terrain. And such a response need not be thought to be mystical nor a matter of displaced religion, if it is connected to information processing molded by our long-term evolution as animals.

Other researchers have tried to isolate further features of landscape – such as mystery and legibility[33] – that shape our responses to natural expanses in terms of a sense, however intuitive and unconscious, of the sorts of experiences we would have – such as ease of locomotion, of orientation, of exploration and so on – in the environment viewed. That is, our perhaps instinctive sense of how it would be to function in a given natural environment may be part of the cause of our emotional arousal with respect to it. A landscape that is very legible – articulated throughout with neat subdivisions – may strike us as hospitable and attractive in part because it imparts such a strong sense of how we might move around and orient ourselves inside of it.

Earlier I sketched a scene in which we found ourselves in an arbor, carpeted by layers of decaying foliage and moss. I imagined that in such a situation we might feel a sense of solace, repose, and homeyness. And such an emotional state might be caused by our tacit recognition of its refuge potential. On this view, I am not saying that we consciously realize that the arbor is a suitable refuge and appreciate it as such. Rather the fact that it is a suitable refuge acts to causally trigger our emotional response which takes the arbor as its particular object and responds to it with a feeling of repose and homeyness, focusing on such features as its enclosure and softness, which features are appropriate to the feeling of solace and homeyness.

Our feeling is not a matter of residual mysticism or religious sentiment, but is perhaps instinctually grounded. Moreover, if such a scenario is plausible for at least some of our emotional responses to nature, then it is not the case that being aroused by nature is always a repressed religious response. Some responses of some observers may be responses rooted in associations of nature with the handiwork of the gods. But other emotional responses, appropriate ones, may have perfectly secular, naturalistic explanations which derive from the kinds of insights that Appleton and others have begun to enumerate.

Admitting that our emotional responses to nature have naturalistic explanations, of course, does not entail a reversion to the natural environmental model of nature appreciation. For such explanations pertain to how our emotional responses may be caused. And when I appreciate a natural expanse by being emotionally aroused by it, the object of my emotional state need not be the recognition of my instinctual response to, for example, prospects. Perhaps one could appreciate nature *à la* Carlson from an evolutionary point-of-view in which the focus of our attention is the interaction of our emotions with the environment as that interaction is understood to be shaped by the forces of evolution. But this is not typically what one has in mind with the notion of being moved by nature.

On being moved by nature

In conclusion: to be moved by nature is to respond to the features of natural expanses – such as scale and texture – with the appropriate emotions. This is one traditional way of appreciating nature. It need not rely upon natural history nor is it a residual form of mysticism. It is one of our characteristic forms of nature appreciation – not reducible without remainder to either science nor religion.

Notes

1 R. W. Hepburn, "Contemporary Aesthetics and the Neglect of Natural Beauty," in his *Wonder and Other Essays* (Edinburgh University Press, 1984). This essay appeared earlier in *British Analytical Philosophy*, eds. B. Williams and A. Montefiore (London: Routledge and Kegan Paul, 1966).
2 See especially: Allen Carlson, "Appreciation and the Natural Environment," in the *Journal of Aesthetics and Art Criticism* 37 (spring, 1979); "Formal Qualities in the Natural Environment," *Journal of Aesthetic Education* 13 (July, 1979); "Nature, Aesthetic Judgment and Objectivity," *Journal of Aesthetics and Art Criticism* 40 (autumn, 1981); "Saito on the Correct Aesthetic Appreciation of Nature," *Journal of Aesthetic Education* 20 (summer, 1986); "On Appreciating Agricultural Landscapes," *Journal of Aesthetics and Art Criticism* (spring, 1985); "Appreciating Art and Appreciating Nature," in this volume; Barry Sadler and Allen Carlson, "Environmental Aesthetics in Interdisciplinary Perspective," in *Environmental Aesthetics: Essays in Interpretation*, eds. Barry Sadler and Allen Carlson (Victoria, British Columbia: University of Victoria, 1982); and Allen Carlson and Barry Sadler, "Towards Models of Environmental Appreciation," in *Environmental Aesthetics*.
3 See Carlson, "Appreciating Agricultural Landscapes."
4 Carlson, "Appreciating Art," in this volume.
5 Carlson, "Appreciation and the Natural Environment," p. 274.
6 Carlson, "Nature, Aesthetic Judgment," p. 25.
7 See, for example, William Lyons, *Emotion* (Cambridge University Press, 1980), especially ch. 4.
8 T. J. Diffey, "Natural Beauty without Metaphysics," in this volume.
9 *Ibid.*
10 Carlson, "Appreciation and the Natural Environment," p. 276.
11 *Ibid.*
12 This is the way that the argument is set up in "Appreciation and the Natural Environment." In "Formal Qualities in the Natural Environment," the object paradigm and the scenery model, it seems to me, both get assimilated under what might be called the formal-qualities model.
13 Carlson, "Appreciation and the Natural Environment," p. 268.
14 *Ibid.*   15 *Ibid.*
16 Carlson, "Formal Qualities," p. 108–9.
17 Carlson, "Appreciation and the Natural Environment," p. 269.

265

18 See for example, Peter Bicknell, *Beauty, Horror and Immensity: Picturesque Landscape in Britain 1750–1850* (Cambridge University Press, 1981).

19 Carlson, "Appreciation and the Natural Environment," p. 271.

20 Carlson, "Formal Qualities," p. 110.

21 Carlson, "Appreciation and the Natural Environment," p. 273.

22 *Ibid.*

23 Francis Sparshott, "Figuring the Ground: Notes on Some Theoretical Problems of the Aesthetic Environment," *Journal of Aesthetic Education*, 6.3 (July 1972).

24 C. D. Broad, "Emotion and Sentiment," in his *Critical Essays in Moral Philosophy* (London: Allen and Unwin, 1971), p. 293.

25 Ronald deSousa, "Self-Deceptive Emotions," in *Explaining Emotions* ed. Amelie Okesenberg Rorty (Berkeley: University of California Press, 1980), p. 285.

26 Carlson, "Nature, Aesthetic Judgment," p. 25.

27 A test suggested by Robert Solomon in his "On Kitsch and Sentimentality," *The Journal of Aesthetics and Art Criticism*, 49.1 (winter 1981): 9.

28 See Immanuel Kant, *The Critique of Judgement*, trans. James Creed Meredith (Oxford: Clarendon Press, 1952), especially the "Analytic of the Sublime."

29 See Carlson, "Appreciating Art," in this volume.

30 Toward the end of "Appreciating Art," Carlson does refer to certain responses to nature, such as awe and wonder, which sound like the type of emotional responses I have been discussing. He thinks that even armed with the natural environment model, we may become aware that nature is still mysterious to us and *other*. And, in consequence, we feel awe and wonder. I do not want to deny that we may come to feel awe and wonder at nature through the process Carlson describes. However, I do not think that this is the only way that we can be overwhelmed with awe in the face of nature. We may, for example, be struck by the scale of nature, without any reference to scientific categories, and be overwhelmed by awe. Thus, though there may be a route to awe through the natural environment model, it is not the only route. There are still other ways in which we may be moved to awe by nature *sans* natural history. Consequently, the account of awe that Carlson offers does not eliminate the more naive model of emotional arousal that I have been defending.

31 Jay Appleton, *The Experience of Landscape* (New York: Wiley, 1975).

32 Jay Appleton, "Prospects and refuges revisited," in *Environmental Aesthetics: Theory, Research & Applications*, ed. Jack L. Nasar (Cambridge University Press, 1988); and Jay Appleton, "Pleasure and the Perception of Habitat: A Conceptual Framework," in *Environmental Aesthetics: Essays in Interpretation.*

33 Stephen Kaplan, "Perception and landscape: conceptions and misconceptions," in *Environmental Aesthetics: Theory*, pp. 49–51. See also Kaplan's "Where cognition and affect meet: a theoretical analysis of preference," in the same volume.

Index

abstraction, 85–8, 91, 96f
accident, 83ff; and 'learned riddle',
  83ff; in forms of nature, 83ff; in
  painting, 10ff
Acconci, Vito, 160–1
Adams, Ansel, 105
Adams, John, 128
Adorno, T. W., 58, 68–9, 74f
adventure, 147f
Aeneas, 164, 165
Aeschylus, 119
aesthetics, 230, 237ff, 228–43,
  229–31; as discipline, 230;
  boundaries of, 229ff; broader
  characterization needed, 195f;
  evaluation, 196; qualities, and
  identity, 2; rhetorical, 99f;
  significance, 189–93; single for art
  and nature, 228–43; symbiosis,
  194f; traditional, and problems,
  229–31
aesthetic appreciation, 214;
  boundaries of, 229ff; nature,
  occasion for, 237; object, 232;
  pleasure, possibility of, 236;
  relevance, 201f
agreement, 45, 46ff
Aidan, Bishop, 1
Alfred, King, 2, 15; and *Historia
  Ecclesiastica Gentis Anglorum*, 2
alien space, 140
Allen, H. G., 146
America, 16

American West, 146
animism, 119
annexation, 7–8; and imagination,
  73; and metaphor, 74; and spirit,
  74; of nature, 71
anthropomorphism, 71, 77–8
anti-art, 218, 221
Antonioni, F., 110
Appleton, Jay, 38, 263, 264
appreciation, 7, 28ff, 31ff, 37, 76;
  aesthetic, 7, 47, and value, 27;
  and annexation, 8; and
  appropriateness, 37, 176; and
  aspectation, 203; and destruction,
  72; and disinterestedness, 28ff,
  199–205, 214; and order,
  208–213; and science, 244–67;
  art, 239; concept of, 199–205;
  content of, 220; contrast between
  art and nature, 199–223; design,
  205–8, 221; different kinds of,
  216; directiveness of, 200f; form
  of, 218; knowledge of object in,
  28ff; nature and order, 217;
  object-oriented, 204f; of art and
  nature, 199–227; of nature and
  art, assimilated, 214ff, and
  disinterestedness, 214; and
  religion, 38; and theism, 215; and
  thought content, 7–8; and truth,
  79; depth of, 38; needs science,
  31f; of art and nature, single
  theory, 32–4; of natural beauty,

267

Index

Index